COUNSELLING
ADOLESCENTS
SCHOOL and AFTER

COUNSELLING ADOLESCENTS
SCHOOL and AFTER

Anne Jones

Kogan
Page

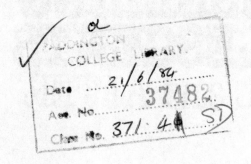
First published in Great Britain in 1977
as *Counselling Adolescents in School* by
Kogan Page Limited, 120 Pentonville Road, London N1 9JN

Reprinted in 1979 with revised bibliography

Second edition published in 1984
as *Counselling Adolescents: School and After*

British Library Cataloguing in Publication Data

Jones, Anne
  Counselling adolescents: school and after. – 2nd ed
  1. Personnel service in secondary education
  – Great Britain
  I. Title
  373.14′0941   LB1620.5

ISBN 0-85038-759-0
ISBN 0-85038-760-4 Pbk

Photoset by AKM Associates (UK) Ltd, Southall, Greater London

Printed in Great Britain
by The Anchor Press Ltd
and bound by Wm Brendon & Son Ltd
both of Tiptree, Essex

Contents

Acknowledgements

I want to thank all those people who helped me in my work as a counsellor and in the writing of this book, in particular, the former head and deputy head of Mayfield School, Dame Margaret Miles and Miss Helen Whale; my fellow counsellor at Mayfield, Mrs Shirley Dunkley, and my casework supervisor, Miss Mary Kernick. I also want to thank my former colleagues at Thomas Calton and Vauxhall Manor Schools, my present colleagues at Cranford Community School and all those other friends and colleagues who have advised, supported, and stimulated me over the years.

I must make it clear that the views expressed in this book are my own and not necessarily those of my education authority or any of the people I have worked with over the years.

Anne Jones

Introduction

This book was originally written as an account of an experiment in counselling adolescents in a secondary school between 1965 and 1971. That part of the text has been abridged but remains substantially as it was written. It is, however, important to realize that it relates to a specific period in time, when I was working as counsellor at Mayfield School. Since then I have added two major sections, one describing the way a counselling approach can serve and enhance both the educational process itself and also the structure and organization of a school. This section is based on my work as deputy head of Thomas Calton School and head of Vauxhall Manor School. In the last section, I describe a counselling approach to the curriculum, with particular reference to Youth Training Schemes (YTS) and prevocational education. This section is based on my experiences at Vauxhall Manor and Cranford Community Schools.

In chapter 1, I related my understanding of counselling to the current ar the move concerns of education, in particultowards prevocational education, experiential learning, and guidance/counselling as part of the common core: what schools are now doing to help young people become adult. I examine the relationship between schools, careers guidance, training schemes, employment and unemployment and attempt to put recent developments into perspective. I remain as convinced as ever that there is a place for counsellors in our schools, though I am glad it is now more recognized that all staff need a chance to develop and use counselling skills. My hope, however, is that this book will help any adult working with young people to do his job better.

For those astute readers who notice that I appear to change sex during the book with alarming rapidity, let me explain that when I talk about the work I did when I was a counsellor I use the feminine case. When I talk about counselling in general, I use the masculine, partly to make the important point that counselling is not a female prerogative — no sex discrimination here!

Finally I must make it clear that where I have quoted from individual comments or cases, I have taken great care to change names and remove identifying details. I have also changed details of the problems, though not in a substantial way, for I wanted the problems to be real, not fantasies invented for effect.

Anne Jones

Chapter 1

Counselling and young people: what now?

When the school counselling movement began in Britain in 1965, it was difficult to foresee what effects it would have. Those of us involved in that development were excited and confident that counselling would add a vitally needed element to the education of the adolescent. What we did not dare to hope for, or even altogether understand at that point was that a 'counselling approach' would eventually be recognized as a fundamental and integrated part of true learning from the cradle to the grave. For make no mistake about it: the developments now happening in education and training for 16-19 will also eventually have a major impact on the way teachers and learners behave in both pre-16 and post-19 age groups.

The magic formula '16-19' appears now to be the key to educational reform. Whilst the rest of the educational system is gloomily contemplating a further spell of cutbacks, and stagnation, in the 16-19 age group we see expansion, growth, the development of new curricula and new methods of teaching and learning. There is excitement and a sense of achievement and purpose amongst the 'teachers' and the taught. The double motivation brought about by 'new hope' and 'new growth' is recognized by others. As a result many people are trying to get in on the act; indeed, there appears to be competition, if not war, between the various contenders for the 16-19 market: ie colleges, schools, training agencies, employers. What is worrying is whether, in this scramble for new business, the whole point of the exercise, namely to build the confidence, competence, coping strategies and practical skills of young people, will get lost.

What is however both ironic and reassuring for those of us who have been in the counselling and guidance field for years, is the sudden appearance as part of the common core in both prevocational education based courses and in Youth Training Schemes (YTS), of such components variously labelled as counselling and guidance, reflecting upon experience, social and life skills, personal effectiveness and personal development. Concepts appear, written into the methodology, such as 'negotiation', 'ownership of skills', 'process skills', 'integration' and 'transferability of skills'[1]. Further, these so called new skills and techniques are not simply for the difficult and the deprived, but are for all, and as such have achieved a new status and respect. Those who imagine that prevocational courses and YTS are only for the failures of the school system will soon realize that they are not only relevant and useful but also

11

desirable for the whole of the 16-19 population (and it could be argued for the whole population). So what are these new skills and techniques?

Fundamentally, they are what some of us have been calling for the last 20 years or so—techniques of guidance and counselling. It certainly makes me feel like Monsieur Jourdain who suddenly realized he had been speaking prose all his life. The new skills and techniques are what we have been talking about all the time, only nobody really heard us. Whilst many of us have long realized the implications of the counselling movement for the education service as a whole, we nevertheless may have made the mistake of appearing to offer counselling as a remedial or even a preventive extra service, rather than a fundamental method of getting people to learn for themselves, take responsibility for themselves, make transitions for themselves, and grow up. But what is important now is to make the connection between what was once and what now is. There is a very great danger that the new initiatives, whether in or out of the education system, will fail to use the wealth of relevant experience which already exists amongst adults responsible for young people in transition. Time and time again teachers are found reinventing the wheel, clutching at straws in an attempt to find out what it is they are supposed to be doing now. In the very same school or college there may be teams of 16-19 teachers demanding in-service training and support, yet not recognizing that on their own staff they have considerable expertise and experience which could be shared with them in a practical way.

Who are these people? Many and various. Obviously the counsellor, the careers teacher or officer, the educational psychologist, the youth worker, and the probation officer; less obviously the drama teacher, some English and humanities teachers, the head or deputy head, the home economics or craft, design and technology teacher, the PE staff, the form tutor, the groundsman or the school nurse.

Not all these people will be able to help: more will depend on the quality of the persons in the post rather than their actual labels or qualifications. Not all that many schools have school counsellors as such, and some of them will take too 'therapeutic' a line for our present purposes. However, the principles on which they have been trained are those on which the new initiatives are based and, if they recognize this, they will be able to help developments a great deal. Many trained counsellors are now disguised as members of the hierarchy, having realized that the system and processes of the school as a whole need working on. They are particularly useful because they have power as well as insight. Careers teachers, educational psychologists, youth workers, careers and probation officers, will again vary in experience and usefulness. However, if they can make the connection between their specific skills and if they can transfer their particular strengths into a more generalizable situation, then they too have an enormous amount to offer, particularly in terms of group work skills and reflecting on experience. And what have the drama, English and humanities teachers been doing all this time? Certainly (if I take my own school as an example) a great deal of role play, group work, evaluative discussion, effective and creative work; what is now called personal development/social and life skills. The craft areas may be precisely the ones in which for years students have been taking a practical task through from the original idea and principles to the finished end product, a requirement of much prevocational work. For years the PE staff and others may have been taking pupils on outward bound residential courses which are marvellous for personal development. Some highly developed tutorial systems also reflect exactly the kind of approaches needed in the new initiatives. Finally, the ancillary staff of any educational institute are, as we know, often better than many of the teaching staff at listening to what young people think and feel.

My purpose in making these assertions, which will or will not be true according to specific local situations, is to try to help us all not to feel *deskilled* in the light of new developments. It is tremendously important to connect past trends with future needs, even if those persons with relevant experience will themselves have to undertake some new learning and evaluation of their work in the context of today. The reformulation of the sum total of one's knowledge, skills and experience in the light of the present situation is not just an invigorating and worthwhile exercise in itself. It is also a capability which everybody will need to develop as the patterns of life, leisure and work change over the next decades. Staff who hold a view of themselves as being 20 years out of date (or who are regarded by others as so being) will gain new self-confidence and esteem from others if they can make this transition. Only if they are capable of making this kind of connection themselves will they be able to help others , whether they are young people or adults in retraining, to do the same.

There are many 'intellectual' guides to the new approaches to 16-19. Paramount amongst these are the outpourings of the Further Education Unit (FEU) which, if you put yourself on its mailing list, will present you with a new booklet about once a month.[2] Despite their jargon, these booklets are not to be derided since they offer a framework for a curriculum and many practical strategies and examples. The first and most influential of these FEU documents is *A Basis for Choice* in which Jack Mansell and his team spell out a framework for curriculum objectives as they see them (see Appendix). *ABC in Action* gives examples of what happened when *A Basis for Choice* was put into practice. The Mansell report is not, in fact, prescriptive but provides a yardstick by which 16-19 curricula (and why not 14-19 or 11-19?) may be measured. This framework has largely influenced both the implementation of the YTS (*one* of the new training initiatives proposed by the Manpower Services Commission [MSC] in 1981) and the curriculum and evaluation of the prevocational courses established by City and Guilds and the Business and Technician Education Council (BTEC). It is important to recognize that in this way Mansell creates a much needed bridge between education and training. It is unfortunate that a similar bridge between schools and further education colleges is not also built. Because the documents come from further education, there is a tendency for those in schools not to know about them (let alone read them) even though they are free to anyone who asks. Further, the documents themselves refer almost entirely to further education even though what they

13

have to say is equally applicable in schools, and particularly pertinent to the 14-16 age group. However, those who now enthusiastically send off for a whole series of FEU papers will find themselves swamped and possibly daunted. There is a particular vocabulary of FEU documentation—some would say jargon, certainly a language of its own—which is off-putting until you have learnt it. My guess is that many practising teachers, and even lecturers, will be looking for less dense, more expansive sources of help. Hamblin's *Guidance 16-19* attempts to meet a practical need, but falls between being a sophisticated and rather directive counselling theory book and a work book.[3] The Leeds counselling and careers development unit has offered various 'life skills books'[4] as indeed has the Careers Research and Advisory Council (CRAC).[5] But by and large few people have explicitly connected by the guidance literature of today with the counselling literature of the past.

It is for this reason that I have revised this book and included more about the young people themselves, their feelings, their needs, their comments, their perceptions, their anxieties, their hopes and their fears. Much of the existing supporting literature is about structures and systems. There is a noticeable lack of comment from young people themselves. Much of the existing literature contains a basic assumption about work, the nature of work and the work ethic, that is, an assumption that work is still the be all and end all of everything. All this '16-19 business' is seen simply as a way of preparing young people for work, if and when they get it. If they still do not get work then there is still a sense of failure, both for the young people and the adults who try to help them. Nobody seems to have worked out what will happen when, as a result of all these initiatives, *all* young people are more mature, confident and competent. Unless we change the basic model or pattern on which work is based, there still will not be enough 'work' in the conventional sense, to go round. But this does not invalidate the new initiatives; it merely changes their focus.

To my mind, we do young people an injustice if we do not recognize and use the skills and qualities that they have and had already before the new initiatives. We must enable them to take responsibility for themselves and the quality of their own lives; to make the transitions in their future lives, whether at work, at home, in the local community or in society, with dignity and pride; and we must abandon the work ethic which devalues unreasonably those who are not in paid work. What people, young and old, need is a feeling of being *useful*, of being able to contribute to society. If the 16-19 initiatives (wherever they are based) fail to do this, then we are simply prolonging adolescent life instead of promoting adult life; we are baby-minding our greatest source of energy, vitality and skill instead of harnessing that energy to the good of our society. And we shall end up either with passive, motiveless young people who reject the work ethic but have nothing to put in its place, or, if our young people are really as capable as I think they are, we shall end up with rebellion and anarchy. However, at the moment I am still hopeful that the YTS will work positively rather than negatively, precisely because of its philosophy and emphasis on the ownership of skills by the trainees and the development of their personal effectiveness.[6]

I should perhaps explain at this point the basis of my authority for having anything to say at all on any of these topics. In the school of which I am now head we have been running prevocational sixth-form courses since September 1981; more of these later. Suffice it to say that I have been a member of one of the teams teaching these students; and I am also a member of the team providing the off-the-job training for British Airways (BA) trainees under a YTS.[7] Further, I am also chairman of the London South and West Area Manpower Board, which has responsibility for approving and monitoring all the schemes in the area. Thus, I am in the fortunate and unusual situation of working simultaneously at a policy and a practical level with the powers that be, the trainees and the trained. This does not give me all the answers, but it does give me a considerable insight into what is happening, both at a macro and a micro level.

For the moment I will content myself with just two observations: first that it is not the MSC which is running the YTS but the managing agents themselves, be they employers, education authorities, voluntary training agencies or joint consortia. The MSC is merely a go-between, a commissioning body, as its name indicates. The Manpower Boards[8], which are representative bodies, decide where the money will be put, and thereafter the managing agency both manages the money and is initially responsible for quality control. So those who carp about the quality of schemes may find they are talking about what is, in fact, *their* responsibility—not someone else's. The second point is that the YTS, particularly in its first years of existence, is bound to be variable in quality, in the same way that schools and colleges are. We can find examples of bad practice in all institutions: HMI secondary survey does not make very reassuring reading for those of us who work in secondary schools.[9] We cannot expect perfection overnight in a scheme of such magnitude as the YTS. What we can and should expect, however, is for managing agents to learn from their experiences, to listen to their trainees, to evaluate, and reflect upon their own teaching and learning experiences and to improve. In other words, we should apply the same principles of learning to ourselves as to our trainees and students.

All this seems to have taken me a long way from my original 'counselling' brief. I regard the pattern of my own development as following very closely the pattern of the counselling movement in the country.

Phase 1: 1964-1971. Preparation for and work as a school counsellor, working on a preventive rather than a remedial model, and working with *all* pupils in an age cohort, but nevertheless being seen as an 'extra' rather than something integral to the whole education process. During this period several counselling courses were established, with emphasis varying from therapeutic to careers guidance. The counselling movement grew in momentum but head teachers were never really brought into it, partly because counsellors were not extra to the teaching quota and partly because they may have held the 'intrinsic' model in their heads ie the view that everybody was a counsellor.

Phase 2: 1971-1978. Working as deputy head (until 1974), then as head

(1974-8) to try to change the *system* and use counselling principles in the structure and organization of a school. During this period the popularity of counselling throughout the country waxed and then waned, but the impact on pastoral care systems and then systems as a whole became noticeable. In particular, the gap between the pastoral and the academic narrowed, and many schools developed active tutorial systems, pastoral curricula and a new integrated role for the form tutor.

Phase 3: 1978-present. Working as head in two different schools trying to set up courses to alter the way pupils learn, to relate what goes on in school more closely to what goes on outside school, and to enable staff and students to make transitions positively. In this last phase the emphasis is back to the practical curriculum—what the pupil/student/trainee actually takes away from his or her total experience .[10] Also in this last phase, at a national level, counselling principles become fully integrated with educational principles. Instead of using specialist counsellors we require all teachers, lecturers and trainees to use counselling skills, and for teachers to be as much aware of process as of content, as much aware of the need to understand and internalize as to remember and recall; and to be able to negotiate with the student/trainee to accept them as they are and work from there, rather than impose something inappropriate upon them. In the past, heads/principals maintained that their staff were 'natural' counsellors, therefore they did not need either training or specialist provision. Now everybody in contact with 16-19s is being asked to acquire these skills which are regarded as so important that they are spelt out in document after document as an essential part of the course.[11] Yet relatively few 16-19 teachers or lecturers have as yet been trained for this, so how do we proceed? Eventually, when more of us have gained confidence in our skills with 16-19s, this movement will affect the rest of the school curriculum and the curriculum for post-19 continuing education and training. To reach that stage, we need to help each other develop the further skills needed.

In the meantime, I still think it could be helpful to look back in some detail over what I mean by the theory and practice of counselling, because I think it illuminates what is happening today and illustrates the techniques and approaches that are needed. To my own amazement much of what I wrote first in my original book is still true and is certainly relevant now. What I have done in this edition of the book, however, is to compress and discard previous material and to add new material from my recent experiences. Nevertheless, what young people have to say is what we really need to hear. So in writing about recent experiences, as I did originally, I have tried to focus on what has been happening to them, their reactions and their feelings.

When the school counselling movement began in 1965 those were expansionist times; for a while it looked as if there would eventually be a counsellor appointed in every school. The principles and concepts of counselling were seized upon with alacrity by many adults working with young people—not just teachers, but also careers officers, youth workers and social workers. There must have been something in the timing of the 'discovery' of the body of knowledge which already existed about counselling which rang a bell with those adults who were seeking to help adolescents in the 60s. The mood then was complex—as indeed it still is. There was a general questioning of the established order, of authority, of moral and social values. There was a feeling among adults sympathetic to young people that adolescents were not given enough to say in their own destiny; they were too often told what to do, expected to conform to the rules 'because I say so'. Adults did not always listen sufficiently to what young people were saying; adults often failed to recognize their 'cry for help'; when they did try to help they too often were over-directive, or offered the help on terms which were unacceptable to young people. In many ways, the situation does not seem to have changed very much!

What is sure is that in 1965, certain counselling concepts—in particular the idea of being 'non-directive', non-judgemental and non-authoritarian—fell like manna not only on the ears of the teaching profession, but also of other agencies dealing with young people. Counselling and all its concepts seemed to be the answer for many of the helping professions.

Unfortunately but perhaps inevitably this was *not* all for the best in the best of all possible worlds. Instead of the steady building up of a truly professional body of counsellors, suddenly everyone was trying his hand, sometimes with unfortunate results. The result of this phase was, in my view, a devaluing of the word 'counselling' which was, and still is, frequently abused and misused; a surfeit of non-directive, non-judgemental, non-authoritarian helpers; considerable role confusion and role diffusion, particularly among teachers and social workers; the emergence of a very confused adolescent group who found the adult world apparently leaning over backwards to please them and not impose on them.

The picture I have just painted is of course exaggerated. We all know adults who were totally untouched by this phase! But those adults who went through it have been grappling since then with the problem of learning how to use their authority as adults, in relationship to adolescents; we have learnt that it does not help young people to grow up if we renounce our own authority, wisdom, experience and judgement as adults. The skill we have to develop consists of using these qualities constructively, not destructively; for example in being sensitive without being sentimental, strong without being overpowering, flexible without being flaccid, loving without being over-involved, gentle without being soft, firm without being rigid, tolerant without being ridiculous. Swinging about on the see-saw of polarization really does not help; we somehow have to learn to manage and to use both 'ends' of ourselves at once if we are really to help at all. This is something young people often see more clearly than we do.

However, the fact that counselling concepts have often been misunderstood and counselling techniques used inappropriately does not mean that they should not be used at all. The conflicts of adolescence (like the conflicts of adulthood!) are still with us, and still offer one of the best opportunities for growth and development that a person ever has. In schools and in society generally we have still not learnt how best to help adolescents use this period of conflict as a basis for growth. In the light of our experiences in the last few years, this may be a good moment to look again at the basic principles of counselling. They are in my view as relevant now as they ever were; an understanding of these principles and some experience in the techniques of counselling are vital to anyone working with young people.

Counselling and pastoral care

Why is it that we still do not have a counsellor appointed to every secondary school? The need is as great as ever, greater in many ways, particularly in an era of inner-urban decline, economic stringency and unemployment. Numbers of children in distress are higher than ever. A single parent, unemployment, chronic ill health, over-crowded and inadequate housing, poverty, lack of care: so many of our pupils battle against these background odds (and survive remarkably well) that those of us who work in inner-city schools begin, alas, to take such handicaps as normal. Add to these social and economic factors the very bleak prospects for employment which face so many of our young people. On the vocational guidance side alone there is more than a full-time job for a counsellor in every secondary school. Even if personal counselling is still considered a frill for the few, vocational guidance is surely a necessity for all.

The reasons why there are no full-time counsellors in all our secondary schools are both positive and negative. The negative reasons are largely economic. There is still no full-scale backing from the Department of Education and Science for this idea. As long as head teachers have to 'give up' a teacher to provide a counsellor, the odds are going to be set against the counsellor. The counsellor and his responsibility allowance will have to be *extra* to the quota for them to be taken up in a big way. Second, the supply of properly selected and trained counsellors is still small, despite the proliferation of training courses over the years and the efforts of such bodies as NICEC[12], which also publishes a very respectable journal of guidance and counselling[13]. It would still be a mistake for the wrong people to take up this kind of work full-time, though many teachers could now be helped to develop their counselling skills.

On the positive side, one reason counsellors have not 'spread' more may relate to their effectiveness. I have always maintained that one of the counsellor's objectives should be to do himself out of a job! Overall the quality of 'pastoral care', of careers advice and of educational guidance has improved enormously over the last 20 years. There is a greater degree of sensitivity and system in these areas now than there was. Many trained counsellors are not working officially as counsellors. They have taken posts in the school hierarchy where they have an opportunity of working on the system as well as with individuals. We can make analogies with other developments which have both a specialist and a generalist phase, for example health education, remedial teaching, and careers education. Are these specialist subjects to be taught and contained within a department, or are they to be taught by everybody 'across the curriculum'? My own view is that in all these areas, including counselling, we still need both approaches. The specialists can help train the staff as a whole as well as doing their own specialist work.

There has now developed in the vast majority of secondary schools a pastoral care system, which is indeed systematic, structured and organized; with points and posts of responsibility allocated to it; with specific tasks to do apart from the day-to-day care and discipline, such as smoothing the transition from primary to secondary school, providing guidance for subject choices, offering careers advice and preparing for the transition from school to work. Within such systems interviews with parents and pupils and contacts with other agencies are conducted with a degree of professional skill and properly recorded; advice is sought from other agencies at a preventive stage, and decisions about pupils' future welfare are properly communicated to the appropriate persons. Indeed in many schools the recording and assessing of social and psychological problems and behavioural difficulties may well be done more meticulously than the assessing of academic progress.

Why is it then that I am still not satisfied? I have already mentioned that there are some institutions and some people who remain untouched by the development of the last decade or so. I am concerned lest in the 'tightening up of standards' of work and behaviour which is with us now, we will lose the gains we have made. There still do exist some teachers who work in a way which is over-rigid and over-controlling. Their pupils either give up and are rejected out of hand, or they become conformist and over-dependent. Their problems come when they leave school and discover that they have been over-protected all their school lives. This extreme of teacher behaviour is just as unhelpful to the adolescent as that of the teacher who overindulges his pupils another way, by forgiving everything and forgetting to teach them to take responsibility for the consequences of their action. In spite of the counselling movement, both these extremes of teacher behaviour still exist and still need working on. Furthermore, the school system can be completely undermined if some staff are operating on a different wavelength from the school as a whole. The mechanisms of the system do not tell you much about the *nature* of the relationships. The system can be about the *control* of pupils or it can be about the *growth* of pupils. True education like true counselling is interested in growth from within, not control from without.

Further, it has been a mistake for a pastoral care system to be *grafted* on to the academic system and split from it as has often been the case. Pupils' learning comes from their total experience of the school, not simply from what goes on in lessons. Some of the messages given out by schools are contradictory and *not* conducive to pupil growth and development. If the 'caring' and the 'learning' parts of the school experience are split, then the pupil may feel himself in a kind of fragmented chaos of which it is difficult to make any sense. Caring and learning need to be integrated; so do loving and making demands on pupils. Something radical has gone wrong here. Teachers are now making a real attempt, in response to popular demands, to achieve 'higher standards'. Yet so often this attempt comes across to the pupils as hysterical meaningless nagging, against which they are well defended. All that happens then is that a larger proportion of the pupil population than before becomes alienated from school. As teachers we have to learn how to convey that because we care about the pupils' progress as *pupils*, we are prepared to make demands on our pupils *and* give them the support and the skills they need to fulfil those demands. This does not demean the pupil. On the contrary, it is putting up with less than a pupil's best which is the real insult. Our job as teachers is to support and encourage the pupil in his battle to do his best and move forward, not to make it so easy for him that he does not bother any more. Teachers often appear to accept shoddy work because they are afraid of upsetting the pupil. Yet cushioning against reality does nothing to help the pupil. As teachers we have to learn how to convey a *total* message; we too often appear to be alternately overindulgent or over-rejecting, because the message is split into two parts. These principles, of being firm because we care, of accepting the pupil without either condoning or rejecting him, of making demands on the pupil so that *he* works it out for himself with our support, are principles which apply equally to teaching and to counselling. They are also principles which still continue to be misunderstood and misapplied, and need a lot of working on if schools are to be anything more than child-minding agencies. In some ways secondary schools seem to prolong childhood rather than promote adulthood.

Where does the form tutor stand now in all this? Often in danger of being split into two separate people, the form tutor and the class teacher. It is clear that form tutors have a vitally important role, especially for pupils with learning problems for whatever reason. Yet the dangers for the conscientious form tutor have been in taking on too much and getting too involved. Teachers are not primarily social workers, friends or even parents to their pupils. How form tutors will understand and take up their role will depend on how well they are trained and co-ordinated in their school. I agree with Michael Marland's concept of the 'tutor ascendant'.[14] The more responsibility they are allowed to exercise, the more responsible they are likely to be. If they make mistakes, never mind, they will learn. We tend to protect both our teachers and our pupils from making mistakes and taking risks; yet this is a most valuable part of learning. Certainly most form tutors are willing and capable of taking on a considerable counselling role if given the support and the opportunity. I suspect that there is still much under-functioning here, largely because of confusion over role and over the delegation of responsibility. The more form tutors understand the true principles of counselling the better. One of those principles lies in the recognition of the boundaries and the limitations of roles.

Counselling and careers

The question of careers advice is one which is even more fraught with difficulties now than it was when the counselling movement began. Careers teachers had of course been established in schools long before then, but the concept of careers guidance, as opposed to advice, was one which developed as part of the counselling movement. 'Guidance programmes' sprang up over the country. In theory at least, the pupil has never been so well prepared for deciding what to do with his future. The underlying problem is that nobody is sure what that future will be. Normally from about the third year on he is given lessons, lectures and individual consultations designed to help him think about his own aptitudes, abilities and personality, his strengths and limitations; to help him choose the right options; to help him find out about as many jobs as possible and the life styles that go with them; to help him make a decision, with the help of the careers teacher and the careers officer, about what he wants to do.

Yet even thus far we find there are snags. First, some schools seem curiously reluctant to differentiate between pupils or to assess their ability objectively. The reluctance comes from a belief in the unreliability of testing procedures, and the negative effects of putting pupils in rank order for those who are not top. Both these points have some validity, yet the corollary, which is that because this is difficult to do well, nothing much is done at all, makes it very hard for a pupil to know how well he is getting on either in relationship to his own potential, or in relationship to his peers. There may well be more mute inglorious Miltons around then ever! If a pupil is to think about his abilities at all usefully, he needs to have more than his own thoughts to work with, however accurate they might happen to be. As far as options and job choices are concerned, the whole exercise may be very remote and second-hand for the pupil. Whose word is he to believe? Which PR firm will take his fancy? And how much will the careers personnel really help him—or will he still prefer to believe what his peers and his parents say about jobs? And *is* it a final choice? Maybe it is just a first choice, and not really all that important.

There are other inherent difficulties in this new sophisticated stage of careers education.[15] Parents and friends, subject teachers, heads of house, form tutors, careers teachers, counsellors, careers officers—all these people, for a start, may be involved in advising or guiding a pupil. What does the pupil make of it all? How consistent or how coherent is what he hears? A further complication, alas only too real, is that jobs for school leavers, with or without qualifications, are getting hard to find. This can unfortunately make careers advice seem like a 'con' designed in part to get better examination results for the school. The desperate exhortations of the teacher to make pupils work harder for qualifications may fall on very deaf ears when pupils know perfectly well that there are not any real prospects regardless of qualifications. There is no doubt that progress has been made in the field of careers education and guidance. There is a lot of hard work going on. But are we working on the right issues? In many ways we may still be missing the point.

In the teaching of reading there is a well worn concept called 'reading readiness'. I suspect that there may be a similar concept in careers guidance. At certain times pupils may be totally unreceptive to guidance because they are working on some other problem. This is not a chronological state so much as a developmental stage. Normally many pupils, especially girls, will have unimaginative and depressed aspirations;[16] they will not take up the range of opportunities open to them even when they are told about them time and time again. They will be unwilling to take the risk of doing something unfamiliar, or to travel far to work, or to move home in order to train or have a better job. What is it that we are or are not doing in schools for this kind of attitude to prevail? Overcoming this kind of attitude takes much more than a few careers lessons. There are now available a few teaching materials which are aimed at these issues.[17] But attitudes here go deep. It is not so much a careers programme but more a way of life that we have to consider.

What schools often underestimate is how much school life contributes to attitudes as well as home life. Schools cannot do everything—but in rightly denying the charge that they can put the wrongs of society right, they sometimes make it sound as if they have *no* contribution at all to make to pupil attitudes. Seven hours a day, five days a week is a considerable amount of time. It is certainly more time than average working parents spend with their family, particularly if they are single parents. The question of the total message conveyed by a school is something of great significance. The processes are just as important as the content.

Much has been said and written over the years about the importance of preparing pupils for life, in particular the importance of 'good working habits' and equally 'learning to make decisions and choices for oneself'. I have a feeling that on both these scores, schools still have hardly begun. When the emphasis in lessons is on academic achievement then the pupil may learn to deliver the goods but not sufficiently develop his own resources. When the emphasis is on 'creativity' and 'individualized research methods' then the pupil may not learn to work in a team to some objective; that is to say, the pupil may have goals of his own (or he may not!) but he may fail to learn to value and respond to the setting of external objectives by his class or school, other than the purely selfish one of passing exams. This may say more about the way schools operate than about the individual child. I am making a rather subtle point which is to do with the overindulgence of the individual and his whims (which may be good, bad or indifferent) and the *lack* of what used to be called 'corporate goals'. This whole tendency is also often reflected in the staffs of schools who work splendidly in individualistic ways, but often in ways which do not fit together to make sense as a whole. At one end of the scale we have the battery-hen approach to education, turning out examination fodder (or examination rejects); at the other end of the scale, we have individuals who may be massively under achieving, but in any case who may not have learnt to use their talents in the service of the school. For school, read any institution in which they may later work.

In a work situation employers do *not* want battery hens—they want to harness and use the constructive energy of their staff. But neither do they want creative geniuses (or uncreative nuisances) who lack a sense of corporate identity and corporate achievement. So this is a big issue of which anyone in careers work needs to be aware. The 'careers programme' will be nothing unless the school as a whole and the staff as a whole are agreed on the importance of this in every aspect of school life. In a seven-hour school day, lessons will take up only four and a half hours or so. What does the pupil learn from the other two and a half hours in school? Who cares what goes on then?

Whether he likes to face this or not, the teacher's job does not end when the lesson is finished. All the time he is in school he is, wittingly or not, conveying a message to the pupils. What kind of message will depend on the school and its corporate ethos. The pupil's basic attitude to adults, to employment, to the world of work and to his future role in society will be much influenced by whatever kind of 'school life' he experiences.[18] This point may seem remote from counselling and careers. It is not. It is part of my overall thesis that the effectiveness of the parts depends upon the functioning of the whole.

As for learning to make choices and decisions, this important area, in terms of helping adolescents become more effective adults, is still often practically untouched in schools. The question of 'subject options' may well be dealt with thoroughly but how much real choice is there, and who actually makes it? As a pupil once said, 'Is this a choice, Miss, or can we do what we like?' Like so many parts of schooling, learning to make choices is *not* a free for all subject. It requires system and planning and above all an understanding on the part of the pupil as to *why* he is being asked to do something. Again this is an idea which can be taken up mistakenly by the teacher, like the English class who were always given a choice of what *kind* of work they wanted to do in English, and nearly always chose 'creative writing'. The result was that they were not sufficiently exposed to other, equally important, kinds of experience in the English language. The skill is not in offering a choice between pease pudding and ice cream; it is perhaps in putting the question another way—making the pupil work out for himself that he does need to develop a certain skill or ability, and having him agree that to make the best of himself he needs to do certain specific learning tasks i.e. what is now called negotiation. If we simply give our pupils a choice between learning or not learning, their choice may be based on the wrong premise. If they understand *why* this piece of work may help them in their development as adults, then they are more likely to take it up. It helps if the teachers themselves believe the piece of work to be useful and they themselves know why it is useful—otherwise the teacher may be pushing into the pupil his own basic doubts about the validity of what he is doing. To my mind this kind of understanding of the purposes of education is essential if the secondary education system is to continue to meet the needs of our young people and our society at all.

So much for 'choice' and purpose within subject lessons. But what about the 'decision-making exercises' of which we all had such hope? Despite all the froth and ferment of ideas, there seems to be very little genuine participation in decision-making in schools *by the pupils* whether simulated (in lessons) or for real (in school). A lot of *teacher* energy has gone into participation and decision-making—alas very often at the expense of the pupil, who may be totally excluded from this process. Indeed teachers may become so obsessed with this that their teaching may suffer. Ironically the pupils may have less real say than ever, and certainly a feeling of not being heard—yet they are the *raison d'être* of any school. What does this teach them about their futures? That the only sure way of getting attention from adults round you is to be a nuisance or to be destructive in some way? Surely the teacher's role here is to be intermediary between the pupil and the school, to interpet the one to the other. The needs of the adults too easily take over from the needs of the pupils. All this has to be worked on if schools are in any way to help their pupils become responsible mature adults.

Another difficulty schools face in relation to careers education is the number of people involved in it. Institutions like NICEC[12] are making a valiant effort to help schools co-ordinate their careers education programmes so that there are some commonly held aims and objectives for each school. It is a big step forward to find the careers teacher no longer struggling on in the careers office alone. I am sure that 'careers' is a subject which should be part of the common core for all pupils, whatever their abilities and ambitions; the old idea of only giving lessons in careers to those who were leaving early is mercifully on the way out. If you involve a large number of teachers in teaching the careers programme, however, you have to spend time and energy building up a common understanding of what it is all for, and *why* it is being done. It is too easy for a desperate head teacher to timetable Miss Bloggs into the team just because she happens to have a free period when 'careers' is being taught. The whole careers programme may be invalidated if neither the teachers nor the pupils understand why they are doing it.

What about alleged pupil boredom? 'I'm not interested in becoming a nurse/engineer/deep sea diver so why bother with it and besides, there aren't any jobs in that.' The pupil may here be questioning a narrowly based 'square peg into square holes' approach to careers education; or conversely the teacher may be failing to convey the purpose of looking at one particular job in detail. The purpose will include consideration of the kind of personality, skills and life style which go with each job, a widening of horizons so that the pupil really does consider all factors[19] and understand how this fits into what are now called occupational families.[20] Even if he does stick to his original decision, it will be an informed decision rather than an ignorant one. Choosing a job is not really like blindman's buff, grabbing the first thing that comes along. Knowing why you *do not* want to do something is as important as realizing how much or how little real choice you actually have. So is making the connections between the skills needed in various jobs.

'Work experience' is another aspect of careers education which needs very careful handling. Rather like 'voluntary work' schemes, work experience can be a meaningless disaster if it is not extremely well handled. Stage one is for a school to get its pupils placed, with a great feeling of relief, for this in itself is no mean organizational feat especially now. But what does it achieve in itself? A rush to work in that particular job because it is the only one the pupil has ever experienced at first hand? A complete rejection of that kind of work by the pupil? A hardening of the arteries of the employer *against* ever taking on pupils again? Or a genuine learning experience for pupils, employers, teachers and schools?[21]

To achieve the latter takes an enormous amount of time. It means a dialogue between the school and the work situation. It means careful preparation of the pupils before they go out, contact and supervision when they are out, some on-going means of recording of impressions, developments and progress, some follow-up work, some feedback from the employers and from the school to the pupil and to each other. Whether the experience should be confined to one job or several, a half day a week, or a whole week at a time, or whatever; who should go? At Cranford we send the whole fifth year out for three weeks simultaneously and their teachers visit them at work. This is helpful to staff, though the argument about teachers needing to have more experience of industry is seductive but more complicated than it first seems. Teachers have been reluctant to take up the CBI 'work experience' schemes for teachers, perhaps because they know full well how destructive it is to their schools if they go away for three weeks. Many teachers, however, have worked in other settings apart from also being husbands and wives, parents, citizens, voters, ratepayers etc so their experience is not as limited as it is sometimes made to sound.

The transition from school to work is another big area which needs to be explored and worked on more explicitly in schools.[22] The real skill in this seems to be to make opportunities for communication and interchange between schools and employers, not confrontation. The dissatisfaction of employers with the finished products of schools is already more legendary than real, as is the so-called inability of schools to deliver the goods. The problem has been that schools have been very busy delivering goods without being clear as to what they are delivering them *for*. Neither are the employers as clear about this as you would imagine from their outcries. Apart from such nonsense as employers still using imperial measures when schools went decimal years ago, I suspect that many of the difficulties arise more than anything else from the state of the economy, the stage of economic growth, and the unemployment situation. In this as in so many issues, there needs to be long, clear-headed discussion and interchange, so that at last reality and commonsense can prevail. What is hard for the teaching profession to face is the success of courses run by such agencies as the MSC in making unemployable young people employable.[23] Whether this trend can possibly continue in the light of the scale of youth unemployment and the YTS remains to be seen.

The 'unemployment' situation for young people is potentially extremely depressing unless we in schools have the courage to make our pupils think about it and be prepared at least to a certain extent for this event at some stage in their lives. There are already some books around to help with this prospect.[24] It is particularly depressing that our society is so concerned with employment that to be without a job is almost like being without a name or an identity. Certainly our status as people should come from being what we are as persons and not just from our job title. Being retired, or 'only a housewife', or only a pupil/student or unemployed—these can be *positive* states, and certainly should not automatically carry the overtones of second class citizen that they so often do carry.

Another important concept in both counselling and careers education, which needs to be taken up more vigorously in schools, is the idea of education and careers development as a life-long process. The decision a pupil makes when he leaves school about what he is going to do with his future is by no means as important as we sometimes make out. Most people are going to change their jobs and the pattern of their lives several times during their lifetime. Sometimes this will be for 'reasons beyond their control', ie no more jobs in their chosen field; sometimes it will be a positive step taken by them out of deliberate choice. Whether this happens by accident or design, it can always be treated as an opportunity for growth by an adult who has a positive, confident approach to life, who is realistically aware of his strengths and weaknesses, who is able to take risks, explore new situations, cope with change and with conflict.

So what are we doing in schools to develop in our pupils these sorts of qualities? Most of our pupils, including the girls, will now have potential *working* lives of some 40 years, though they are likely to have periods of not working and also to retire earlier. For this time-span the thought of doing one job is not only boring, it is also unrealistic. So many adults who did not enjoy school particularly blossom at a later stage in their lives and suddenly develop new interests and aptitudes, be they hobbies or jobs. So one of our tasks in school is to help our young people see themselves as whole persons, with leisure, family and community lives to lead as well as jobs to do; to help our young people realize that very few decisions about careers are irrevocable, if they are prepared to start again; to help them know how to start again later, when they are ready, *not* to reject them out of hand if they cannot take advantage of the educational opportunities given to them when they are at school; *not* to overvalue academic achievement so that this becomes the only yardstick for 'success', for it patently is not; to use methods of teaching our young people, which enable them to grow and develop their resources, *not* methods which merely contain and control; to respect and value our pupils so that they have sufficient self-esteem to face the world; to avoid over-projecting or overpraising our pupils which may give them a false idea of their own importance and ability; to provide some experiences of stress and conflict to enable our pupils to learn to cope with these with our *support* but not our intervention; to give our pupils *genuine* opportunities for taking responsibility for their own actions and facing the consequences; *not* to iron out all the difficulties of being adolescent, but to help our pupils work at them for themselves.

To me this is what schools are about. These are counselling objectives, careers objectives, educational objectives. I hope that you will be able to see these objectives behind what I say in the rest of this book. In the next and succeeding chapters I recount in quite simple terms the work I did first as a counsellor, then as a deputy and then as a head teacher. The details relate to the ways things were then and what happened then. The principles upon which the work was based remain true; so do the pupils' feelings. Although what I wrote was originally geared towards the teacher who was interested in developing counselling skills, now it seems to me that it can be usefully taken up by any adult working in a professional way with young persons in transition, particularly on the point of growing up.

References

1. *A New Training Initiative* (1981) MSC. May
   Foundation Training Issues (1982) Institute of Manpower Studies. February
   Youth Skills Project (1983) Institute of Manpower Studies
   Training for Skill Ownership: Learning to Take it With You (1983) Institute of Manpower Studies
2. *A Basis for Choice* (1979) Further Education Curriculum Review and Development Unit (FEU) July
   ABC in Action (1981) FEU September
   Developing Social and Life Skills (1981) FEU January
   Vocational Preparation (1981) FEU April
   see Bibliography for fuller list
3. Hamblin, D *Guidance 16-19* (1983) Basil Blackwell
4. Hopson, B and Scally, M *Lifeskills Teaching* (1981) McGraw Hill
   Lifeskills Associates *Lifeskills Teaching Magazine* from Ashling, Back Church Lane, Leeds LS16 8DN
   Barry Hopson is the Director, the Counselling and Career Development Unit, University of Leeds
5. The Careers Research and Advisory Centre (CRAC) Bateman Street, Cambridge
6. *The Youth Training Scheme: Scheme Design and Content* (1983) YTS. April
7. Watts, A G ed (1982) *Schools, YOPs and the New Training Initiative* CRAC
8. *Guide to the Work of the Area Manpower Board* (1983) MSC. March
9. *HMI: Aspects of Secondary education* (1979), HMSO
10. *The Practical Curriculum* (1981), Schools Council, working paper 70 Methuen Educational
11. *Youth Training Scheme: Scheme Design and Content* (1983) YTS. April
12. NICEC
    The National Institute for Careers Education and Counselling, Bateman Street, Cambridge
13. *The British Journal of Guidance and Counselling*, CRAC
14. Marland, M (1974) *Pastoral Care*, Heinemann
15. Avent, C (1974) *Practical Approaches to Careers Education* Hobsons Press
16. *Training Opportunities for Women* (1975) Training Services Agency
17. Jones, A, Marsh, J and Watts, AG The Life Style Series
    i) *Male and Female: Choosing your Role in Modern Society* (1974) Hobsons Press
    ii) *Living Choices: Home and Family in Modern Society* (1976) Hobsons Press
    iii) *Time to Spare: Leisure in Modern Society* (1980) Hobsons Press
18. Bazalgette, J *School Life and Work Life: A Study of Transition in the Inner City* (1978) Hutchinson
19. A technique promoted by Edward de Bono's thinking lessons (CORT, Cambridge)
20. *Occupational Training Families* Institute of Manpower Studies, see also *Youth Skills Project* (1981) and *Training for Skill Ownership* (1983)
21. Watts, A G ed (1983) *Work Experience and Schools* Heinemann organization on schools series
    Eggleston, J ed (1982) *Work Experience in Secondary Schools* Routledge and Kegan Paul
22. Carter, M (1972) *Home School and Work* Penguin (see also ref 18)
    Maizels, J (1970) *Adolescent Needs and the Transition from School to Work* Athlone Press
23. Vocational Preparation for Young People (1975) Training Services Agency
24. Lawrie, P (1976) *On the Dole* Kogan Page
    Dauncey, G (1983) *Facing Unemployment* Hobsons Press

Chapter 2

The advent of the counsellor

I began my work as a school counsellor in 1965. At that time the idea of school counselling was new to Britain, so new in fact that I would often be mistaken for a kind of local politician. Friends and acquaintances who were interested in education would always begin by asking me why I was needed. What could a counsellor do that a form teacher couldn't do? Don't British teachers take a pride in looking after the whole pupil, not just in teaching their subject? So I shall begin with these questions.

It is true that counselling in schools was not altogether new; what was new was the establishment of the counsellor as a new professional species with professional skills. In October 1965, courses for training school counsellors (who must be trained teachers with five years' teaching experience) were set up at the University of Reading and Keele. Since then others have mushroomed throughout the country. The thrust from below was there, but the pull from above never came. There is still no official policy, no national directive, no frame of reference, no statutory duties or powers laid down about school counselling. The original counsellors had a great deal of freedom from red tape but at the same time enormous scope for damaging as well as promoting the well-being of school students.

It was therefore not surprising that the advent of the professional school counsellor was hailed with mixed feelings. In part this is because the counsellor's role was ill defined and badly understood. Many regarded the superimposition of the counsellor on the educational structure as an unnecessary extravagance in an age when economic and academic resources are scarce. Some regarded the counsellor with over-enthusiasm as a magical cure-all; some regarded counselling as a bandwagon for the ambitious or unsuccessful teacher to jump on; some saw the counsellor as a threat, someone making a takeover bid for the powers of the conscientious form teacher, the careers officer and the child guidance clinic. The fact that school counselling was an American import only added to our resistance; we marked our defiance by spelling the word with a double l: counsellor, not counselor.

The subject of counselling was emotionally explosive in the educational world, triggering off conflict and ambivalence even in those who purported to sympathize with the movement. Few of us understood what the counsellor was trying to do, and even the counsellors themselves were not agreed upon this.

There were probably as many different schemes of counselling in the country as there were counsellors. Indeed sceptics were tempted to say of counselling as Eysenck has said of psychotherapy, that 'it is an unidentified technique applied to unspecified problems with unpredictable outcomes.' A natural distrust of the unknown, a fear of being made somehow to appear inadequate or diminished by the counsellor made us all wary; it was tempting to fall back on the security of tried and tested routines, backed by economic argument, to avoid facing the immensely complicated issues and implications which the whole idea of school counsellors involved.

Any simple definition of counselling is bound to be misleading and incomplete. In chapter 3 the nature of counselling is discussed at greater length. But it is important to any understanding of this book to attempt a definition at this stage. Basically counselling is an enabling process, designed to help an individual come to terms with his life and grow to greater maturity through learning to take responsibility and to make decisions for himself. In modern connotation, counselling is not meant to denote a process of advice-giving, of *telling* someone what to do, but rather of providing the conditions under which an individual will be able to make up his mind what, if anything, he should do. Sometimes an individual needs help of a specific nature, for example objective information about a job or about his own limitations and capabilities; sometimes he needs simply to talk out in a calm, relaxed atmosphere his innermost thoughts. Counselling is not of course a word to be used exclusively in the context; this is the kind of service that the Marriage Guidance Council provides through its counsellors for those with marital problems; counselling also has much in common with what social workers call casework.

In the past the role of the counsellor was fulfilled in the community spontaneously by a variety of people: the priest, the doctor, a relative, a godparent, the school master: someone who had a certain detachment or objectivity and to whom qualities of wisdom, understanding and experience were attributed. In schools these roles have always been filled intuitively by certain members of staff, not necessarily the pupil's own form teacher or house tutor, but often someone associated less with authority, perhaps a matron, an art master or a home economics mistress. The problem now is that for various reasons, such as the breakdown of the extended family network and the pace and pressures of modern living, it is sometimes difficult for individuals to get guidance when they need it. At the same time that life has become more and more complex, the structure of society has become decreasingly supportive to the individual. Man's social role, moral code, the pattern of his family life, his work and his leisure are in a constant state of evolution.

By analogy, in schools we find mirrored the same dilemmas and complexities as in society. Teachers may be interested in helping their individual charges but they do not always have the time, the opportunity or the skills to do so fully. The reorganization of secondary schools so that time is given on the timetable for tutorial, careers guidance, and study skills work recognizes this fact.[1]

The tutor who takes on a counselling role has three main functions: educational guidance (help with subject choice and academic progress), vocational guidance (help in choosing or finding a job or career) and personal guidance (help with any personal problem). Counselling is really a technique used in guidance and is most relevant to personal guidance. The three threads of guidance are of course inextricably entwined, though it seems that this is one of the factors which makes for the semantic and practical dilemmas faced in defining the counselling. It *is* possible to distinguish between vocational guidance (which is closely linked with educational guidance) and personal guidance, or counselling. A person who wants vocational guidance may need counselling at a personal level before he can make an objective decision, but not necessarily so. It is asking a lot of a tutor or counsellor to expect him to combine the great technical knowledge of job content and opportunities, skill in testing, slotting, evaluating and recording abilities required of the educational/vocational counsellor, with the much more passive yet exacting role of personal counsellor. What may happen when the two roles are combined is that the tutor or counsellor is not able, through lack of time, to fulfil his non-evaluative, non-directive listening role. The more direct vocational guidance role, with its tangible results in the shape of record cards and decisions, may take over. Anyone who attempts vocational guidance should be acquainted with and be able to use counselling techniques; indeed vocational counsellors *should* use counselling techniques, but because of pressures of time they may not always be able to counsel as much as they would wish or as much as their clients need. All school students need vocational guidance; only a small proportion need personal counselling, but for this small proportion it is very important for their future well-being that their needs are not overlooked. Hence the argument for the specialist careers teacher and counsellor to supplement the work of the tutor.

Guidance services in British schools

Let us look now and examine the provision in English schools for educational, vocational and personal guidance. Most of the responsibility for guidance lies in fact with the form tutor. He in turn is supported and directed in his work by the house or year master and the head teacher. When necessary he can call on the services of the educational psychologist, the careers teacher and the education welfare officer to provide the supplementary specialist skills and knowledge he lacks.

The English system of diffused responsibility for guidance has the merits of providing an elaborate network of care for the individual and of making use of whatever talents in this respect that the staff may have. The snag is that it is an amateur system and a random system. It depends on the inspired intuitive gifts of the teacher, and is based on the assumption that all teachers are gifted in this direction, which is patently not always the case. True, it provides safeguards for the individual: the head of year can make up for deficiencies in the form tutor, and the head can provide support for the head of year. But it is the form tutor who is fundamentally in the key position here and this important fact is not always realized or accepted. Reorganization of schools into larger comprehensive units means that heads have to delegate more to heads of year who in turn must delegate to form tutors. But effective delegation has to include some specification of the role and duties involved in 'pastoral care' and some training for this role. How often is this thoroughly done?[2]

If we were to do a job analysis of what the form tutor actually does, we would find that he makes of his job what he will, according to his age, aptitude and ability. Dinner money is taken, registers are marked, attendance slips are filled in, reports are produced on time, but over and above these tangible tasks is a whole range of activity which may or may not take place. Hence the dilemma many schools face in deciding whether, how and when to introduce a full tutorial programme which is allocated proper 'lesson' time.

Pastoral care is a concept which is now out-of-date. While most form teachers provide a high standard of pupil care, it is also true that some teachers have little interest in this aspect of their work, and some have little talent for it, even though they may be interested in it: notwithstanding these may all be good teachers. All form tutors, whatever their intuitive skills, could be helped to be more effective, more perceptive and more objective in their approach to their charges if their initial training prepared them more thoroughly for this role,[3] and if they regularly discussed their role and their problems in groups within schools. Schemes of this kind do exist, particularly if there is an active tutorial programme, but not as a part of standard educational practice. Those interested in the training of teachers through groups should read Elizabeth Richardson's sensitive account of her work in the Department of Education at Bristol.[4] This is a quite different approach from the 'group games' people now so often play.[5]

Training in professional skills, for heads, heads of year and teachers alike, should include experience in groups to bring a heightened awareness of the emotional forces at play in any school situation. It should also include study and experience of interview techniques, with particular emphasis on the art of listening, and an understanding of counselling techniques.

Educational guidance

In an attempt to overcome the pastoral-academic split, in many secondary schools, educational guidance is undertaken by the form tutor, supported by the head of the year. By educational guidance I mean not only help with choice of subjects but also the maintenance of systematic and objective records of a student's attainment and development.

Pupils arrive at secondary school with a primary school profile which may form the beginning of their secondary school record card, and which usually gives an objective measurement or grade for certain abilities. We do not normally ask the secondary teacher to give sophisticated individual tests of intelligence and attainment; this is the job of the educational psychologist, who will test children at the request of the school in cases where the teacher suspects either that a pupil's work is falling below its potential or that a pupil is strained because he is pushing himself beyond his capabilities. Whether the educational psychologist is used in this testing capacity as much as he might be depends on a number of factors: whether the psychologist himself believes in tests, how busy the psychologist is with 'more serious' cases, how much confidence the teacher has in putting forward a problem case. Many teachers find real difficulty in deciding when a child needs educational testing and therefore only ask for it in extreme cases when they are absolutely sure of themselves, and not afraid either of making themselves look ridiculous or of wasting the psychologist's time. A lot of us feel rather the same about doctors: it is not enough that they provide a service, we must be confident enough to use it.

This line of argument assumes that objective measurement of ability is an important component in educational guidance. Not everyone would agree that it is. There are certainly moments in a pupil's school career when such impartial information would be invaluable. For example, if pupils have to choose between courses, it is relevant to know whether this pupil is potentially university, college of education, A level, O level or CSE material. But an experienced teacher will claim here that he is able to tell where a pupil's abilities place him in the spectrum of choice, and he may well be right. He will also claim that the pupil may not have reached his full potential yet, and that to make a rigid cut-off point would be unfair. Certainly a form teacher who has known both pupil and staff over a period of time will understand more than any outsider the true meaning of a B+ for Miss Smith in geography and a C+ for Mr Burns in mathematics. But it is possible to make a mistake in placing even though a school's policy may be to keep course choice as revocable and flexible as possible. The important point here, surely, is to spot the under achievers, to find out why they are under achievers and to help them to fulfil their potential.

Devising more sophisticated profile systems and keeping them properly filled in are tasks which could be allotted to a school counsellor and take up a lot of his time. But before we embark upon such a scheme we have to ask why we need these records; if we need them, how can we best ensure that they are to be useful, and if they are to be useful, who should keep them. There is no reason why schools should not devise records schemes to be filled in by form teachers; indeed this is what already often happens. In other words, more sophisticated recording and profiling mechanisms are important topics to be considered in the running of comprehensive schools, but they are not conclusive arguments for the introduction of school counsellors.[6]

Whoever is responsible for guiding the pupil with his choices, be he head of year, form tutor or counsellor, needs to remember that a student likes to feel he has had some say in the matter. Schools which have experimented with pupils writing their own reports have found this very beneficial to pupil learning, especially when time has been found for follow up discussion with the tutor.[7]

Vocational guidance

Decisions made through guidance do of course have vital implications for vocational guidance and this is why it is so important for these inseparable processes to be continuous and on-going throughout a child's school life. Crisis-counselling of school leavers is generally regarded by the careers service as an unsatisfactory process of limited value. Thorough vocational guidance involves not just careers advisers, whoever they may be, but the whole education of the individual. More attention needs to be given not just to providing more information about jobs at an earlier stage but also to providing more opportunity for schoolchildren to make decisions and, most subtle of all, to motivating them to want to study, stay on, do well. And we must remember that it is not enough to motivate the children if their parents do not share these aspirations. These I think are points which teachers are in a position to influence more than they realize. Whatever the answers to these problems— and there is no simple solution—it is certain that there is need and scope for better vocational guidance in schools. If we accept this we then have to decide whether it should be co-ordinated by the all-purpose counsellor, by a specialist occupational counsellor, by a school based careers officer, or by a careers teacher.[8] But the person who takes on this role will have to spend a lot of time working with form tutors and heads of year to ensure that they understand, share and help to implement what the school is trying to do, as well as investigating and co-ordinating the work that goes on throughout the curriculum. Team work is essential here.

Personal guidance

What about the provision of personal guidance under our existing system? Like the other types of guidance, its provision is patchy, not sufficiently structured into the official fabric of school life and dependent in quality very largely on the attitudes and personality of the head, house or year staff and form tutors. The official organs of personal guidance for students at risk are the child guidance clinics for psychological problems and the welfare services, notably the social services, for social problems. In many areas these services are not able to do as much preventive work as they would like for a number of reasons. These are community services and parents who are worried can make direct and confidential contact with them, but parents do not always know this. Heads too are sometimes insufficiently informed about the nature and purpose of the services and sceptical of their value: the research in the Plowden Report on this topic, although done in primary schools long ago, is probably relevant here.[9] Both services, particulary the school psychological services, are understaffed. Most child guidance clinics either have a waiting list, or schools think they have a waiting list and therefore hesitate to use them. In any case problem children are often referred when their problems have reached such magnitude that the pupils concerned are disrupting in some way the smooth functioning of school life. Teachers may find it difficult to decide when a child's behaviour requires the attention of a psychiatrist and hesitate to approach the educational psychologist for a second opinion in the same way that they may hesitate to approach him about testing: that is unless they are very confident, unless the head is particularly sympathetic to the psychological services and unless the psychologist is known to the staff, liked by the staff and seen to perform a useful function either by referring children to the child guidance clinic or by counselling children and their parents. At a time when educational psychologists are in such short supply, they are simply not in school often enough to advise and reassure a member of staff with an embryonic problem child. This is where the specialist counsellor can be useful.

Theoretically the education welfare officer is the person who can advise the school about social welfare services and which agency to use. The Plowden Report research here again shows the education welfare officer service to be understaffed both in quality and quantity and that its former role of 'attendance officer' looms large. Schools may be lucky enough to have an outstanding welfare officer attached to them; if not they have to depend on their own knowledge of the social services and their own contacts with them, which may be very good or may be minimal. What is more, whatever information heads and deputies manage to glean about the present tangle of social welfare services is not always passed on to the form teacher. Teachers may not often have the opportunity for contact with outside welfare agencies and their knowledge of them may become theoretical and clouded. Obvious social problems are dealt with, but is this enough? Could more preventive work be done in schools?

The form tutor

Let us look for a moment at an 'ideal' form tutor: sensitive, aware of his own limitations, he has the interests of his pupils uppermost in his mind, without getting over-involved in their problems; he is constantly aware of the emotional undercurrents in his form and able to forestall problems before they develop; he does not hesitate to ask advice from his head of year or head, and he brings in experts such as educational psychologists and careers officers at the earliest opportunity. He thus combines the best in guidance with a balanced overall view of the pupil and continuity of care.

Many form tutors achieve all this and more; many understandably fall short of this ideal. Most heads learn quickly to accept the limitations of their staff, to make the best of the qualities their staff do have by a subtle balance of staff characteristics throughout each academic year and an intricate network of safeguards, provided through other personnel such as heads of year, to see that individual pupils suffer as little as possible. But what happens when heads have practically no choice of form tutor? With the present numbers of teachers in schools, it is likely that heads will have to use most full-time staff as form tutors, yet not all of these will be entirely enthusiastic about or suited for this role.

Continuity of care is another myth which befuddles our thinking about the role of the form teacher. Some schools as a matter of policy institute continuity of care in an attempt to counterbalance effects of size and impersonality. Thus a child may keep the same head of year all his school life and the same form tutor for two or three years at a time. There is no simple way out of this dilemma: the important principle is to structure the system of care so that an individual child has a choice of adults with whom to relate who know him sufficiently well to see him in perspective. Thus a blockage in a relationship with one teacher or the sudden departure of another would not leave a child either feeling victimized or thinking that nobody really knows him or cares for him.

If we accept that form tutors could improve the quality of the personal care they provide if they were given more specific training for this role, and if they had both knowledge and experience of counselling techniques, we must also accept that it is unlikely even then that they would be able to serve all the needs of every individual in their care. We have to face even in the most outstanding form teacher limitations placed upon him by his other roles. His first job after all is to teach and he does not have time to be all things to all his form members. Furthermore his other roles in the structure of the school community may limit his counselling potential in the eyes of his pupils.

First the question of time. Form tutors are normally given very little free time with their form. Some may not even teach all the members of their form and their contact with them may be therefore limited to morning and afternoon registration. More and more schools have established 'tutorial periods' to help overcome this particular problem, but even now this kind of form time is often spent in a rather embarrassed way in quizzes, debates and just doing homework. Even good tutorial programming does not always ensure a one to one relationship between the tutor and the pupil. Few form teachers systematically interview every member of their form at regular intervals and contact with parents is even more haphazard. A child will be summoned for interview by form or year head normally only in certain prescribed circumstances: if the child is in trouble, if he is to be sent on an errand or asked to perform some duty, if he is to be asked for some information.

Let us suppose that the child wishes to talk about something that is bothering him. First he has to pluck up the courage to make an approach, and this in itself is not easy. Unless a specific time is set aside for the interview, it is quite possible that the child will not be able to get round to his real problem because the bell for the next lesson has gone and teacher and child alike have a duty to move on. Moreover it takes an exceptionally perceptive or unharassed teacher to see that a simple statement may be the cue for a need for a longer chat.

Take for example the statement: 'My sister's having a baby tomorrow.' A busy teacher might reply, 'How nice for you. Would you mind sitting down while I take the register?' A less harassed teacher will ask a few questions about it and remember to ask a few more after the baby is born. But what the child may really need is not for someone to ask her questions, but someone to *listen* to her. What she may really need is to express her own fears and worries about childbirth, her own insecurity and ambivalence in the face of this new rival within the family. To be able to do this the pupil needs to talk to someone who is not in a hurry, who is giving all his attention to the interview and who is not worrying about the fact that he is late for his next lesson and that there will be a rumpus in the classroom. There is no reason why the form teacher should not suggest a meeting during lunch hour or after school to continue the discussion, but unless this is a recognized, expected and established pattern of school procedure, it is unlikely to be either suggested or used to any great extent. In any case, teachers often have staff meetings of various kinds after school and little 'free' time.

There are other factors too which may block the possibility of real communication between form teacher and form pupil. The form teacher's duty to look after his form is subordinate in fact to his duty to teach his subject and his duty to see that the children in his charge keep the school rules and regulations, work hard and do not waste time. The strength of the teacher's authoritarian role will depend on how democratically the school is run, and how tolerant and permissive is the teacher's basic personality. But however flexible and fearless the teacher, he will still have to demand conformity from his pupils on certain points, whatever his beliefs, if he is to do his job. He is likely in any case to be perceived by his pupils as an instrument of authority; indeed if he is not perceived in this way he may be doing a disservice to schools, pupils and himself alike by undermining the school disciplinary system. But because of the teacher's authority, his role as a potential counsellor may have certain limits. Rebels and drop-outs may find it particularly hard to turn to him either because he stands for what they oppose or because they realize his more liberal tendencies but do not want to put him in a dilemma. Children recognize, sometimes more than we credit, the limitations of our roles.

Another factor which may block the form teacher's counselling potential is his judgemental role. Teachers are constantly asked to make judgements on their pupils by assessing their academic work, their industriousness, their behaviour, their potential and their personality. True there has been in many schools a swing away from percentages and positions but it is important for the school, the pupil and his parents to have some idea of the progress the pupil is making, both in relation to his own potential and by comparison with his peers. Assessments of behaviour or personality are bound to reflect the teacher's own attitudes and prejudices. Pupils are therefore not going to reveal to teachers, unless they can help it, information that may be damaging to their image and prejudicial to their reputations.

The same sort of behaviour is to be observed in the relationship between any employee and his boss; in the school situation between the teacher and the head, and between parent and head too. 'Such a good teacher,' the head may say, in all sincerity. 'She takes such an interest in her children.' Or 'Such a good mother; she understands her daughter so well.' This may not be how the child concerned feels.

Most of us present some kind of façade to those in authority over us. We may do this consciously or unconsciously. When we break through the façade, it is either because we trust the person concerned enough to know they will not hold it against us, or because we have ceased to care what they think about us. Clearly parents and form teachers should know their children well enough to see through the outer image, simply because they have contact with them every day. But this conclusion does not necessarily follow; unless we are emotionally disturbed and our feelings are so strong that we can no longer control them, most of us reserve the horrors of our innermost thoughts for those few people we can trust sufficiently not to use them in evidence against us or our families.

So although children may need to talk to someone, they may not turn to their teacher, not only because they perceive the teacher's judgemental role. Another factor may be that they cannot be sure that what they tell in confidence will be kept confidential. Children recognize that teachers are liable to react to pieces of confidential information like most other human beings. Either they will want to pass this information on, because they feel it important to know everything about the child; or they will want to act upon this information because it provokes in them anxieties of their own and feelings of concern for the child which can only be dissipated by 'doing something'. For example a child might tell a teacher that her parents are unhappily married and that her father beats her mother up every Friday. Supposing this information to be true, all it tells you about *the child* is that she is worried and that she needs, at this moment, a little extra sympathy and support, and a chance to talk over her feelings. Once she has done this the relevance of the information to an understanding of the child is diminished; if such information became common knowledge among the staff it could lead to a stereotyping of the image of the child's family and a distortion of the child's own image which would do nothing to help her. Or supposing a child confides that her father has been making incestuous advances towards her. If this is true and incest has taken place, then it is a case for the law. If it is not true, but really a fantasy in the child's mind, built upon her own desires, then premature action can only make matters worse. Clearly a child in this situation needs a lot of help, but the help must come from someone with professional skills and the time for dealing with such a situation.

Comment

If we look at existing school guidance services we see that *educational guidance* is at present undertaken by heads of year and form tutors who could be helped by more training to improve their skills for this role. There is relatively little choice of subject within most schools' curricula. Educational psychologists can be used for educational testing, or more teachers trained to do this work. *Vocational guidance* is not sufficiently linked with educational guidance and motivation or the curriculum as a whole. The careers service has not at the moment adequate supplies of skilled manpower to provide a careers counsellor for each large school. We have to decide whether to train more teachers for this specific role or simply increase the size of the careers service. In the area of *personal guidance* not all teachers have talents for helping individuals with their problems and those who do could improve their techniques with more training and self-awareness. Form tutors have considerable potential as counsellors but there are limits to their counselling role partly because of their other roles in the structure of the school and partly because they have so little spare time. Normal children do nevertheless have a need at times to form a relationship and to talk out their problems and conflicts with an adult who can listen sympathetically and respect their confidences and whose role is no way either authoritarian or judgemental. More curriculum time needs to be made available for these processes. The counsellor has a role in supporting and training tutors who do want to take a counselling role and who have time for it. There is, however, also a need for a counsellor as a backstop with more time, experience and specific skills. The move towards 'tutorial' programmes and social education programmes[10] is to be welcomed but does not obviate these potential role conflicts or time constraints. The need for staff development and support becomes even stronger.

References

1. Hamblin, D (1983) *Teaching Study Skills* Basil Blackwell
   Active Tutorial Work Books 1-5 Lancashire Education Authority (1980,81). Basil Blackwell
   Button, L (1982) *Group Tutoring for the Form Tutor* Hodder & Stoughton
2. See the journal of NAPCE (The National Association of Pastoral Care in Education) for examples of how this might be done.
3. *HMI: Teaching in Schools: The Content of Initial Training* (1982) DES
   HMI: The New Teacher in School (1982) HMSO
   This reveals that even now training in pastoral care/the role of the form tutor receives scant attention in most initial training courses.
4. Richardson, E (1967) *Group Study for Teachers* Routledge and Kegan Paul
5. eg Donna Brandes and Howard Phillips (1979) *Gamester's Handbook* Hutchinson
6. Pearce, B (1979) *Personal Record Keeping in Schools* Counselling and career development unit, Leeds
   Balogh, J (1982) *Profile Reports for School Leavers* Longman for Schools Council
   A Review of Issues and Practice in the Use and Development of Student Profiles: (1982) FEU September
7. Adams, E and Burgess, T *Outcomes of Education* (1980) Macmillan
8. Hayes, J and Hopson, B (1972) *Careers Guidance: The Role of the School in Vocational Development* Heinemann Educational
9. *Children and their Primary Schools* (1967) The Plowden Report HMSO
10. (i) David, K (1982) *Personal and Social Education in Secondary Schools* Longman for Schools Council
    (ii) Button, L (1982) *Group Tutoring for the Form Teacher* Hodder & Stoughton Educational

Chapter 3

What is counselling?

In this chapter I want to discuss the meaning and nature of counselling at greater length. Although many teachers now attempt some counselling at the same time as recognizing that some individual students need more help than they can provide in the time available to them, others postulate gloomily a kind of Parkinson's law of counselling: adolescent problems expand to occupy the number of counsellors available. Leave adolescents alone, they say, and their problems will sort themselves out with the fullness of time. Is this so? Is counselling simply a soft option for the malingering drop-out? The truth is that individual counselling is not all that comfortable a process, since it demands searching self-examination. Any counsellor worth his salt should be able to recognize when he is being abused, rather than used. Furthermore he will expect his clients to come as much from the good and the brave as from the bad and the ugly: the adolescents who are most at risk are not always the ones who show it most.

Many teachers remain confused about the nature of counselling. This is hardly surprising when so many different kinds of people claim to be counsellors. Counselling is fashionable, and that for a start puts some people off it. Teachers, doctors, social workers, psychologists, youth leaders, marriage guiders and ministers of religion all lay claim to the counselling role. Whether in fact they really do counsel, or merely think they do, will depend on many factors. The kind of help called counselling may in fact range from advice-giving to psychotherapy. The school counsellor may sometimes give advice, though this is no justification for his existence since teachers give advice very readily. Equally he may occasionally work at a psychotherapeutic level, though he would be unwise to attempt this without himself being expertly guided. But his basic role is somewhere between these two extremes. Leona Tyler has defined the aim of psychotherapy as personality change.[1] The school counsellor is more concerned with the development of what is, then with fundamental change; with the here and now more than with the deep and distant past; with making the best of a situation as it actually is, rather than with altering the way of the world. If anything changes through counselling, it is not the fabric of the client's life and personality so much as his feelings and his attitudes towards himself and others, and his degree of acceptance of himself and the world he lives in.

Adolescents in school and in society have to face many problems of adjustment and identity;[2] they have to learn to be independent, to make decisions for themselves, to take responsibility, to weather a crisis, sometimes to live with a difficult situation. Many adolescents survive this stormy period much strengthened by their experience and without needing to talk to a counsellor individually about their problems. They will doubtless benefit from group discussions and exercises on these topics but that is another matter. The counsellor's role is to give support to adolescents in transition who want to talk about it. The counsellor's role is not to cover over the adolescent's difficulties, but to help him to face his problems and grow to greater maturity through them. Thus the foundation of a more integrated and balanced adulthood may be laid. Counselling is therefore appropriate for adolescents who are basically sound in mind and body, but who need help at certain stages of their development. This is not to say that their problems are not serious or real. Conflict may cause depression or despair in an adolescent, which may prevent him from taking action or being decisive, or doing his school work properly. But the problem is only part of a passing phase in the adolescent's growth and situation; it is a transitory developmental or situational problem, not a fundamental impairment of his personality. All young people need an opportunity to talk whether they take it or not.

A simple illustration might make this point clearer. June may be feeling bewildered and hurt because her mother has married again. June cannot accept her stepfather in her deceased father's role. As a result she is moping about at home and not getting much out of her vocational sixth-form course. She is not developing interests and activities with friends of her own age, she is doing nothing to help herself out of this despondency and she is rejecting her mother's efforts to help her. It is no good telling June to pull herself together. She will not be able to pull herself together until she has come to terms with her feelings, understood what has happened, realized that no fairy godmother is going to alter the situation and accepted that no one is trying to hurt *her*—her parents desperately want her to be happy; and that it is in her power to make the best or the worst of this situation. A sense of perspective will not come until June feels secure in herself and in the people she needs; this security may not come until she has expressed her violent feelings. She may be afraid to express her anger to her mother in case she loses her altogether. The counsellor's role is to provide the conditions in which June can begin to express her real self. The counsellor does not tell her to be sensible, to take a grip on herself. The counsellor is not trying to repair an inability to make relationships with people, because up to this time June has not found this difficult. The counsellor is simply trying to help June release and use her own resources for coping with life and take some constructive action on her own behalf. But June does *have* resources of her own; she is *capable* of taking action. Through taking responsibility herself, June develops and strengthens her ability to cope with difficult situations, an ability which will stand her in good stead when she is an adult. She has not buried her problem only to have it re-occur at a later stage in a different form, perhaps when she marries or has her first child. She has not had her problem solved by someone else, which would prevent her learning how to solve problems. Through her relationship with the person counselling her she has faced her problem, she has worked through her feelings and she has learnt something useful about herself and the world.

Theories of counselling

There is a vast body of American and British literature on counselling theory and technique, which is best read at first hand.[3,4,5] The main debate between the theorists concerns the amount of direction the counsellor should give the content of the interview. It is generally agreed that the quality of the relationship between counsellor and client is of fundamental importance; that among the goals of counselling are 'self-understanding, self-awareness, self-acceptance, self-determination'. But are these goals best achieved by non-directive, directive or eclectic counselling techniques? *Non-directive counsellors*, inspired by the work of Carl Rogers,[6,7] put the onus of direction vey much on the individual; the client must be allowed to talk about what he wants to talk about. The relationship between the counsellor and his client is in itself therapeutic and brings the freedom for the client to make his own decisions and grow towards maturity. *Directive counsellors* are more purposeful. They lead the client through an examination of his problem, go through the possible consequences of various courses of action, help the client try out various new solutions. The client is still making the decisions but the choice is largely directed by the experience and the expertise of the counsellor.[8] *Eclectic counsellors* use whatever method they feel best suits the needs of the client, arguing that some pupils, because of their age, inexperience or personality, need more specific help in making a decision than others.[9] More recently client problems have been seen as learning problems and the counsellor's job has been defined as 'helping his client learn more effective ways of solving his own problems'; that is, to learn more adaptive and constructive modes of behaviour.[10] It is this mode which is particularly appropriate in the current climate.

I know from my own experience how confusing it can be for a teacher, first to come across the highly technical literature about counselling theory, second to try to reconcile these philosophies with his own philosophy and personality, third to integrate what he has learnt in theory with what he does in practice. We must not forget that, in fact, theories of counselling have much in common and their differences are mostly in emphasis. They have as their basis the interaction between two people, one of whom is trying to help the other. With what purpose, by which means and with what effect will depend above all on the personalities of the two persons concerned and to a lesser extent on theories and techniques. Ultimately the counsellor functions not according to a book, but according to himself, yet in a disciplined, informed and professional manner. In this next section I shall use the word counsellor to mean a person counselling, not necessarily the person labelled a counsellor.

The elements in a counselling relationship

What are the ingredients which make up the relationship between the counsellor and his client? These ingredients are not exclusive to a counselling relationship: they might be found in any relationship between two individuals, and the fact that they are often missing is at the root of many problems between people. In family life, at work and in school, we are more likely to thrive if our relationships with the people near to us are based on mutual liking, trust, respect, tolerance and genuine concern. In the school setting the kind of relationship which exists between head and pupils, teachers and pupils, teachers and teachers, pupils and pupils, teachers and parents, affects not only the atmosphere of the school, but the amount of education that goes on. It is a sobering thought to recall how often, not intentionally, but because we are not thinking about what we are doing, we unwittingly crush instead of encourage, criticize instead of praise, belittle instead of believe, advise instead of listen, co-exist instead of communicate. Although we may not all be counsellors, or want to be counsellors, we can all learn from a consideration of what is involved in a counselling relationship.

Rapport

First there must *be* a relationship between the person counselling and his client. That might sound self-evident, but it is possible for two people to be together, to be talking, without there being any communication of feeling between them. The plays of Pinter and NF Simpson for example illustrate vividly some extreme cases of non-interaction. It may take time for a relationship to be established between counsellor and client, but they may quickly make rapport with each other, that is, recognize that there is, in their response to each other, a basis for building up a relationship. But for a fruitful relationship to be established, the client must want a relationship with the counsellor, and the counsellor must want to help the client, and feel that he can help him, in other words there is negotiation. Let us suppose for example that John is sent for counselling because he is unruly, aggressive and rude. If John himself either does not want or does not see the need for any help from anybody, then the counsellor may not be able to form a helpful relationship with John. He may after a while, if he is sufficiently skilled or lucky, inspire enough confidence in John for him to change his mind. But counselling will not really begin until John admits his need. If John has decided that he needs help, but the counsellor appears bored or disinterested in what he is saying, if the counsellor is thinking, 'What a dreadful type. I can quite see why no one can handle him. How on earth can I be expected to do anything with a case like this?' then there is not a sound basis for a counselling relationship. John will sense the lack of confidence and respect in the counsellor, and will not feel the warmth, trust and security in the relationship which he needs to be able to talk about how he really feels: to be able to admit for example that behind his aggressive defiance he feels unsure of himself, unloved and unwanted.

Respect for the individual

It is important that the person counselling should recognize John as an individual, as a person in his own right, and not by a stereotyped tag such as 'that long-haired lout in 5.E' or 'Brian's naughty brother' or 'one of that gang that wrecks everyone's lessons'. Recognition as an individual implies a uniqueness which is important to a sense of individual worth and self-respect. The counsellor can communicate this by showing respect for John: by being punctual and courteous, by calling John by name and by remembering the details of what John has already told him. It is insulting to John if the counsellor has to rummage through masses of notes in order to recall him, or if the counsellor confuses him with somebody else or asks about something John has already explained. The counsellor must stop and make time to review details of John's case before the interview if he cannot trust his memory; though if the counsellor does forget, it is better for him to explain than to pretend. The relationship must be as genuine as possible.

Acceptance

It is vital for the counsellor to accept the client as he is, warts and all, not only on certain conditions. If we look at John again, we see that part of his problem is that his mother is always saying, in effect, 'I won't love you unless you do as I say'. The teachers have been saying the same thing in their way, withdrawing rewards unless certain conditions are met. 'You won't go on this outing unless you behave' or 'I can't have you in this class unless you keep quiet.' This is reasonable enough for the sake of the class as a whole, but it is not going to cure John's behaviour, and is more likely to have the effect of reinforcing his sense of failure and worthlessness. The aim of the counsellor is to hold nothing against John, in no way to judge or prejudge him. He takes John as he is, without either condoning or criticizing his various misdemeanours. But the acceptance must be genuine, and come from within the counsellor. John will not be deceived if the counsellor is inwardly shocked, sceptical or suspicious. But if John feels genuine acceptance from the counsellor, he will feel less threatened by the interview situation; he will become less defensive and some of the blocks to the communication of feeling will be removed.

Empathy

The kind of response which John needs from the counsellor is called empathy, which must be distinguished from sympathy and pity. Feeling sorry for John can have the effect of making him feel more sorry for himself, which is not constructive. Sympathy is a self-centred emotion: the counsellor knows how he would feel if his mother didn't love him, but how does that help John? John needs empathy: the counsellor tries to understand how John feels in this situation. He understands John's feelings of hostility, despair, aggression, anxiety, defiance and guilt and John feels that he understands or that he really is trying to understand.

Trust

John is not going to tell the counsellor much unless he trusts him. A counsellor who is not trustworthy will have a bad reputation among the pupils, and this will undermine all that he is trying to do. Even if the counsellor is generally liked, trusted and respected by the pupils, John has to be sure for himself that the counsellor is trustworthy. This means that at first he will not tell the counsellor very much, and if the counsellor presses for intimate truths, he may meet with rebuff. First the relationship between John and his counsellor has to be established, the counsellor tested out. The counsellor has to reassure John as to who he is, why he is there, what the expectations and the limits of their relationship are. He has to do this in a way which John can understand, that is without recourse to psychological terminology, which could either be incomprehensible or intimidating. John must know for example that if he says his mother is lazy and selfish, the counsellor will not pass this on to his mother: to do this would damage John's relationship with his mother, and the aim of the counselling is quite the opposite—to improve this relationship. Both the counsellor and John realize that these statements are only partially true, that they express John's despair and anger at his mother's inability to reassure him of her love. Similarly John must know that the counsellor will not pass on this information to the teaching staff because, in fact, John loves his mother very much and does not want to blacken her name; he needs to express his hostility towards her to someone he can trust, but that is all. John also needs to be able to say that he hates school, that he cannot tolerate this teacher, that it is all unfair: but he must trust the counsellor not to pass this on to the school; otherwise his life there will become even more intolerable. John has to trust the counsellor sufficiently to start to ventilate his true feelings before he can begin to get his problem into perspective: when he has done this, he may be ready to consider his own part in it all and to what extent his own attitudes, his own expectations of others and of himself and his own behaviour are influencing his life.

Confidentiality

It is on the question of confidentiality that the form tutor and the official counsellor may have to behave differently and this role difference may affect outcomes. One of the first points the counsellor must explain to John then is the principle of confidentiality. He must make it clear that he will not pass on to anyone anything which is told him in confidence without John's agreement. This must include not only sensational facts like the time John found his mother in bed with his 'uncle' Bob, but feelings, like John's deprecatory attitudes to those in authority over him. (The staff know about those already, but there is no need for the counsellor to reinforce their hostility towards John.) However John will not be helped unless something of what he is feeling is communicated to his parents and his teachers. Ideally John will undertake this himself and then there are no problems of misrepresentation. But often John will need the help of the counsellor in doing this; the counsellor can pave the way for a more sympathetic reception of the new improved John. So the counsellor may say to John, 'I think it might be helpful for your teacher to know that you are finding life at home rather a strain, particularly as your father is away'. If John agrees but does not want to talk about it himself, the counsellor gets his permission to talk this over with the form teacher. The permission to talk is part of the respect shown by the counsellor for John. The form teacher says that he knew already that John had problems at home: yes, it must be very hard for a strong virile young man like John not to see his father; mother seemed to be finding it very hard to cope the last time John was in trouble and she was sent for by the head. Perhaps we need to handle John in a different way? The counsellor does not tell the teacher what to do, but tries to harness his sympathy for and understanding of John, feelings which have rather disappeared in the strain and exasperation of dealing with him daily.

What about seeing mother? Again there is no doubt that this can be extremely valuable to the counsellor, both to gain greater insight into John and to assess his problems realistically and also to help the mother to think more of John's point of view. But is it valuable to John? Only if John agrees that this would be helpful. If the interview is against his will, then it will destroy the bond of trust and respect between him and the counsellor; it will cause alienation not communication. If John agrees to the interview, the counsellor may find that both before and after John needs reassuring that the interview was in his best interests, and not a part of a new alliance of mother and counsellor against him.

Supposing during the course of counselling John tells the counsellor that he has 'got a girl into trouble' and that she is under the age of consent. Where a law has been broken, or where there is moral or physical danger to an individual, then the counsellor has a duty to society, the school and John's family to consider. It is only fair for the counsellor to make this clear at the very outset, so that if John tells him about this, he knows that action may be taken: perhaps this is what John wants and all he is asking for is some courage in facing up to his responsibilities in this. With the counsellor's support John may be able himself to tell the appropriate persons what has happened and face the consequences of his action or he may ask the counsellor to help him communicate the truth. But this can be done discreetly and tactfully by involving only those people who really need to know about this incident, avoiding publicity and panic and thus retaining John's dignity as far as possible. He is punishable within the law, but there is no need to make a public scapegoat of him as well. Indeed if John gains the strength to shoulder his responsibility the incident can be turned to constructive rather than destructive use. But before the counsellor does anything at all about this particular kind of incident, not only does he get John's agreement but he makes perfectly sure that this *is* the truth and not something John has made up because of his great need to demonstrate his manliness. If it is true but John refuses to give permission for action to be taken, then the counsellor may feel he has a duty to society to act nevertheless; but again as a mark of his respect for John he does not do this without first telling John what he is going to do and why. In my experience it has never been necessary to go against a child's wishes in this sort of case. Each case has to be judged on its merits and the point at which the counsellor feels conflict between his duty to society and his duty to the boy will depend on the disposition of the counsellor and the terms of reference under which he is working. The unattached youth worker may feel more freedom than the counsellor working within an institution. There is no golden rule, but it is my belief that the counsellor should make clear his legal and ethical position at the outset, so that someone like John is not lulled into revealing all and then is 'shopped'. This is unethical and untenable. The counsellor is not a spy service for the authorities and his first duty is to the individual child. The counsellor has therefore to be sufficiently strong in himself not to have to relieve his own anxiety or pass the buck of responsibility by taking premature unnecessary or unethical action. But it should be very rare indeed for the counsellor not to get the co-operation of his client.

Testing

Suppose during counselling it emerges that John would like to know whether he is capable of going to university, and a psychological test may be useful. John has asked for this because he has already grown to the point where he can take constructive action on his own behalf. Some counsellors prefer not to undertake testing themselves, even under these conditions; they feel that psychological testing is likely to hinder the progress of the counselling relationship, by putting the counsellor in an evaluating judgemental role, which may inhibit the client's freedom to express his feelings; they regard testing as the job of the educational psychologist or psychometrist. Whoever administers the test, its purpose is to help the client; the information obtained by the counsellor is for the use of the client himself. There is obviously a place for testing in schools, but not necessarily within the counselling relationship unless the client wants it.

The counselling interview

What is the counsellor doing during his interviews with John? Basically he is listening. This is not as easy as it sounds. The teacher exhausted from chalk and talk might think enviously of the counsellor sitting listening in a cosy one-to-one relationship. It is easier in one way only: the counsellor is giving his attention to the needs of one person instead of 20 or 30, and he is not trying to teach facts as well as encourage the weak, stimulate the strong and discipline the unruly. But the quality of the listening relationship between the counsellor and his client is at a deeper and therefore more demanding level than any classroom interaction; and there is no respite, none of the mechanical tasks such as setting homework or giving out books, none of the changes of tempo such as posing a problem for the class to solve in groups, which bring in the classroom the necessary breathing space for the teacher to gather together his thoughts and his strength.

When the counsellor is listening to John, he needs to give his full attention, body and soul, all the time. He is not just listening to what John is saying, he is trying to feel the feelings behind the words and he is observing the way John is sitting and looking. Nails being bitten, fingers tapping, fists clenched, lips trembling, eyes downcast or averted, cheeks pale or flushed, shoulders hunched or feet shuffling: these are all indications of John's feelings. What is more, the counsellor has to remember that this works both ways and that John is looking at him: John is liable to interpret the counsellor's behaviour too. If the counsellor is looking out of the window, rustling through files, yawning or coughing, taking notes assiduously, watching the clock, looking glazed or doodling, John may well think the counsellor is bored or disinterested in what he is saying. 'Just listening' requires great discipline and concentration on the part of the counsellor. The wise counsellor does not take on too many clients in too short a time, and gives himself time to breathe, think and reflect between each interview.

One important problem counsellors have to face is how to be emphatic, to show 'non-possessive warmth' without becoming over-involved with their clients. However detached and professional the counsellor thinks he is, he is bound to be involved with John to an extent. Whether he likes it or not his personality and own attitudes are bound to be having an effect on John. It seems to me that there must be involvement between John and the counsellor for anything to happen at all.[11] The danger point is reached when the counsellor is meeting his own needs through the interview as well as, or instead of, John's. When the counsellor himself feels angry with John's mother or the staff, and John, sensing this, thinks of the counsellor as an ally against the rest instead of someone who understands the point of view of both camps, then the counsellor becomes an alienator rather than a communicator. If the counsellor's own pride or need for success or results is at stake, then he risks pushing John into a solution which John does not accept for himself and which ultimately does not work for this reason. The counsellor is inevitably involved with the client but in a disciplined, professional way. Of course counsellors have needs: they may need to protect or to dominate, to be liked, to be systematic and orderly, or to be needed. It is to be hoped however that the counsellor's personal needs will be met primarily in his own private life, and such needs as do overspill into the counselling situation will be recognized by him and kept under his control. Clearly this is no easy task, which is one reason why counsellors themselves need regular discussion of their work. Listening without interrupting, without leaping to conclusions, without leading the discussion away from what John really wants to talk about is difficult, and may be particularly difficult for someone who has taught and is used to a more dominant and active role. An inexperienced, nervous or anxious counsellor may find himself doing most of the talking: asking questions instead of letting John talk, filling in embarrassing silences with a change of subject, asking for information when what he really wants to hear about is John's feelings. John himself may avoid those topics that are painful to him initially, but he is more likely to talk about them if he is allowed to come to them in his own time and is not pressed when he needs silences to formulate what is so difficult to express.

The counsellor's first task is to let John talk, to let John feel that he is accepted and respected, to establish a relationship. He has to try to understand what John is saying, to see John and the people in John's life as John sees them, not as he himself would see them. He may need to restate to John what he thinks John has said in order to check this. Initially he is not concerned with the external truth so much as John's view of the world. He has to resist explaining to John prematurely what he thinks are the mechanisms of John's behaviour: for a start he may be wrong, particularly if he does this too soon, and in any case John may be more usefully helped to work this out for himself over a period of time. Interpretation may be frightening and unacceptable to John, and only cause him to block even more the path to the truth.

During the interview, the counsellor has very little time to work out what is happening, and often it is only in retrospect that he and perhaps John can begin to see what it was all about. Listening to a tape-recording of an interview can be a rewarding way of improving counselling techniques though this can only be done if the client agrees and is not inhibited by the presence of a machine. Otherwise writing a verbatim account of an interview can help a counsellor to perceive his most glaring technical defects and to understand what has happened.

What does counselling achieve?

We have discussed some of the qualities in a counselling relationship and we have said so far that the role of the counsellor is to get John to talk about his feelings and his problems with the aim of achieving greater self-understanding and self-acceptance. What happens next? What effect does this have on John? Sceptics might say that all John has learnt is to talk about his problems, and that this in itself is not going to alter John's problems or his behaviour in any way. But the point is that John's problems and John's social situation may be unalterable, and perhaps the only factor that can be altered is John's perception of his situation, which may be distorted. John's behaviour cannot begin to take a turn for the better until he understands the stresses in his life and becomes confident enough to be able to tolerate them. Then he may well begin to try out new patterns of behaviour, to make decisions, to take action on his own behalf. In this sense counselling may facilitate the learning of new behaviour patterns. But first the *mens sana* may need extra attention to achieve the balanced, tolerant view of life necessary for constructive and purposeful action and experiment. Those of us who have taught know from our own experience that some children *will* improve if they are exhorted or threatened, punished or rewarded. We may get results this way, though we should question how much these methods help our charges to grow up, to mature, to become responsible. But there are certainly other pupils who respond to none of these approaches. These children above all may need the particular kind of attention, the completely different kind of approach which the counsellor can provide because of his special role.

How can the counsellor establish a normal healthy 'preventive' service which is accepted and used spontaneously by pupils? It is not an easy task. Young people are unlikely to turn to someone they do not know at all: they only have the counsellor's word for it that he is trustworthy and respects confidences, and they mostly need more reassurance than that. If the counsellor teaches as well as counsels, he will be better known; he will have been tested out in the classroom situation and assessed by his charges. But the teacher/counsellor runs the risk of being perceived as an instrument of authority by the pupils and himself feeling conflict between his two roles. If he is nevertheless successful to an extent, he may well find his colleagues jealous of his achievements. The issue of whether counsellors should teach as well is one which provokes intense debate in the teaching profession and convincing arguments on either side. If we accept that the counsellor should not teach, then we have to think of a way for the counsellor to make contact with all the pupils, to be able to explain the nature and purpose of his service, to show that it is both normal and healthy to need and use such a service at times, to be tested out and assessed by the pupils. It is not enough for the counsellor to address a year or even a form and tell them why he is there: most of what he says will not be taken in and may leave the impression that his service is somehow abnormal. Once he is really established, word will get round as to how he operates and how trustworthy or helpful he is. But until that point, what can he do to establish rapport and trust with his future clients?

One way of doing this is for the counsellor to run a series of group discussions on human relationships. This is something we tried in the school where I worked as counsellor. As a result of discussion groups about a third of the pupils came for counselling of their own accord.

References

 1. Tyler, L (1961) *The Work of the Counselor* Appleton Century Crofts
 2. Erickson, E (1968) *Identity: Youth and Crisis* Faber and Faber
 3. Stefflre, B *ed* (1965) *Theories of Counseling* McGraw Hill
 4. Proctor, B (1978) *Counselling Shop* Burnett Books in association with Andre Deutsch
 5. Warters, J (1964) *Techniques of Counselling* McGraw Hill
 6. Rogers, C (1951) *Client Centred Therapy* Houghton Mifflin
 7. Rogers, C (1961) *On Becoming a Person* Houghton Mifflin
 8. Williamson, E (1950) *Counseling Adolescents* McGraw Hill
 9. Hamrin, S and Paulson, B (1950) *Counseling Adolescents* Science Research Associates
10. Krumboltz, J *ed* (1966) *Revolution in Counseling* Houghton Mifflin
11. Halmos, P (1965) *The Faith of the Counsellors* Constable

Chapter 4

Establishing a counselling service

In this chapter I want to describe the counselling service established at Mayfield Comprehensive School in 1965. In spite of everything I have experienced since, I still feel that there is a need for a service of this kind in a comprehensive school or college of further education. The basic framework of the counselling scheme we devised was simple. It was designed to encourage self-referrals as much as possible; by this I mean that the students themselves come voluntarily and spontaneously for help when they thought they needed help. Obviously teaching staff suggested to certain girls that they might like to come for counselling, but they were never forced to see the counsellor. Because of this emphasis, the counsellors did not help every girl who needed help, only those who wanted help. Effective counselling at any level depends upon the co-operation of the client. Giving the pupils themselves the responsibility and the opportunity of deciding whether to come for counselling helped to ensure this co-operation.

Part of the problem for the counsellor is to define realistic aims which are within the limits of his capabilities and, furthermore, to learn to use constructively the resources of his colleagues on the staff, and within the community welfare services. His role is not at all defined, and different counsellors may evolve different but equally valid schemes, all of which will have certain advantages and certain limitations.

In this chapter I want to describe the particular scheme of counselling which evolved over a period of time in the girls' comprehensive school where I worked. There were at that time two part-time counsellors on the staff. We each took specific responsibility for half the girls in the school, ie 1000 each, but in fact we concentrated our main efforts on the third year girls, who were all given an opportunity to talk to us. Of the 180 third year girls assigned to each counsellor, only about 20 per annum were counselled in any depth, though many others came once or twice. Thus the actual, as opposed to the potential, caseload of each counsellor was not very large. I offer our scheme for critical scrutiny in the belief that some parts of it will be useful, other parts may be discarded or improved, but that most of it will be of interest as an early working model.

It seems important, to give our scheme any coherence, to begin by explaining something of the organization of the school at that time, the reasons why counselling was introduced, and how and why the counselling scheme was devised.

The organization of the school

The school itself was a large comprehensive for girls in an urban area. It is fortunate in that it was comprehensive in three ways; socio-economic, intellectual and cultural. It contained a healthy mixture of girls with widely different social backgrounds and of various nationalities, and there was a balanced intake of intellectual ability, with no shortage of highly intelligent girls. In other words it was not a school which draws on one housing estate or one stratum of society, and it was not intellectually impoverished.

The school was unstreamed, with a 12 form entry, that is, 360 girls in each academic year. Each form of 30 girls was put in the charge of a form tutor who was responsible for their pastoral care. Her role was clearly specified by the head; the phrase 'form tutor' rather than 'form teacher' was used to denote the extent of her responsibility for each individual. The form tutor stayed with her form for at least three years. The 12 form tutors in each year were in turn responsible to the year mistress who looked after the 360 girls in her charge throughout their school career. The deputy head concerned herself especially with the third and fourth years, the head with all the other years. Thus there was a continuity of care and consistency of concern for each individual girl. The children had a great sense of belonging both to their tutor group and their year; this identification with a small group provided for the children a stable and secure home base which was both a refuge and a strength to them. The children very often confided in their tutors, and the tutors themselves talked over their problems with the senior staff.

The system of pastoral care was therefore, as in most schools, carefully thought out and actively used. The fact that the head and the staff decided this was not enough is in itself testimony to their sensitivity and deep concern in this field. They felt that in addition there was a place for someone to *supplement* the work of the form tutor. The form tutors recognized that they did not have time amidst their many other duties to give sufficient attention to the few girls in each form with serious problems. They also recognized that some children might want to talk to someone outside the structure of the school system, someone who would listen but who would not be bound by virtue of her office to take disciplinary action. This is not to say that girls do not confide in their form tutor; some do and some confide in a subject teacher but just a few need the reassurance of someone who can be trusted with confidential information, who is outside the disciplinary role.

It was important that the head and staff themselves thought of the idea originally, and really wanted a counsellor. Pioneering any new job is no easy task, but the task was made simpler because of the co-operation and support of the head and her staff. Goodwill, acceptance and positive regard from colleagues are as important to the work of the counsellor as to any individual. Staff attitudes to counselling are readily conveyed to pupils and had they been negative could easily have undermined the system. It is not every teacher who can easily share her children and bear not to know everything about them; yet this ability to let go the child to the counsellor, in the ultimate interest of the child, was one of the most helpful staff characteristics.

Aims and principles

When we first began to discuss our scheme in October 1964 we thought of counselling as a way of promoting positive mental health. The head itself had taken an active part in a conference on this subject organized by the National Association for Mental Health in 1963 and I had recently completed training as a Marriage Guidance Education Counsellor. We found that we had similar objectives in mind, all of which were concerned with mental health:

(1) to help individuals through temporary crises
(2) to help adolescents with normal developmental problems
(3) to note signs of abnormal disturbance at the earliest stages
(4) to refer cases needing specialist treatment at the earliest possible opportunity
(5) to help communications within and between the school, the home, the community and its resources
(6) to support teachers who are helping individuals in their care but who themselves want reassurance and guidance.

Before we actually began our counselling experiment in September 1965 several further important points were established. These were the principles of confidentiality, availability and acceptability.

Confidentiality

This has already been discussed in chapter 3. A client-centred service can be on no other basis but that of absolute trust between counsellor and pupil. For the counsellor to reveal what is confidential is not only unethical, but also completely undermines the service provided. The counsellor's reputation for trustworthiness or otherwise will have serious repercussions on the effectiveness of the counselling service. Confidentiality is sometimes hard for teaching colleagues to accept, yet it is possible for a counsellor to communicate with them in general terms and in a positive way without breaking confidentiality; it is however *impossible* for a counsellor to help her clients to express their feelings fully if they are not confident of her integrity.

Availability

The principle of availability is linked closely with the idea of encouraging self-referrals rather than staff-referrals. Most counselling interviews had to be arranged with an official appointment: this seems essential for smooth administration, also less disruptive for classes and less irritating for teachers. The form tutor handed out an appointment slip which served as an official pass for leaving a particular lesson to come for counselling. But because we feared certain girls might be put off by this official red tape, we always made it clear that the counsellor could be contacted directly in her room, before or after school or between lessons. Problems do not fit neatly into timetables; good communication with the counsellor demands that she should be accessible. She cannot however take on every client who knocks on her door, there and then. An acute crisis may not be the best moment to begin constructive counselling: the form teacher may have to bear the brunt of the emotional outburst while the counsellor reassures the child that she can have an appointment in the near future. When the emotional storm has passed, the child may be in a better position to look at its underlying causes.

Acceptability

To begin to function at all adequately the counsellor has to be accepted not only by the pupils but also by the staff, parents and social welfare services agencies. Gaining acceptance from all these groups takes time. We had to begin with the immediate environment. We set up discussion groups to gain acceptance from our potential clients, the girls. To gain acceptance from the staff, we had to make it clear that the counsellor's role was *different* from the form tutors' and that the counsellor was in no way taking over the year mistresses' or form tutors' responsibility for the pupils but that she was simply a supplementary benefit providing an ancillary service of a completely different kind.

Role limitations

From the beginning we set certain limitations on the counsellor's role: she would not teach; she would not undertake vocational guidance, educational guidance or psychological testing. Our reasons for making these decisions were simple and practical.

No teaching

The counsellor would not teach because she would not have time to teach; to do so would take her away from her main purpose, counselling. She would not have time to teach because she was going to begin, experimentally, on a part-time basis. Even if she had time to teach, there was the possibility of this causing confusion about her role both for herself and for the pupils. In a school as large as ours the teaching role would not particularly help the counsellor to know her clients in their normal setting, for she would only be able to teach a small proportion of them. In any case it is arguable whether it is a good idea for the counsellor to risk prejudicing her view of the child through classroom experience. Because of her peripheral role, the counsellor walks a delicate tightrope across many boundaries. There is some respite for the counsellor in not having to face the additional conflict of the dual role of teacher/counsellor.

There are disadvantages too. For example the counsellor has relatively little light relief and may get out of touch with normality. For the girls in our school however we were able to define the counsellor's role as different from the teacher's role. Thus the counsellor was accepted by the teaching staff as a colleague, which is essential, yet in the girls' eyes was perceived as someone standing slightly apart from the school 'system'. This made it easier for the girls to talk, in confidence, about problems which they imagined might affront or worry unduly someone in a position of authority. The counsellor is not 'agin the government': this would make her a destructive and damaging force within the school. But she did not feel for example that she must enforce school regulations at all costs. *Not* teaching helped to free her from this kind of subtle pressure within herself to enforce conformity.

No vocational guidance

In the school there were two careers mistresses. The careers room was open daily before and after school. The careers officers of the local careers office came into the school from the third year onwards. Much was done to help the girls make wise vocational decisions. Deciding that the counsellor should not provide vocational guidance did not mean that we felt no more could be done in this field. It meant that we recognized that if the counsellor undertook vocational guidance she would probably have little time left for the personal problems which may well lie at the base of a vocational problem; vocational guidance is easier and more effective when the client is free from emotional strain and conflict. It is also a highly skilled and specialized job in a technical sense. It requires considerable knowledge not only of job qualifications and conditions but of developing national manpower trends and local fluctuations in job opportunities. In other words, we respected the careers officers' specialized training and skills for providing this kind of service, and recognized that our role was not to compete with their expertise but to be supportive to it. It is true that there is a case for having more vocational guidance in schools; but the counsellor who undertakes this has to recognize that the burden of paper work and administration which may accrue as a result may prevent his having time for or even perceiving the extent of the fundamental personal problems of his clients. The counsellor must decide what he is most able to do and apportion his time accordingly. In our case we decided that the counsellor would refer to the careers teachers or careers officer any cases needing vocational guidance.

No educational guidance

We also decided that the counsellor should not undertake educational guidance for similar reasons: an effective system of guidance already existed; to undertake educational guidance would be time-consuming and might divert the counsellor from clients' more basic problems; the year mistresses and form tutors, guided by the head and deputy head, were in a better position than the counsellor to help pupils with their choices of subject and course, because they had a more balanced overall view of the individual's work, progress and behaviour over a period of time. Because of her non-teaching role, the counsellor was at a disadvantage in assessing pupils' abilities realistically. Where completely objective assessment of a pupil's abilities was required, then the educational psychologist was asked to administer appropriate tests. The range of choice in the middle school was limited compared with that in an American high school. One of the aims of the school was to keep individuals' options open as long as possible within the confines and restrictions of the further education system and the needs of those who really did want to take specialized vocational courses while still at school. The decision we made then was that the counsellor was not necessarily the person best suited to provide educational guidance and that her limited time and talents were more urgently needed elsewhere—namely in the realm of personal problems.

The role of the counsellor *vis-à-vis* the child guidance clinic had to be worked out most carefully. The existing system was that referrals to the child guidance clinic could in obvious cases be made direct by the school with parental agreement, or by parents. More often the educational psychologist attached to the local child guidance clinic who visited the school regularly would be asked to assess, sometimes to test, children about whom the staff were worried and to make recommendations for action where appropriate. The educational psychologist continued to be used by the school exactly as before: staff referred to her directly and occupied her time fully. What the counselling service did was to provide another source of referral, based on what the girls felt about themselves. For what was interesting and disturbing about the system of self-referrals we established was the number of serious problems which came to light which otherwise might have gone undetected and unsolved. These were, in particular, girls whose work and behaviour were not remarkable in any way who may have been functioning in school quite adequately, yet who in fact had serious problems. 'She could do better': this category of girl may have been covering up a mild depression or difficult social situation. This may have been *why* she was not giving her best.

Counsellors do not replace educational psychologists: they need them for advice and guidance. They in turn support the work of the school psychological services by helping with early detection and referral of serious problems. We found the existence of a counselling service improved, not undermined, the relationship between the school and the child guidance clinic. We have found the support of the school psychological services essential to the proper functioning of our work. We defined the work of the counsellor as closely allied to that of the psychological and welfare services but to do with a different category of children. Our work was with 'normal' children, in the broadest sense, theirs with children needing more highly specialized treatment. We knew that there is no such thing as 'normal'. What we meant by this loose term is simply that our province was children who do not need any kind of special education in the environment most appropriate for their age, ability and aptitude but who needed some supportive counselling at times to give them the assurance and peace of mind necessary for full development of their potential. When we discovered a child with problems needing more specialized or expert attention than we could provide, then we made referrals; at all times we consulted the experts to make sure that we were not trying to carry or sustain problems which we were not able to help constructively. If for any reason (such as parental refusal) we were not able to bring in the specialist help required, then we ourselves consulted the specialists for guidance.

Reaching our clients

Having established that the counsellor would not undertake teaching, psychological testing, vocational or educational guidance, but would concentrate on the personal problems of the normal individual, we had to think of a way for the counsellor to reach these individuals. One possibility was for the counsellor to sit in her room, labelled *Advice Centre*, and to wait for customers to come. We felt that whereas in the community setting this kind of approach can be fruitful (as for example in the consultation centres at Hampstead, Brent, Notting Hill, Bristol etc) in the school setting all but the most extrovert might be daunted initially, until the service had been proven. It would be difficult to communicate the aims and frame of reference of the scheme; an assembly of pupils addressed by the counsellor might have some effect but we felt that even this would leave the majority of the pupils sceptical and confused about the nature, the value and the trustworthiness of the service. This approach was too passive; the 'ever open door' and the mass communication meeting could be tried and were tried but were not enough in themselves.

Another way of reaching clients might be for form tutors to refer to the counsellor, girls who were causing them some concern. There were two objections to this scheme: first there was a danger that the counsellor might be used by the form teacher as a punishment or threat. The girl might see the counsellor as just another arm of the law and refuse to co-operate. An experienced counsellor would be aware of the dangers of manipulation by pupil or teacher; a skilled counsellor might be able to overcome any initial hostility or misapprehension in the client. But in certain cases the co-operation of the client would not be forthcoming, which would make counselling impossible. Second the children who were causing the form teacher most concern were not necessarily the ones needing the most extra attention. Law breakers, window breakers, paper throwers, rabble rousers are easy enough to spot; so are teacher's pets, complete isolaters, weepers and wailers. Even some of these categories of difficult child are sometimes not brought to the attention of authority until more than one teacher is suffering at their hands, and the problem in no way discredits the ability of the teacher to control a class. Given that even the most obvious problem children may not be helped in the earliest stages of their difficulties, because of the teacher's fear of appearing or being inadequate, we had to face the further point that some problems are not obvious. Children may be labouring under quite serious stresses and strains which for personal reasons they may cover up in public. Form teachers may be aware of this of course but it cannot be assumed *automatically* that the form teacher's judgement of which children need counselling will tally absolutely with the children's actual needs. It is highly likely that the form teacher's judgement will be right but this cannot be assumed. It is rather like asking a teacher to send forward for X-ray only the children she thinks might have TB. If a screening service is to be reliable, everyone must be screened. The advantage of the counsellor's seeing everyone was that the children had the opportunity of expressing their difficulties, if any, for themselves. When they did this they were in effect asking the counsellor for help, which meant that she might be able to help them. If she unearthed problems she could not help, at least she was able to bring in the appropriate specialist.

This brings us to the consideration of a scheme in which the counsellor simply interviews everybody. If the counsellor's reputation is already established, and if he is equipped with extraordinary personal qualities, or a good screening tool (ie a test for picking out potentially disturbed children), this method could achieve good results. We rejected it because we felt that it was to inquisitorial and that girls might not respond to sudden questioning by a complete stranger even though the stranger reassured them with promises of confidentiality. Psychiatric screening based on a few key questions might well be something to combine with a school medical, conducted in the presence of and with the agreement of the parent: the ethic of the medical profession is generally understood and patients are used to being asked personal questions by doctors and giving routine answers to them. We felt that the role and ethic of the counsellor was not then sufficiently understood or accepted to justify systematic questioning: we felt that girls and parents might object, and might object with reason, to being asked questions about their private lives by a counsellor. If pupils or parents tell us voluntarily about their problems, this is a completely different matter.

Any other objection to the routine question and answer interview was the effect it might have on any potential counselling relationship. Apart from the suspicion or hostility which might be aroused in the client, it also puts the counsellor, from the very beginning, in a judgemental, expert role. Administering a questionnaire is an impersonal objective activity which avoids the necessity of making a relationship: it is a less strenuous activity for the counsellor but it does not promote the formation of a relationship which is so essential to counselling itself. Asking questions in a friendly chat is a more personalized way of getting information but is liable not to elicit the whole truth because it is unlikely that any bond of trust and confidence will be established with the counsellor in a few minutes, except in a minority of cases. Someone who has come forward for counselling does not mind giving information, but this is because she has already demonstrated this intention and her good faith by seeking an interview.

So whilst we accepted that it was important for the counsellor to interview every child at some stage during her school career, we felt that the value of the interview could be enhanced if the counsellor already knew all the pupils well enough for them to trust her and to *want* to confide in her. Teaching an ordinary school subject would bring the counsellor in touch with only a few pupils. Teaching religious education might be another way of making brief contact with a large number of pupils, though the religious education teacher has to spread himself throughout so many classes for so few periods a week that he may find he has little opportunity of getting to know his pupils individually; he will in any case probably be regarded, whatever he is really like, as being a staunch supporter of law and order and a maintainer of the *status quo*. He has an important role to play in a school: but because of his association with religion, pupils in fact may not express their true feelings to him as much as he may think.

Thus although religious education teaching could be a way for the counsellor to make contact with pupils, an even freer and less authority-loaded approach might be through discussions on human relationships. This we decided would be our way of making contact with pupils, explaining our role, being tested out by the pupils and beginning to establish the rapport which could form the basis of a counselling relationship later, if necessary. This approach most satisfied our aim of establishing a service which was neither too passive nor obtrusive upon personal liberty, a service which gave an equal chance for every individual to ask for help if and when she should need it. It was no accident that we decided to use group discussion of human relationships in this way, for two reasons. Both myself and my colleague, who joined me a term after I began, were trained as Marriage Guidance Education Counsellors. It was this training which helped us more than anything else to formulate the conceptual frame of reference upon which our experiment was based and which led us naturally to think of group work with children as a way of making contact with them and explaining our role. The second reason we began in this way was that the school already used outside speakers for discussion groups about human relationships with the third year girls.

From our experience of taking similar discussions in schools, on behalf of the Marriage Guidance Council, we knew that often girls would come up afterwards with a pressing personal problem. Because we were 'just visiting' we were unable to help them in any sustained way. Being permanently attached to a school meant that our group work could be more thorough because we would have more sessions with smaller groups, and that we would be able to give a series of counselling interviews for those who asked for help and for as long as they wished. Furthermore these would be self-referrals which we regarded as of fundamental importance to the working of the scheme.

Taking over and extending something already established made our scheme immediately more acceptable and comprehensible to staff and students; the fact that previously it had been thought necessary to use outside speakers in this role, to allow absolute freedom of discussion, helped us to preserve the role of outsider—a role which had frustrating limitations at times but which certainly encouraged girls, individually and in groups, to speak freely.

The structuring of the groups

In deciding to continue the discussions already established with the third year girls (aged 13-14) we bore in mind the following considerations. Some girls are ready for this sort of discussion before the third year, others not till later, but by and large this is the year when the onset of puberty brings in its wake a whole host of developmental problems, many of which manifest themselves in difficult behaviour. The little girl of yesteryear may suddenly become a demonic siren, fluctuating between insolent independence and desperate dependence. She does not know how to handle her new self and quite often neither do we. But she is certainly growing conscious of her own sexuality and glad to join in discussions which deal not just with the facts of life, which have already been covered in human biology, but with her own feelings, her hopes and fears, her illusions and her expectations. Her problems may not be primarily how to deal with the opposite sex, so much as how to gain her independence and what to do with it when she has it. Growing up physically brings with it a whole new set of difficulties in learning how to relate to people: at home, at school, with the opposite sex and in society. This is what our group discussions were really all about.

In the third year of the school there were 12 forms, each containing about 30 girls aged 13-14 years. Six forms (that is about 180 girls) were allocated to each of the two counsellors, who then took responsibility for these particular girls throughout their school life. As the academic year divides into six half terms, each counsellor devoted half a term to concentrated work with each of the six forms for whom she was responsible. We spent the first three weeks of the half term in group discussions, sometimes taking a double session, sometimes taking one morning and one afternoon session of the same day. The second three weeks were for individual counselling. In all, the form missed six lessons to come to the discussions. Which lessons they missed was worked out carefully with the staff, who mostly recognized that this was not an insuperable blow to their syllabus and might reap rewards in other ways.

We did not see the whole of each form at a time: there were approximately 30 girls in each form and this is too many for an effective group discussion in which all members could feel sufficiently free and confident to participate. Each form was therefore divided into two groups of 15; even this was rather too many and three groups of 10 would be better. But with limited time at our disposal we had to make a practical decision: to do the group work more thoroughly would leave even less time for work with individuals. This way we also disrupted fewer lessons, probably to the relief of the teaching staff. At least it can be argued that our discussions did not take up a disproportionate amount of time or get adolescent problems out of perspective.

The division into groups

We did not divide the girls into their groups of 15; the girls divided *themselves*, by a simple sociometric technique. Just before the group work was to begin, the form teacher explained something of what the discussions over the next few weeks would be about and what a counsellor is. She then picked out two girls, both popular, but quite different kinds of girls; she may choose Mary, who represents the quieter, 'sensible' element in the form, and Marilyn, who represents the boisterous, 'sexy' set. Both girls might be mature, or maturing fast, but in different ways. The rest of the form then decided for themselves which group they wanted to join.

We found by experimenting that this method had certain advantages over the teacher's own groupings. The teacher can judge physical and social maturity, but the other important factor to take into account is the natural groupings of friends, the social networks in each form. There will probably be more than two natural groups in each form, but provided they understand something of the nature of the groups, the girls were very good judges of where they belonged. Of the two resultant groups, one might be marginally more mature, more blatantly 'sexy', but both were based on an existing network of relationships, which greatly helps the cohesiveness of the groups. The girls were more relaxed, more able to bring out their real feelings among people they knew and trusted already. Just occasionally we were faced with one wild, garrulous group, and one passive inarticulate group, but more normally there was a developmental spread in each group. We certainly preferred this to a group divided alphabetically or completely randomly by the form tutor. Our self-selection method avoided also a feeling that the groups had been graded into the haves and have nots, which was certainly not the intention but which had been expressed by groups chosen by the form teacher. Our self-selection method not only brought us a more cohesive group, but demonstrated from the very beginning our willingness to let adolescents take responsibility for themselves.

The physical structuring of the groups

We did not have counselling rooms specifically and permanently set aside for our use. We borrowed rooms from other departments for our exclusive use on the days we were in school. Thus the girls knew where to find us when they wanted to come for individual counselling. If they had an urgent problem they knew that they could catch us to make an appointment in our rooms between lessons, or before or after school. The rooms were not specially or luxuriously appointed, and this was of no great importance. What was important was that they were not cluttered with rows of desks, they were small, they were not overlooked by passers-by: this helped to ensure a degree of informality, privacy and security. The girls sat in a circle of chairs, without desks, and the counsellor was a part of this circle.

The physical structure of the group is important. By making herself a part of the circle, instead of being ensconced on a throne or dais, or installed behind a desk, the counsellor diminished to an extent the tendency the group might have to regard her as the leader and the expert. The discussions were then more likely to be centred on the needs of the group and less dominated by the counsellor. The circular structure ensured that every member had an equal chance of participating, of seeing everybody; of being involved, and that nobody was, by some quirk of fate, forced to take a back seat, allowed to hide behind someone else or put into a dominant position which upset the balance of the group.

In the first group discussion it was vital for the counsellor to explain her job, her role, her way of working; she told the group that in all they would meet six times during the next three weeks and that after that they would be able to come for individual counselling if they so wished. She explained about confidentiality, she encouraged the group to express what they really felt rather than what they thought they ought to feel, reassuring them that the contents of the discussion would not be passed on to the staff or their parents; and that the counsellor herself would not mind what is said, that no subject is taboo if this is what the group really wants to discuss. The group probably did not believe this at first; the counsellor would probably find that the group brought up some sensational 'shocking' subjects in order to test this out. If the counsellor survived this, the group would then begin to have sufficient confidence in her to talk more normally about their real problems.

What actually went on in the group discussions is such a fascinating and vast topic that to discuss it in detail now would divert me from my present task which is to lay bare the bones of our scheme. All I want to do now is to make a few points about the group discussions. It did not really matter what the girls discussed in the group. There was no syllabus and there were very few 'red herrings' because the aim of the group discussions is not to put across certain information but to allow the girls to talk about their feelings. 'Red herrings' might occur when one girl dominated the group with a long personal story which acted as a damper to the expression of feelings by others, when the group was too dependent on the counsellor or when two particular girls took up a dialogue to the exclusion of all others. But these were not blockages of subject matter so much as blockages of psychological mechanism.

We must distinguish between the kind of group work undertaken by counsellors and that sometimes undertaken by teachers. A skilful teacher may manipulate a group to argue out a case and to come to a logical conclusion; but it is the conclusion that the teacher has wanted the group to reach—the 'right' answer, based on facts. He has not put words into people's mouths, but he has asked the right questions at the right times. This technique of innocent ignorance is a valuable teaching tool. 'But why do you think he did that?' 'How did it get there in the first place?' In group counselling this technique has little place. The counsellor is not manipulating the group for his own end, to make them believe 'the facts', because he is not dealing with facts but with feelings and these are necessarily subjective and individual. The teacher who leads group counselling discussions must therefore be prepared to allow discussion which may go against his own views; he must be prepared *not* to come in at the end—*deus ex machina*—with the right answer. He must have a view but he must be able to tolerate that not everybody need share it. The teacher in the classroom can air his views without necessarily having them questioned and an uncomfortable challenger can soon be cut down to size with sleight of tongue. The counsellor cannot do this if the group is to be at all free.

Given that we spent at most two out of six sessions answering and discussing questions to do with love, sex, sexual behaviour and related social problems, it must be evident that these topics were given relatively scant treatment. It would be possible to spend an academic term or year discussing each and every issue properly. Many of the topics raised in our groups, such as the meaning of love, the purpose of marriage, abortion, homosexuality, are brought up in discussion in the teaching of other subjects: human biology, religious education and English in particular. We thought it important that the whole staff should be involved in this, as indeed they were, and we valued the spontaneous discussion which arises from the study of a set text or the debate of a moral principle in lessons. But the purposes of these discussions may be different from ours. Our discussions were to give the girls the opportunity to discuss freely those few things they might feel unable to ask their parents or their form teacher; to help them not to be afraid to communicate their feelings to adults; to lay the foundations of a relationship between them and the counsellor to the end that they will feel sufficient confidence in the counsellor to come for help when they need it; to give the girls an opportunity of testing out the counsellor, of deciding whether they like and trust her; to give the counsellor an opportunity of seeing how a girl behaves in her peer group.

This last point is important for the non-teaching counsellor; the group work provided her with a brief glimpse of the way the girls relate to each other. It is doubtful whether a teacher/counsellor would teach everybody who came for counselling, and so for him too, group work could be useful. A counsellor who has taken a group six times is not going to have anywhere near such an accurate picture of the child's general behaviour as the counsellor who has taught a child for a year or so. But then, if the counsellor is trying to see the world as the client sees it, he is likely to find this easier if his view is not prejudiced by the classroom experience; if Joan is the ringleader of the group which undermines your lessons, it is difficult to help her as objectively as you would wish. The counsellor in the group discussions has the advantage of not needing to enforce discipline, rules or punishment and this makes it easier to view the group, however many troublemakers it contains, with a certain objective benevolence. But he can notice certain things about individuals in the group. In our groups we might notice that Mary never said a word, and did not appear to have a mate. We might observe that June needed to be dominant in the group, that Molly got very emotional in discussion, that Kate opted out and that Pat always tried to sit next to the counsellor. There may not be very much significance in these observations: type-casting by the counsellor on such flimsy evidence could be damaging and misleading. But we bore our observations in mind when we saw the girls individually.

The autobiographical note

Every girl in the third year, then, was seen by one or other of the counsellors for six discussions about human relationships. In the fourth or fifth discussion group, we asked the girls to write an unstructured autobiographical note. We explained carefully that the purpose of the note was to enable the counsellor to get to know them in order to be able to help them if and when necessary. We stressed that the note was for our own use and would not be shown to their teachers or parents without the individual's permission. We said that they could tell us much or as little as they liked about themselves and their families. Our reasons for this permissive approach were these: we knew that some families resent any intrusion into their private lives and we respected this right to keep one's private life private. For example, a girl might want to keep secret from everybody, including us, the fact that her parents are separated, possibly because this was the wish of her parents.

We asked the girls to tell us, if they wanted to, something about their parents, their brothers and sisters (with ages), the way they spend their spare time, what they wanted to do when they left school and anything else they thought would interest us and help us to get to know and understand them. This last open-ended clause was one which often brought, much to our surprise, the written expression of a serious problem. More normally, the note was relatively guarded and the problem, if any, was left to the face-to-face interviews. A few girls expressed their feelings more easily on paper than verbally but this was not usually the case. When we first began doing this we asked for the autobiographical note in the second or third meeting. Later we changed this to the fourth or fifth. The difference in the kind of remarks made was amazing. Clearly even by the second or third session the girls were not sure how much they trusted the counsellor. By the time they got to the fourth or fifth session, and assuming they were ever going to trust the counsellor, they were feeling more certain.

The autobiographical notes provided a wealth of illuminating comments on life which I propose to discuss later. For the moment all I want to say is that the autobiographical note was *not* a reliable indicator of whether a girl needed help. The quality of the note was greatly influenced by such factors as the girl's ability to write, and how reserved she was generally. Some girls are guarded in what they write and understandably so. Some notes are surprisingly emotional and dramatic and the counsellor has to be careful not to read too much into them. Because the note was voluntary there was no knowing whether information, significant or insignificant, had been suppressed or concealed, distorted, exaggerated or simply omitted. Were we trying to get a systematic factual picture of the background of each girl, we should not allow them to write an unstructured note, we should administer a questionnaire. What we were interested in was not so much the facts of a girl's life, but the way she felt about people and things in her life. It therefore did not matter to us initially whether the girl was exaggerating, or how much she was hiding. This is something which emerged if and when she came for counselling interviews.

Having the autobiographical note in hand did however help the counsellors to remember which girl is which. Without them we would quickly have forgotten the little we had gleaned about the girls in the six discussion groups. It gave us a peg on which to hang our own impressions of the girls; this was particularly important in discussions with staff. It also helped to refresh our memories when a girl returned for counselling spontaneously two or three years after she had been in our groups. The girl's emotional situation may have completely changed by then but it is obviously more encouraging and reassuring to the child if the counsellor remembers something about her life. Even if the counsellor did not remember her particularly well the girl felt that the counsellor knew her and cared about her, and this attitude facilitated the establishment of a counselling relationship.

The standard interview

In the last of the six sessions with the counsellor every member of the group was interviewed briefly. The purpose of the interview was to establish whether the child wanted to come for further counselling. Each child was given an equal chance of stating this in private. We did not ask those who want to come for further counselling to put up their hands or sign a list. We felt that not only would this contradict our aim of showing respect for each individual child, but that it would also not bring us the right customers. The rowdy, unruly element in each form was not going to admit publicly that it wanted help. The shy or withdrawn children might not feel sufficient confidence to show their needs in front of others. In the brief interview the child was not jumping on to a bandwagon—she was stating her preference without being sure what her friends were doing. While the interviews were being conducted the rest of the group discussed any remaining issues or finished reading the books or the Marriage Guidance Council pamphlets which the counsellor had lent them.

Both counsellors were fortunate in having a room for discussion groups which is divided from the main thoroughfares by a small lobby. This lobby was useful both as a secluded waiting room for clients and also for this routine interview. At this stage there was only time for a short interview of five minutes or less. This was not the moment to begin counselling proper as there were too many pressures of time and too many people to see. There were few cases so urgent that they could not wait for a proper appointment. Where a girl had stated in her autobiographical note that she had a problem, it was simply a case of reassuring her as to how soon an appointment for a counselling interview could be arranged. Some girls gave no indication of any problem either on paper on in the group, and most of these, after a few minutes' chat, said there was nothing they wanted to talk over at greater length. They were reminded that they could always come back later if they changed their minds: occasionally they did this.

Some girls wrote rather inadequate notes and the counsellor checked over details such as the ages of brothers and sisters. The counsellor might notice for example that there was no mention of dad, and would ask about him. If it turned out that he was dead, or was not living with his family for some reason, the counsellor would tread gently, giving the girl an opportunity to talk more, but at the same time trying not to reopen old wounds which might have healed over. What was missing in the autobiographical note could often be as important as what was expressed: but if a point was not mentioned precisely because it was a sore point, and a confidential one at that, the counsellor respected the girl's right to keep her family life to herself and did not press too hard. Some of the girls stood out from the way they behaved in the group as being in need of extra care and attention, but not all the most hard-bitten young misses wanted to turn to the counsellor for help. We might give extra encouragement to those *we* thought need our help to come for counselling but we certainly did not in any way force them to come, because we did not think we would be able to help them on these terms. We did not in any case normally undertake supportive work with girls who were already in care, on probation or seeing a psychiatrist unless we were asked to do so by the agency concerned. Quite a few girls slipped through our net because of this permissive non-directive approach of ours but at least we *were* another net, and we did counsel a lot of girls whose needs had passed unnoticed up to that point.

Individual problems

My records show that in a form of 30 there were usually about 10 who ask for counselling. What kind of problems did they bring forward? Obviously there was no set pattern but we can give an approximate breakdown of numbers. Some six girls had transitory developmental problems, particularly conflicts with parents about going out and having boyfriends. Two or three might have problems which were serious and disturbing but not to the extent of making their behaviour abnormal. These might be girls with home backgrounds which were genuinely difficult and hard to tolerate without support: marital disharmony, financial worries, overcrowding, aged grandparents, sibling rivalry, a handicapped brother or sister. One or two girls had problems which were better referred to the child guidance clinic or social services. This was excluding those already benefiting from these special services. In particular many of the girls we found we could help were the 'could do betters'. They might not be much trouble, they might not be withdrawn or isolated, but they did need help if they were to do themselves justice. Merely stating that a child could do better does not help her to improve, and may even discourage her. If we feel a child could do better we need to ask why, and to try to get at the root cause.

We were well aware that it would be unrealistic to expect any one counsellor to suit the needs of every individual child. Some individuals prefer to turn to some other member of staff when they need to talk or they may decide to keep their problems to themselves. In the groups the girls had the opportunity to judge for themselves to what extent they thought this particular counsellor was empathic, understanding, permissive, non-authoritarian, non-judgemental, trustworthy and genuine. On the basis of their assessment the girls decided whether to use the counselling service. Some never needed to use the service and some never wanted to. Some did not need it just then, but they came back to the counsellor one, two or three years after the group discussions at a stage when they did want counselling. When girls who have been through our groups were referred to us later by staff, our task was again made easier.

The group work thus formed the basis of the relationship between the girl and the counsellor and increased thereafter the effectiveness of both self-referrals and staff-referrals because the role, aims, and methods of the counsellor were understood. They were understood not because the counsellor has explained them but because she was tested and known. Because it was normal for girls to come for counselling after the groups, going to see the counsellor did not become shameful or odd. Many girls went to see the counsellor and a child did not have to have 'terrible problems' to qualify. Girls who came for individual counselling did so in lesson time with an official appointment, and for as long as they wished. Most girls needed to come only once or twice; but in each form there would one or two at least who needed regular counselling over a long period of time.

Relationships between the school staff and the counsellor

What did the teachers think about counselling? How did the counsellors fit into the organization of the school? How did staff feel about letting girls out of lessons for group discussions and then, again, for individual counselling? The description of our counselling scheme would be incomplete without some explanation of how it fitted into the organization of the school as a whole.

In describing the way we built up and worked out the teacher/counsellor relationship over a period of time, I shall attempt also to answer some of the many questions, both practical and personal, which counselling raises in teachers' minds. On the practical side, teachers whose pupils miss lessons to go for counselling are bound to ask whether the time is being wisely spent. Why not fit counselling into the lunch hour or after school? What effect does it have on a pupil's academic progress to be singled out for counselling? Can the counsellor guarantee that this pupil will work better and learn more in future? Isn't the counsellor simply encouraging children to wallow in self-pity? What can the counsellor do, in such a short time, which is any better or any different from what everyone else has already tried? *Why* can't the counsellor sort out this problem (even though no one else has): what is the counsellor *for*? Is there not a danger that some pupils will just use the counsellor as another way of getting out of lessons?

On a personal level teachers may feel, though not very often voice, deeper anxieties. What is Jane saying about *them*? Is she criticizing them or their teaching methods? What will the counsellor do with this information? Supposing she believes it, supposing it is true, supposing she passes it on to the 'powers that be'?

These personal anxieties coupled with general scepticism about what counselling might achieve may lead to even more questions. *Why* won't the counsellor tell the staff about Jane's family's background? Why is Jennifer going to see the counsellor? What is wrong with her? Who is this counsellor anyway?

One of the threads in the teacher's ambivalent feelings about the counsellor is the fear of being criticized by pupils. This fear is hardly ever expressed by staff, at a conscious level, yet is a well justified fear, for girls very often *do* make criticisms of staff or the way the school is run, in the same way that they run down their parents. There may well therefore exist in a school which has a counsellor a feeling among the staff that the counsellor is loaded with a lot of damaging information which, although exaggerated and one-sided, might be used against a member of staff. Until teachers are able to see for themselves not only that this does not happen, but also that the counsellor does not hold grudges or anything else against them and that he respects and values them as individuals, then they are bound to have mixed feelings about him.

The head and his senior colleagues can clearly pave the way for the counsellor and without their support the counsellor is lost. But in the day-to-day work of the school, the quality of the actual teacher/counsellor relationship can subtly influence for better or for worse what the teacher is trying to do in the classroom and what the counsellor is trying to do in the counselling room.

It is therefore an important part of any counsellor's job to dispel any fears and misconceptions about himself; to define realistically, in as far as he is able, the limits and limitations of his job and himself; in other words, to form good relationships, to communicate his objectives, to create an atmosphere of trust and positive regard between himself and his colleagues. If he is not able to do this he should not be a counsellor. If he is anything of a counsellor, his colleagues will respond readily to his approach and give him the reassurance and co-operation he needs to function properly. His colleagues will respond even more sympathetically if he is prepared to admit his own doubts, worries and uncertainties from the beginning and share them.

Staff who are left in ignorance of what a counsellor is trying to do are not to be blamed if they react adversely. Those who imagine that the counsellor is a panacea for all ills will quickly be disappointed. Those who are inwardly resentful of the counsellor will seize triumphantly upon examples of what the counsellor is failing to achieve, not realizing that they are judging success solely from a teacher's viewpoint, not from a counsellor's. But how else can they be expected to make judgements if the counsellor has not explained his viewpoint? Those who are willing to give the counsellor a trial run before pronouncing judgement will also be disappointed unless the counsellor has taken great care to gain their sympathy for and the understanding of his work and methods.

Thus the sorts of questions teachers ask publicly, privately and inwardly when faced with a counsellor for the first time are often based on a series of false expectations which *ipso facto* are bound to lead to dissatisfaction with the counsellor. The new counsellor may be caricatured mentally as an almighty power or as a ridiculous mouse. It is natural for staff to have mixed feelings about the counsellor at first but if this rate of fantasy and disillusion continues, it simply means that the counsellor is not doing the job properly.

In the early stage of the development of counselling, the onus of proof as to what a counsellor is rested with the counsellors. Everybody has been to school and everybody knows (or thinks he knows) what a teacher's job is. Nobody knew exactly what a counsellor's job was and it was up to the counsellor to demonstrate this constantly.

A counsellor who assumes that others understand his work is making a false assumption. He must tell the staff what he is trying to do and why; to adapt the old teaching adage, 'He must tell them, he must tell them again and he must tell them he's told them.' What is more, the counsellor must be seen to be what he claims to be; ultimately the service will be used or misused according to its quality. In the meantime while the service is being established it is important for the counsellor himself to disclaim any impression or illusion that he is either superhuman or omnipotent, for he certainly is neither. He is just one member of a team of people, each with a complementary and supplementary role. The counsellor who has given the impression that *he* will solve the children's problems is asking to be discredited; the teacher who has sent a child to the counsellor because he is difficult and finds that after several weeks' counselling the child is not better but more difficult than ever is liable to be very annoyed with the counsellor. It is important therefore for staff to realize for example that it is not uncommon for a pupil's behaviour to deteriorate after counselling has begun, partly because the pupil may be releasing and trying to come to terms with feelings he finds uncomfortable to face. It is important also for staff to accept that there is no guarantee of success unless the pupil himself wants to improve. Counselling does not obviate the necessity for ordinary classroom discipline, which should continue as usual.

A counsellor who has not educated the staff about his role and methods is at fault. To establish the teacher/counsellor relationship takes as much care and time, if not more, as establishing a viable pupil/counsellor relationship. Even if the counsellor is under no illusions about what he can achieve, it may happen that despite his protestations and definitions, certain staff will persist in regarding him as someone who will 'cure' problems. The answer here is for the teacher and counsellor to talk over a problem together and work out in discussion their respective roles. This stops the teacher from devaluing his own importance. It helps him to see the counsellor in perspective—as someone who can be useful but who has decidedly limited value and virtually no powers at all.

In order to maintain good relationships with the staff it is important for a counsellor to point out at all times the difference if any between their expectations and his practice. For example staff, like the children, may try to manipulate the counsellor: 'This girl wants to leave and she should not. Could you sort her out?' 'This girl has a very close relationship with her boyfriend. Could you find out what they are up to?' When the counsellor neither persuades the girl to stay on at school nor reports on her sexual behaviour, resentment may well set in unless the counsellor has already explained that his role is neither to persuade children to take certain courses of action nor to spy on their private lives.

Having a counsellor on the staff does not prevent teachers using for themselves the techniques of persuasion and direct questioning. But a counsellor who is really the arm of the law in subtle disguise is doing his clients a grave disservice. His first duty is to serve the needs of his clients; he must therefore resist the pressures of his environment to use his service as another, albeit subtle, way of enforcing conformity. The counsellor may hope that after counselling, a child will, as part of his growing maturity, come to accept the responsibilities of the society in which he lives. But there is no built-in guarantee.

The teacher/counsellor relationship in our school went through a series of phases, rather like many a marriage: first the honeymoon, then a short period of semi-illusionment when harsh reality begins to temper over-idealism, then finally a realistic working relationship in which the strengths and weaknesses of both partners were perceived, accepted and blended as harmoniously and constructively as possible.

The counsellor's arrival was hailed with great enthusiasm and a feeling that at last something would be done directly and early with girls who had problems. The counsellor herself shared this euphoric and optimistic mood. The head and the senior staff gave her the warmest of welcomes and did a lot of groundwork in advance. Before the counsellor arrived the head had discussed the idea and the scheme with the staff, individually and collectively; the counsellor had individual discussions with key members of the staff, and with all the third year form tutors with whom she was going to deal in particular. The work began enthusiastically. By the end of the first term an important difference of approach between the teaching staff and the counsellor was apparent. The staff wanted to know what could be done to help a particular individual. The counsellor could only say that there was nothing to be *done*; everything that could be done had already been done (such as providing free dinners, arranging a school journey etc). What the girl needed was warm but firm relationships with the adults in her life, tasks to do which she could achieve, praise and encouragement for her, avoidance (if possible) of situations in which her negative qualities would be stressed—yet on the other hand no 'extra soft' treatment. In other words the counsellor's approach was less practical and tangible than the teachers' and almost entirely to do with the quality of the relationships between the individual and the people in her life.

The way the teachers handle their relationships with their pupils is something so bound up with their own attitudes and attributes that it is something the counsellor cannot *tell* them to change, any more than she can tell the children to change. This approach is both tactless and ineffectual. It would in any case assume that the counsellor knew the answers and herself had 'superior' attitudes—neither of which is true.

The reaction of the staff to the realization that the counsellor was herself as human and limited as anyone else was a kind of double-take; annoyance that this person didn't have a simple answer to a complicated question, and that after all the buck still rested with them; then a dawning of positive feelings. If the counsellor does not know the answer then the teacher is still herself the most important person *vis-à-vis* the child; it is the teacher who spends most of her time with the pupil and the counsellor is very much a fringe benefit. The overall responsibility for the child therefore still rests with the teacher; thus the counsellor does not undermine the teacher/pupil relationship. A parallel may be drawn with the counsellor/client relationship. If the counsellor takes over the responsibility of the child or of the teacher, she is not helping them to be more responsible or to take responsibility for themselves, yet in both spheres this is one of her objectives.

The teacher who faces the full extent of her responsibility for a child may in fact increase her own respect for herself as an effective form teacher; through believing in herself in this role, she may *be* a more effective form teacher. The counsellor's role is not to tell her what to do, but exactly as with the clients to get her to talk about what she thinks she might do, to air her feelings, her doubts, her attitudes, her reasons. With teachers as with clients, the counsellor does not know the answer, and it would not really help if she did. The teachers work out their own answers but with the additional sense of perspective, clarity or insight brought about by having voiced their thoughts. The counsellor is not the only person who can provide this non-rebounding sounding board within a school. But again, as with clients, the non-authoritarian, non-judgemental role of the counsellor is occasionally helpful. If you tell your boss you are making a mess of things you may think rightly or wrongly that she will not be able to give you a very good reference; if you can trust the counsellor not to reveal what she is told then there are no repercussions for one's status or future prospects.

At the beginning of the second year of our experiment the counsellors were aware of some hostile undercurrents; it seemed important to face up to these feelings. We arranged a meeting with the third year tutors, during which a great deal of hostility was expressed towards the child guidance clinic, hostility which was in fact really about the counselling service. There was a feeling that nothing changed, nobody improved after treatment, 'they' didn't tell you how to handle a child, 'they' wouldn't tell you anything because everything was confidential, so how could you help?

We realized that in our desire to establish a confidential client-centred service, we had at this stage neglected our relationship with the staff. We had been on good terms with the staff but we had not worked out our relationship with them sufficiently and we had not communicated with them well enough, so afraid were we of damaging our relationship with the pupils. This explosive meeting cleared the air for everybody. Through the discussion the staff began to see more clearly what the counsellors were trying to do. From that moment the staff and the counsellors began to perceive each other more realistically. By the end of the second year of the experiment, the staff began to use the counsellors extremely well, and the counsellors began to use the resources of the staff as a whole more effectively in the service of their clients. Realism had set in.

As a result of the group discussion the counsellors realized that it was not good enough to assume good relationships and good communication with the staff. Good communication needs proper channels of communication and the only way to ensure proper channels of communication is with official structure and timetabling. A chance meeting over lunch or in the staffroom is not the moment to begin serious discussion of an individual. For a start nothing so important should be left to chance or it might never happen. Second, a hasty public interchange provides neither the calm nor the privacy essential for a well considered discussion of a child's needs. A rash, off the cuff comment about a child by a counsellor or by a teacher may well give an incomplete or false impression which is damaging to the child, particularly if the comment is also overheard by a member of staff sitting nearby who is even less acquainted with the whole truth.

It was for these reasons that we began to structure most carefully the staff/counsellor contacts. Naturally there is informal contact at break, over lunch and between lessons, but if there is something serious and lengthy to discuss, then the counsellor may use the social occasion to make an appointment for a proper discussion, rather than embark on something complicated in a few hasty moments. Sometimes the counsellor arranges to see a certain member of staff at break. The advantage of working in this way is that teacher and counsellor are able to give thought to the discussion in advance. In particular the counsellor has decided professionally, not on the spur of the moment, how much she is able to say about a child, and what the purpose of the discussion is.

It would be wrong to give the impression here that the counsellors never talk to the staff except by arrangement. It is essential for the counsellor to seize every opportunity for communicating with teaching colleagues, to miss no opportunity for saying, 'And how is Naomi?' Teachers will sometimes spontaneously proffer the information that a client or former client is going through a bad patch; prompting by the counsellor forms an extra safety net. More important than the interchange of information is the maintenance of a warm, trusting relationship between the teacher and counsellor, and a feeling that both are working together for the good of the child.

As a result of setting up proper channels of teacher/counsellor communication, staff attitudes to counselling became more realistic. This was partly a function of time. Whatever system is adopted, the efficacy of a counselling service will not be accepted by the staff overnight. We found that it took the best part of two years for the service to be realistically perceived, emotionally accepted and wisely used. Apart from the few members of staff who had always been sceptical of the service and steered clear of the counsellors, the staff/counsellor relationship continued to grow in strength and understanding. It was not only that the staff understood what the counsellors were trying to do, but that the counsellors too were beginning to have a clearer idea of their function.

The organization of staff/counsellor relationships in the school

Thus alongside the system of group discussions organized for third year girls there was a careful scheme of staff contact. At the beginning of each academic year the head introduced the counsellors to the staff as a whole and explained their role. The mistress in charge of the third year called a meeting of all third year tutors after school at which the counsellors again explained the pattern of the group work, their role and way of working. Any questions were answered or discussed. This again was not enough: approximately half a term was spent with each form and so form tutors whose forms were to be seen at the end of the academic year would have forgotten what it was all about by then. It was also more conducive to a good teacher/counsellor relationship for the counsellor to see the tutor individually again before starting work with her form. So the counsellor made contact with the form tutor just before the group discussions with her form began to remind her again of the scheme; to explain how to get the girls to divide into groups and why; to discuss which lessons it is most practical for the girls to miss in order to come for discussions; to ask the form tutor to negotiate and excuse these alterations in timetable for the next three weeks; to discuss in general terms what this particular form was like. Sometimes the form tutor would tell the counsellor which girls to look out for. But this is not always helpful to the counselling relationship as it can have the effect of inhibiting or prejudicing the counsellor. On the whole it was preferable to take the group without prior knowledge.

After the three weeks of discussion groups and the preliminary interview the counsellor spent one or two periods discussing the form with the year mistress and form tutor. This is something which was not done in the beginning except rather casually. The year mistress and the form tutor were the people most intimately concerned with the day-to-day life of the individual pupil. They had a good impression of what a girl was like and whether she showed any signs of strain and they could provide the counsellor with useful reality based information which helped the counsellor in assessing whether there was a need for a referral. By seeing both key personnel at once the counsellor ensured that the level of communication with each was the same. This avoided the situation of one member of the trio saying—or feeling—'But you didn't tell me about that particular difficulty. If I'd known, I could have done more'. The year mistress and the form tutor contributed their impressions freely to the discussion, the counsellor only said what did not break confidentiality, though she may well have had a child's permission to pass on information on a confidential basis if this really seemed appropriate and helpful.

More often than not the year mistress and form tutor knew a lot more than the counsellor about the child's background. If they came out with the facts that Betty's parents were separated, that there were six children, that Betty was always late for school and looked tired and undernourished, then there was little point in the counsellor keeping this information, which the girl has not explained in confidence, as if it were a deadly secret. It might be something which the staff responsible for the child already know, but which is *not* common knowledge. The form tutor usually knew whether a girl was coping with her life or finding it a strain, though she might not always know why. Sometimes a girl whom the form teacher knew needed extra help wrote a very non-committal note, and might not come forward for counselling. In this case counselling was thrust upon her, though the form tutor might decide to make a more determined and direct approach herself to get to the root of her troubles. Because a girl does not choose to come for counselling does not mean that no one can help her. She may prefer to talk to someone else, or she may already be under the wing of a social worker.

The triangular discussions were held in the counsellor's room, not in the staffroom; this was to ensure greater privacy and a relaxed atmosphere. Every member of each form was discussed though in most cases there was little to say. In order to establish what was already known about each girl the counsellor asked the staff to talk first. The counsellor had already checked with the girl concerned whether the school knows about separated parents or a handicapped brother or whatever it was; thus the counsellor knew whether it was important to the girl that this family secret be kept secret. Occasionally parents have confided in the form tutor without the girl's knowledge and so the tutor told the counsellor what the counsellor would otherwise have kept secret. It might be important to the girl's own pride and self-esteem to feel her home life and school life are kept separate, even if in fact they are not. In this rather delicate situation, the counsellor had to remember that betraying confidences is not just a question of relating facts: if she is lulled into a sense of false security by thinking that the staff already know about this particular child and that there was little point therefore in being discreet, she had to remember not to reveal attitudes or opinions which might be more a betrayal than the hard facts.

The discussion between the year mistress, form tutor and counsellor took place after the group discussions had ended and all the girls had had their brief routine interview. This was a good time for the contact, because the counsellor had not yet begun counselling proper. It was natural for staff to want to know *why* a child wanted to come for counselling, particularly if it is someone rather unexpected. At this stage all the counsellor knew was that Jenny wanted to come for counselling but she did not really know why. It was therefore easier for the counsellor to withstand the pressures of the staff's natural curiosity. If later on it was appropriate for the tutor to know why Jenny was being counselled the counsellor would tell her why with the child's permission. Without doubt it was the counsellor's duty, in the interests of the child, to *communicate* with the form teacher; bad communication might set up hostility, resentment or jealousy in the tutor, which in turn could adversely affect the child. But communicating did not mean telling all; the staff were not led to expect an explanation of why a girl was coming for counselling, and if they received an explanation it was because it was something that they knew already or that the child did not mind their knowing.

After the discussion of each form the counsellor kept in touch with the form tutor. The counsellor depended on the tutor to let her know of any particular developments in the work or behaviour of her clients or former clients. The discussion of a child could help both teacher and counsellor to develop their insight about her. The form tutor also helped the counsellor by handing out appointment slips to the girls and excusing them from lessons when they come for individual counselling.

The appointment slips were written out and distributed by the deputy head. This was logical as she had particular responsibility for the third and fourth years with whom the counsellors mostly worked; she also had particular responsibility for the timetable. Thus in one action she kept track of both the counsellors and the counselled. She had an opportunity to check on the way the counsellor was spending her time; she was also able to check that a girl did not repeatedly miss the same lesson. The counsellor did in fact write out a suggested timetable and list of appointments which was usually accepted.

The official blessing given to the appointment by this arrangement helped the staff to accept that this was a genuine excuse which was therefore not to be questioned. The appointment slip, which the girl took with her to the lesson she was to miss, also acted as an official pass for getting out of the lesson. This avoided any suspicion that going to see Mrs Jones was a euphemism for having a smoke or roaming the corridors. If a spontaneous interview had to be arranged the counsellor herself wrote a note to excuse the girl from her lesson. When a girl asked to leave a lesson the staff did not ask the girl why, though they might well ask themselves this question. Any complaints about lessons being missed went through the form tutor to the deputy head if necessary. These were not very frequent; when they did occur they were usually for good reasons and the timetable was adjusted accordingly. The departure of a girl for an official counselling session was intended to be treated as unobtrusively as possible. As far as it was possible to ascertain by questioning staff and pupils individual counselling was normally accepted without annoyance from the staff or gossip from the girls. The longer the service had been established and proved, the more this was likely to be the case.

Counselling and school records

It is pertinent to ask at this stage what contribution the counsellors made to the school records and what happened to all the valuable information they collected about the girls. In many counselling schemes, the counsellor himself takes responsibility for setting up and maintaining the school record cards; he collects and collates information from the primary school, interviews all pupils in the first year and adds his own comments plus any information about pupils' backgrounds to the card. This can be a very useful function, but it is not a function which is compatible with the particular kind of counselling service we established in our school. The existing system of official record-keeping was that the primary school profile, the interview notes, and any correspondence between home and school were kept in filing cabinets along with a new record card of each girl's academic and social progress which is maintained by form tutors. Form tutors had access to the records of their form; any particularly confidential matters were restricted to the medical records which were kept locked in the medical room and were not accessible to tutors without special permission.

The counsellor's records were kept separate from the other records and were regarded as completely confidential. The autobiographical notes were written by the girls on this understanding; they were never on any account shown to members of staff however innocuous they might be. The counsellor's own case notes were equally confidential, their purpose being to help the counsellor remember and understand the details of her client's case. The counsellors had a filing cabinet which locks, and to which no other member of staff had access; this includes the head who accepted, in a way not all heads would accept, that she did not have to know everything about each and every child. It is important to add here that the head and deputy head knew a great deal about many girls which they too keep confidential. Unless the girl concerned however happens to be on the counsellor's books there is little point in their passing on information. If the counsellor is already seeing a girl it seems unlikely that she would not be told about the matter directly by the girl. Confidentiality works both ways. Discretion is by no means the prerogative of the counsellor.

The counsellors rarely added anything to the official records of the school because they were extremely cautious about the possible effects of labelling children as problems. If children are generally difficult the school is already well aware of this; if they are generally well adjusted there is no need to cast doubts on this by alluding to their problems. In a case where action, such as referral to a specialist agency, is taken, then this is usually known to the school and noted accordingly. In cases where the problem can be sorted out between the client and the counsellor and is entirely private and personal (that is, in no way affecting the girl's school life) no note at all is made in the school records. Form tutors knew of course which of their girls come to see the counsellor. Tutors were asked to let the counsellor know if the girls became involved with any other agency. The counsellor then advised whether it was in the girl's interest for her to contact the agency with the child's permission. This kind of co-operation was particularly important with the careers officer and the school doctor. The counsellors, guided by the form tutors, tried not to miss an opportunity for constructive communication where it is in the girl's interest and with the girl's blessing.

Teachers do not always accept readily the idea of confidential counsellor records. There is a strong view within the teaching profession that the counsellor is doing a grave disservice by sitting on all the valuable information she has gathered. Teachers argue, with good reason, that they cannot help a child if they do not know what is the matter; that if they understood a child's problems, they could deal with them more sympathetically. But in the first place the counsellor is not in any way coming between or taking over the normal means of communication between teacher and pupil: it is still an important part of each form tutor's duty to get to know her pupils as well as possible. In the second place a child with problems is not necessarily helped by being treated any differently from other children, either more leniently or more punitively. Fair and equal treatment for all would surely be one of the first demands of any pupil power movement.

The conflicts provoked among teachers by the concept of confidentiality are usually out of proportion. Form tutors are usually well informed about their pupils' backgrounds, which reduces the amount of truly confidential information to a small proportion. There is never any point in burdening the staff with information which has no bearing at all on the way the child is behaving in school; when it is relevant to school behaviour it is very rare (never, in my experience) for the counsellor not to get the child's permission to explain the situation; or better still to get the child to say something herself.

Confidentiality does not equal non-communication. It is possible to communicate to staff that a child is having a difficult time at home without going into details, though there *is* a danger that hinting darkly at problems might set a form tutor's imagination boggling into fantasies more horrific than reality. It is best to get the child's permission for a straightforward honest statement. The communication of irrelevant knowledge can be both useless and damaging to the individual; the communication of confidential knowledge to staff merely provides them with a blunt weapon. If they are told they must not use this knowledge they are then left with a feeling of frustration and impotence; if they are tempted to use or unwittingly use what they are told in confidence there is a betrayal of the individual. If the matter really is confidential it is confidential; a compromise of half truth helps neither the pupil nor the staff.

If we take any educational issue it is clear that there are advantages and disadvantages in every scheme. If we think of streaming versus non-streaming or house groups versus year groups for example we must admit that there are good arguments for and against each side.

Our confidential self-referral service had certain advantages: our clients wanted to be helped and they trusted us. When they talked freely it was precisely because they were confident of our trustworthiness. If they were not confident of our integrity they would not talk. If they did not mind the staff knowing they would talk to them; they might talk to a counsellor as well because she had more time.

One of the disadvantages of our scheme was in the very few cases when a girl actually said, 'I can tell you this because you have said you won't tell anyone, and you mustn't—otherwise I won't tell you'. At some stage, preferably at the beginning, the counsellor has to make it clear that because of the child's age and the counsellor's responsibility to the child, to her family, to the school and to society, there *is* a limit to the amount of explosive material the counsellor can accept and sit on passively. On the other hand if the counsellor has the strength not to take precipitate action she may find that the client will change her mind later and ask for something to be done. The prohibition was more to test out the counsellor than to prevent action.

If for any reason the client does lose confidence in the counsellor, then there is no hope of further counselling until confidence has been restored. With staff-referrals the counsellor/client relationship is generally more tenuous at first, for the pupil may imagine that the staff are trying to manipulate her through the counsellor. When staff and counsellor are both involved in helping a particular child it is important not to confuse their different roles. The staff may need to take punitive action or to send for a parent because of a girl's bad behaviour. If the girl becomes confused and thinks this has come about because she has talked to the counsellor, then the counselling relationship is lost. Plain dealing rather than double dealing usually clears up this kind of confusion, though a girl who is ambivalent about getting help may well seize on any opportunity to avoid facing her own problems.

Although our service was basically designed to encourage self-referrals, staff-referrals were often made. We found that referrals made in the first and second years were not always as effective as referrals of older girls. This was partly because the girls were young and less able to take responsibility for themselves in the way we would like; partly because they were not quite sure who or what the counsellor is, although this had been explained to them by staff and counsellors. Any girl who had been through the third year groups had a good idea of the way the counsellor works. For example Sandra was referred by the staff in the fourth year for 'playing truant, being disobedient and generally getting into trouble'. Had she not been a member of a group the previous year when she had, in fact, been calm and relatively trouble-free, it is highly likely that she would have sat sullen and uncommunicative before yet another adult who looked as if she was going to 'deal' with her. She knew the counsellor already and knew the terms of reference under which the counsellor worked and she was able to communicate very quickly the kind of strain she was feeling in her relationship with her family. This is something she had not made clear in the disciplinary setting. She needed to go to the child guidance clinic; the interview with the counsellor confirmed what the school already suspected—that there was more to this than adolescent high spirits. A referral to the clinic was made forthwith, the girl herself accepting the need for this kind of help.

This example shows that the counsellor can miss many opportunities for helping girls unless she is backed up by the staff. The staff can help enormously by reminding girls who are having difficulties about the counselling service: if the girl then accepts that counselling might be useful, progress can be made. If the girl does not like the idea of counselling or the counsellor, then some other solution, as in the days *before* counsellors existed, has to be tried. Counselling is only one of many possible solutions to any problem, and may not always be appropriate. It is an extra source of help, but it is by no means a cure-all.

Criticism of staff and school organization

What does a counsellor do if a group or an individual begins to criticize the school regime or individual members of staff? This may be what the girls themselves want to know, which is why they are trying it on. The counsellor's way of dealing with it will be astutely judged by the girls. The counsellor who is so insecure as to sacrifice her own integrity and professional standards in order to be popular and 'in' with the girls is not only disloyal to her teaching colleagues she is also soon seen through by the pupils who will not respect her for her lack of standards. In this situation the objectivity of the counsellor is of paramount importance. Her way of dealing with the situation is simple and firm: she does not become involved; she does not take sides but remains outside; she may ask a few questions designed to provoke a consideration of the feelings of the staff or the reasoning behind the ruling but she puts the responsibility for action firmly back with the individuals concerned. On no account does she take upon herself the role of trade union negotiator. If the grievance is genuine, the children's own appointed leader can take the matter up with the authorities concerned or raise the issue in school council. It is amazing how many grievances disappear spontaneously at this point. When it became known on the third year bush telegraph that there was no joy in trying to get the counsellor to support the children against the staff, then baiting the counsellor lost its appeal. Most children understand and accept readily the way the school is run and why. Those who do feel unjustly treated may on reflection be able to see how their own behaviour and attitudes have contributed to this. Raising this kind of issue with the counsellor is therefore an uncomfortable process for it brings the individual up against her own limitations and does not allow the school to remain a convenient scapegoat.

Personal criticisms of members of staff usually reflect the emotional needs of the pupils more than the attributes of the teacher herself. This becomes clear when the same member of staff is praised by one pupil and criticized by another, perhaps even for the same quality, such as being strict. Occasionally a teacher may be the victim of antagonism really intended for an unsatisfactory mother. The pupil/teacher relationship in such a case can be the source of great strain and conflict, not only for the individuals concerned but for the whole class. This tension can be relieved if the child is able to ventilate her strong feelings. The counsellor recognizes these feelings for what they are: not the true situation necessarily but an expression of the child's emotional needs. If the cause for concern really lay within the teacher, then the majority of the form would feel this way. Once the child has expressed her anger she may begin to get the situation into perspective. If the child tries to manipulate the counsellor to side against the teacher she will soon stop when she finds it gets her nowhere.

The teacher who is being used as an emotional scapegoat by a pupil must find this a great worry and even begin to lose confidence. It can therefore be reassuring to the teacher if she has the courage to face the counsellor with her side of the problem, to realize that this is not simply a case of bad handling on her part but something much more complex. The counsellor can help restore the teacher's self-confidence and sense of perspective as well as the pupil's; the counsellor does this in the same way as she helps the pupil—that is, not by prescribing the answer but by listening to what she says, accepting and respecting her as a person with professional skills. The teacher who has a difficult child to deal with may be afraid to reveal the extent of her difficulties in case it makes her appear inadequate. The counsellor can make a helpful comment to open the way to communication. By facing the issue the teacher may be able to assess more realistically the way the pupil is playing on an emotional weak point of hers and gain the strength to deal more resiliently as well as more sympathetically with this particular pupil.

What does the counsellor do if several pupils criticize a member of staff independently of each other and when there does appear to be some justification in the accusations? Does the counsellor report this to the head? She certainly does not. This sort of breach of confidence would be completely unprofessional; it would also be unnecessary. Any counsellor who imagines that the head and her senior colleagues are not aware of the strengths and weaknesses of members of staff is suffering from delusions of grandeur. It is part of the head's job to know her staff, to develop and inspire the best in them. The counsellor is not going to improve staff performance any more than children's by reporting them to the authorities. This kind of judgemental role can only undermine the teacher/counsellor relationship. The counsellor must not use what the children have said about a teacher, partly because it may be a distortion of the truth, partly because this does nothing to improve teacher/pupil relationships. If the member of staff concerned comes to the counsellor to talk about her difficulties this must be kept as confidential as any interview with a girl.

It is only when a teacher brings forward to the counsellor some of the problems she is facing in the classroom that the counsellor has any role to play in improving staff performance. But the counsellor's role in the situation is not to be overlooked. The counsellor who has learnt to work discreetly and unobtrusively with staff may do much, indirectly, to help the staff develop their own strengths and minimize their own weaknesses. By keeping in touch with the staff the counsellor also ensures that she herself does not forget the difficulties of the classroom situation; she does not know the answers any more than they do but these can be worked out in discussion.

Staff/group discussions

Sometimes a particular girl causes trouble with everybody who teaches her. This may be a girl who is not particularly amenable to counselling. In this sort of situation we found it invaluable to get together all the members of staff who taught the girl. In one notable case a second year girl, Barbara, was causing great concern. She was very sensitive to any mild rebuke and would respond to any direction by any teacher with a great show of aggression and fuss. Every member of staff was suffering at her hands, except for the drama and housecraft teachers in whose lessons there was a greater degree of freedom and self-expression. The staff meeting was held after school, over cups of tea. The counsellor said that it was difficult to get at the root of this particular girl's problems, and that it might help in understanding Barbara if everybody would say something about her. One by one staff listed misdeeds, annoyances, rudeness, belligerence. The counsellor began to regret having convened the meeting, fearing that the discussion was simply inflaming bad feelings against Barbara. Then suddenly there came a great wave of sympathy for Barbara; one after the other the staff expressed concern for how Barbara must feel in this position of being constantly criticized and devalued. The counsellor said that it was best to wait and see how Barbara developed from then on; if nothing changed there would have to be a referral to the child guidance clinic.

The extraordinary thing was that from that moment Barbara began to improve. Why was this? She grew up a little and this helped; she was also greatly helped by the staff as a whole, who mustered just that little extra tolerance needed to carry her over this passing phase. There is nothing so depressing and so reinforcing of one's sense of worthlessness as being constantly criticized. The staff tried, not to be lenient with her, but to look for the good in her and avoid collisions between their authority and her need to assert her own. In this case it had proved impossible to work with Barbara's attitudes to her social environment; it proved worthwhile working with the attitudes of the school to Barbara. These are not necessarily mutually exclusive processes; in some cases it is worth trying both. It is worth noting that in neither approach is the counsellor altering Barbara's *actual* environment—the counsellor is not a juggler of externals.

The counsellor's role in school policy

Although in our scheme we took great care to keep the counsellor outside the main stream of school organization and discipline we realized that to insulate the counsellor totally from school policy did not help her to help her clients. She must not identify with the school powers, but she must not be so isolated from them as to become alienated. If she is to assess what is normal behaviour in a client, she must know what is normally expected of her and why. The counsellor who herself does not know or understand what school policy is may quite unwittingly make a comment which goes against the objectives of the school. It makes it harder for her to retain the neutrality and objectivity she claims, if she only hears the children's remarks about what is going on. The counsellor has to keep her feet on the ground, even if she does not use them very much. Whether or not the counsellor agrees with everything the school is doing she has, like all the staff, a duty not to undermine what the school is trying to achieve. The easiest way for her to understand this is for her to attend and participate in staff meetings or discussions. It may even be helpful to the staff for her opinion to be sought on some new organizational scheme: the counsellor's role as outside observer of the school's social structure gives her an opportunity for an objective assessment of the effects of policy on social behaviour. The counsellor may be wrong, but it is both healthier and more constructive for her to put forward her view for consideration alongside the views of the rest of the staff.

The counsellor then has a useful viewpoint to contribute on decisions of policy and should therefore participate in staff discussions. On the other hand, general staff meetings are not the moment for the counsellor to add to the general discussion of an individual child. This risks misrepresentation, distortion and breach of confidentiality. A properly convened discussion is a different matter. If the counsellor does contribute to discussions on school policy the only danger for her clients is that she will begin to identify too closely with the school system and start to succumb to pressures to make children conform. If the counsellor is aware of this possible side effect, she is more likely to retain her objectivity and sense of perspective.

Conclusion

It is entirely natural for teachers to feel ambivalent about counselling at first. The counsellor too will feel insecure and needs the full support of the head and staff in setting up a counselling scheme. Consultation at all times is essential to ensure good communication and good relationships.

However the goodwill and support of the staff are not enough to ensure a constructive working relationship between staff and counsellor. The counsellor has to take the initiative in defining and explaining at every opportunity her role and function. There needs to be regular discussion, properly convened, between appropriate members of staff and the counsellor, to ensure the maximum co-operation, understanding and efficiency. Co-operation with the staff at every level does not go against the counsellor's role as a trustworthy outsider, provided the counsellor is sufficiently disciplined professionally to remain objective. Through working out together their complementary roles, the teacher and counsellor are both able to help the individual child more. Discussing his own difficulties with a counsellor sometimes helps a teacher to improve his own self-insight and techniques of pastoral care. Members of staff who have natural counselling skills can continue to deploy them, with the added self-assurance and effectiveness gained from their discussion with the counsellor. This relieves the counsellor of the burden of dealing with cases which can be perfectly well handled by form tutors; it enhances the role of the form tutor; it spreads the effects of the counsellor's specialized training skills and philosophy throughout the staff, thus ensuring an even greater unity of purpose between teacher and counsellor and leaving the counsellor more time to deal with those cases in which his specialized training and his role as outsider are important to and needed by the client. Thus the counsellor's work with the staff is almost as important as the work with the children in furthering his general objectives. A relationship between staff and counsellor built on mutual respect, confidence, trust and reciprocal co-operation is essential to an effective counselling service. A counsellor who neglects relationships with the staff is doing his clients a grave disservice.

Chapter 5

The adolescent world

How do young people see the rest of us? How do they feel about the way we behave, the way we handle them? What are their hopes and fears, their needs and their problems, real and imagined? Having explained the mechanics of our counselling service, and the ways in which we established a working relationship with the girls and with the staff, I want now to discuss the pupils' feelings and problems. There is a great deal of overlap between the problems expressed in the groups and the problems expressed by individuals; thus the sorts of comments made in groups and in the autobiographical notes can form a useful background to individual problems; they can also give non-adolescents greater insight into the adolescent's feelings. They provide a glimpse of the various ways young people currently view the adult world. It is not easy for adults to keep in touch with the 'teen scene' at a realistic level. Some adults are rather intimidated by the modern adolescent, some are jealous, some bewildered, some belligerent, some reactionary, others are permissive to the point of appearing not to care what happens. It is hoped that the comments made by the girls in their autobiographical notes will illustrate the kinds of feelings and problems experienced by normal adolescent girls who do not need counselling. Most of the comments speak for themselves, though they would repay close scrutiny and detailed discussion. In quoting these notes I have been careful to remove any details which would make them identifiable. The spelling and phrasing are given as in the originals. I think they give a vivid and valid view of the way young people feel. James Hemmings's book *Problems of Adolescent Girls*, based largely on letters girls wrote to magazines, has a similar flavour and reveals a similar range of problems.[1]

Parents

I have to be in by eight o'clock every single night. My dad's very strict—I wanted to go to a party but my dad wouldn't let me. My mum won't let me do anything and I get sick and tired of it but I know its for my own good but she treats me like a five year old. My mum worries about me with boys in case anything happens, and I could hate her sometimes but I feel sorry for my dad.

I don't think they like me as much as my sisters because I get blamed for everything.

I find that I get fed-up with my parents when they start to row and this usually leaves me with no place to go to get out of the house.

When it comes to getting up in the mornings, both my parents start calling me and shouting at me. My dad bellows at me as if he were still in the RAF.

One thing I hate about my mum, say if there's boys standing outside the verandah or in the streets, she starts up a fight with me and sought of chucks me out and tries to show me up in front of them. I've got that feeling that she don't seem to want me to grow up, like not going out with boys, she sought of seems to think I go out of my way to go out with them, but I have not been out with a boy yet.

My mum is very strict and sometimes I go to bed at 8 o'clock and read to get away from her. If I go out before tea, I have to be back by 6 o'clock and I'm not aloud out any more.

I am staying on at school. It was my own decision. As my mum said, only I know what I want to do.

My mother can be very nagging if she wants to. I can't stand this and it usually ends with me walking out of the room.

I am allowed out whenever I want to which is not very often as there is not any clubs or dances where I live and you usually have to travel to get anywhere interesting.

My life is quite unhappy as my parents keep on at me.

I smoke and my mum knows, because what is the use of doing it behind their backs so you might as well do it in front of them.

My dad is very nice to me sometimes but suddenly changes and goes all moody. I'm not yet allowed to go out with boys but I always do and we always have rows over this.

My parents are rather old and getting rather moany—my mother is nearly always moany especially in the morning. My father I hardly ever see. I get on alright with my father because he is always nice to me and hardly ever grumbles. My mother though, always says don't do this, don't do that and so I always feel as though I'm in the wrong.

My mother is strange in a way, one minute she is helpful and will say things like 'never you mind, you're growing up' and the next minute she will go off in a flying temper because I am growing up. I know this is because she is starting the change, but it doesn't help and I never know what mood she will be in. Every now and then she gets into a temper because I never go out. I would like to, but somehow I just can't mix and make friends.

My mother and father don't trust me at night.

My mum goes to work and so we all have to muck in with the jobs: this is usually where the fights occur.

My dad goes mad when I stop out with boys. I am not allowed to go anywhere unless there is a reason.

My mother don't mind me going out with boys but she hits me when I come in late.

My father's not bad, but he's only interested in my education and my mother don't like me going around with boys. I have three boy friends.

My mother worries a lot and she is always fussing.

My mother wants me to have every opportunity possible where education is concerned as she did not have opportunities when she was at school. I find we don't understand each other very well.

I never lie to my father as I think this only makes one untrustworthy and he respects me for this.

My parents quite often get on my nerves when they don't understand our modern ways.

I look after myself really and I'm just in the house at night. When I am old enough I want to leave home.

I find it hard to please both my parents at once.

My mother works part-time. My father disagrees with her work as he thinks she should be at home in case of emergency.

I don't know if its my imagination or not but I think my parents honestly don't understand children.

I am the only child. My parents and I discuss things and we do not have any real secrets from each other. If I ask them anything they answer it whatever it may be. I find it very easy to talk to my parents especially my mother. They are very understanding and fair. I don't think they spoil me, and if there is something I do not want to do and they want me to do, they say, that I must do it and if I don't they get annoyed.

Comment

Although negative comments about parents were the exception rather than the rule, nevertheless it seems that it is not easy for parents to deal with their teenage children or vice versa. Many of the complaints made were clearly reality based and not just symptoms of adolescent rebellion. Over-possessiveness, jealousy, moodiness, bad temper, rivalry, constant nagging, anxiety, lack of affection or communication, favouritism of other siblings, apparent indifference — these are the sorts of characteristics which make for problem parents: usually there was no comment, occasionally a positive comment. Nevertheless these examples, though highly coloured, are typical of the way many adolescents see their parents. The group discussion confirmed this.

Siblings

My three sisters are married so there is just me and my brother. He's always bossing me around and telling me off.

I have one brother who is seventeen years old and we do not get along very well, we are always arguing and fighting but he always wins the fighting for he is much stronger.

My little brother is a mongolian child. This upsets me when people joke about it.

I have one sister but long for an older brother but naturally this was not possible as I was the first child born.

My brother's at work. He's alright, but he gets a bit moody, still probably its because he hasn't really got a girl-friend.

My elder sister of 16 is very handy as she takes the same size as I do and I am nearly always on the borrow.

My sister is 11. She is always causing trouble for me. She will do something and blame it on to me. When my mother goes out she will never do a thing I ask her. Every time she passes me she kicks and hits me. But my parents take no notice of what I say.

My sister is 8 and quite a problem because she asks about babies and where they come from and I wonder if I tell her too much sometimes.

I have one sister who is 20. She is bossy and seems to think that I am lazy, stupid and horrible. She also tries to and does hit me, but seeing as I am growing up to her height, every time she goes to hit me, I warn her off.

My sister is 7 and she often gets on my nerves, so much in fact that I could wring her neck.

I don't get on well with my brother. I am treated as the baby of the family and I rather resent this.

My younger brother is spoilt by my mother, most probably because he is the youngest and she can't fuss my elder brother and me, he usually gets away with a lot of things whereas my brother and I don't.

I hate my brother because he is always showing off when my mates call for me.

I am not as clever as my sister, but I find it very difficult to make my parents, especially my mother, understand.

My sister is a nuisance as she plays her records after me everywhere I go and she shares a bedroom with me and dirties it up, and also when I decide to go to bed late she stays up too and annoys me. She writes on my books and scribbles on my pictures. She is 8. My big brother is 19. I like him because he tells me whether to get different clothes and whether they suit me, he lets me use his record player, tape recorder and records.

I share my bedroom with my sister and this sometimes causes trouble between her and myself, her being neat and tidy and I not up to her standards.

I've got one brother who is 19, he sometimes gets on my nerves although I become very friendly towards him roundabout Xmas time and my birthday.

Comment

In my experience the pupils who wrote the longest pieces about their siblings did not feel the problems as much as it appeared, and having expressed themselves in this dramatic way they had relieved their feelings and did not want to dwell on them longer. Where problems with siblings appear to be serious they are more usually symptoms of problems in relationship with parents. The pupils who verbalize their negative feelings so easily are usually equally able to look at the positive side and cheerfully admit for example that they for their part provoke their siblings beyond endurance and deserve all the bad treatment they get. Most of the pupils had not got their problems out of proportion and if and when they elaborated them to interest me, they usually left it at that. I have not in fact quoted cases which led to sustained supportive work.

Grandparents

My nan won't let me play pop music because she can't stand it.

I live with my nan also. I find her moans are dreadful to hear. I am told I do not do enough for my mother. Sometimes I get so wild I stalk out of the room.

One thing I can't stand is being told I'm talking rubbish just because I'm younger than the person I'm talking to and I don't like people making excuses for old people and saying, 'Well, she's old you know.'

Nan's very nice but she too often reminds me that if it wasn't for her she doesn't know where I would be. This only happens when she's annoyed with me and I don't want to do something for her. Still I expect she's entitled to be like that. Apart from her occasional moans she's very nice and kind and generous.

We all get on, except with Nan. She treats everyone like slaves, dominates all the money and only dishes it out as she sees fit. She gives me lots of money and I suppose she loves me, but I feel that if she would stop making everyone else's life a misery that I might love her in return.

I am the only child and my parents and I live with my father's mother. This is not a bind to us like it would be to some people, but I couldn't imagine living without my grandmother.

My sister and I do not get on very well with my grandad. He is always telling us of what he used to do when he was young, and was always in at 8.30. And now he expects me to do the same. He always wants to know where we are going and who we are going with, what time we will be back.

Comment

In fact only one or two pupils in each form have grandparents as well as parents to contend with. The girls' comments speak for themselves.

Friends

I go around with one friend. We go out to parties and enjoy ourselves, but she is a blond and very pretty and all the boys look at her, but I find her personality very boring. The boys that do speak to her find out what she is like and then don't think so much of her.

I am very shy, especially when there are boys about. I go all hot and get butterflies in my tummy, but I do like them.

I do not go out with boys although I notice them. I expect I shall start going out with them next year. At the moment I feel I am a little too young.

I have a big problem though, so many boys say they like me, but I don't like them.

I have a boy-friend who is much older than me. My mother does not know about him and I am afraid she will stop me seeing him if she knows. He knows I am only 13.

I like boys, but I am very left out when in a group of girls, and probably thats why I do not go out a lot.

I am very boy-shy. Perhaps this is because there are not many young people of my age where I live. The people are 19-20 or over, or about 6 years old and under.

My interests (if you can call it that) are mostly boys. I get on well with boys, and I go out with a boy, but it isn't all that serious. I am an anajetic person, as my mum says, I never get tired.

Really I don't think I'm a very nice person to know because I talk too much to people I know and yet I'm very shy to anyone else.

I get on well with people and like meeting them but I can't stand moany people, or people of our age or older who think themselves better than us. I can talk to people, but sometimes get tongue-tied with a nice boy.

I am a virgin and want to stay that way till I'm married. Sometimes when I go out with a boy I do get sort of spasms and do feel sexy, but I've found that I can control myself.

I haven't got a boy-friend although I do go out in a group with boys, but we don't often pair off.

The only thing is, I have to look after my brother and take him for a walk. This sometimes stops me from going out with boys because they want to go out at about 6 o'clock, but I have to look after my brother at that time, and this is every night I have to do this. I would like to get married when I am 19 years old.

I have no trouble with friends out of school, but in school I seem to be the odd one out. The girls in my form seem to think its not right for me not to go out with boys and not to wear make-up.

I have lots of friends out of school, but my best friend and I have known each other for nearly twelve years. She lives on the fifth floor of my block and we get on quite well together because we like the same things. I like boys, especially one that lives up the hill to me. In the holidays my friends and I go down the park or we go swimming. Sometimes I go out in the evenings but it is a bit boring at night round our way. We might go in my friend's house or just walk about and have a laugh and talk to some boys.

Comment

Despite much sophisticated bravado, on average only half a dozen girls in each form had boyfriends in the specific or sexual sense. But my impression of the girls in each form of 30 was that only half went out at all and of these, half went out with girls or in a mixed crowd and half had boyfriends. Very few indeed had serious boyfriends who lasted more than a few weeks and the ones who did appeared to regard them primarily as good companions and to have what was basically an asexual relationship. This would not of course be true for older adolescents.

Sparetime activities

At night I am allowed to go out but there is nowhere to go.

I like walking through the Park on a Summer's day.

I am allowed out when I want to which is not very often as there is not any clubs or dances where I live and you usually have to travel to get anywhere interesting.

I usually stay in and do my homework. Its a bit of a bore because I don't know anyone who lives near me—in the holidays its terrible.

I have a job on Saturdays, but as you are not going to show this to anyone, I can tell you because I am slightly under age.

I don't go out because there's nothing to do, only pictures.

I love strawberries and ice-cream, modern clothes, pop-music and boys. I hate spaghetti and school, going visiting my aunts, and doing homework.

I like ballet-dancing. My sister often says that I won't stick at it but I like it too much to give it up.

I go out most nights a week, on Wednesdays I go to evening class and on Fridays to a Youth Club.

I don't go out because I tend to worry about my homework and so I stay in and do it. I think we shouldn't have homework, especially over the weekend, because if you are going away you have got your homework to worry about, and not only that, we spend five days at school a week, writing and so they should give us a rest.

I like needlework, reading and listening to records. I like boys but my mum won't let me go out with them.

When I am not working or reading, I take dogs or babys for a walk with my friends, my favourite sport is swimming.

I have not got many interests because I do not have time for them. I like watching TV.

I like ice skating, needlework and dancing but not going swimming. I like listening to pop records and I like meeting new friends of both sexes.

I love horse riding. I go to the stables every day.

My hobbies are reading, sleeping, going for walks with friends and having a laugh.

Comment

Most of the pupils claimed not to go out very much, and to spend most of their spare time watching television. Some appeared to have time to go out every night, some were too busy doing homework. The most disturbing comments were those about the lack of amenities in the area. In some cases this was the rationalization of a desire not to face the world, but more often it was true. The other problem was the parental veto: some half a dozen girls in each form were not allowed to go out at all, not even with girlfriends. They may not have set about asking very determinedly; most were happy to accept this housebound state at this age, but not when they were over 16.

Ambitions

When I leave school I would like to be a computer operator but I shall have to work hard for this.

I don't know what to do when I leave school. I am staying on but I dislike school.

I would like an intelligent and easy going husband, a bit like me in some ways, a couple of children and some animals.

My ambition was to become a vet, but that idea went down the drain when I found the studying that had to be done.

My ambition is to work with horses.

I haven't a clue what I want to be but I shall be glad when I leave.

I would not like to be very famous, but I would like to have a lot of money so I could buy the things I like and go to the places I want to go. I feel terribly tied down at school. I know my work is very important for my future but sometimes I feel like just giving up and going out to work. I would never do this but sometimes it is very tempting.

When I leave school I'd like to be an air hostess I think, but I keep changing my mind.

We want to emigrate to Canada, that is, us girls and mum, but my dad doesn't.

I do not know what I want to do when I leave school, but I want to stay on to the seventh year to take A levels if I can.

I did want to be a tipest but I am not brainey enough.

I really am set on being an actress when I leave school although my parents don't agree. I can see their point, insecurity and so on. But I would hate to be stuck in an office in front of a typewriter. I feel this would bore me. I would be willing to work very hard to achieve my ambition though it may seem only a childish dream.

Comment

Most of the pupils did not know what they wanted to do when they left school, which is hardly surprising at their age. Most suggestions were, in line with Thelma Vennes' research, realistic and not particularly exciting or ambitious.[2] A few had unrealistic aims, particularly non-whites: aspiring doctors with no hope of O levels, would-be ballet dancers who were totally untrained and quite the wrong shape anyway. This category of pupil needs skilful handling.

Adolescent moods and general comments

I hate my name and I don't know what I want to do when I leave school. I like horseriding and swimming but I am not good at either of these things. I don't like homework and injections. I also disslike school doctors and school medicals. I am fat and tall and I am not very good in sliming.

I have a quick temper. I am quiet and shy.

I have had a rotten past. I was in a home most of my younger years.

My trouble is that I have a quick temper and I don't mean to argue but I get so annoyed that I can't help it. I bite my nails when I'm reading a book or watching television, but mostly when I'm nervous.

I am fat and I know I am fat. I am very self-conscious in the presence of men. I hope I will grow out of it.

My sisters and I are always argueing because I have a quick temper and they keep teasing me.

I bite my nails through nervousness, despite efforts to stop. I have moods when I get shy but I can usually hold my own and I'm usually happy and friendly.

I dislike cheese, people who always get embarrassed, men who think girls should be feminine, girls who are so thick skinned that they don't believe you when you say you don't like them. I like most people, drink, school (more or less) money, and pop groups.

My moods change far too rapidly for my liking.

One thing I hate, really hate is the dentist. Even the mention of it I burst into tears.

I have hundreds of secrets, just small things, things that would seem silly if I told my family, but they mean a lot to me. I seem to day-dream a lot.

I bite my nails through nervousness. This has something to do with school. In holidays they begin to grow but as soon as I come back to school I can't stop.

Since I came to secondary school, I have changed very much. I used to be timid and shy but now I have come well out of my shell, but I think I'm not such a nice person as I used to be.

I don't believe in marriage.

I get shy in front of people very easily and they often think I'm quiet but once they've gone I'm alright and I'm my normal self.

Have you eny idears how I could look my age becous I am very small for my age.

I dislike overbearing people, snobs, spoilt children, talk backs—people who become your friend and then talk about you behind your back, sweets, white coffee, my mother sometimes, my sister most of the time, the neighbours, racialism, prejudice, war, history. I like everything not listed above, especially my mum when I don't dislike her.

Comment

Not all the pupils commented on their moods — they were not specifically asked to do so. What was interesting about their comments is the number who expressed grave self-doubts, which were largely unjustified; those who worried about being fat were, at most, simply rather luscious and nubile. Those who claimed to have violent tempers appeared to be quiet and calm. Those who patently *were* fat and aggressive did not usually comment on this on paper: either the point was too sensitive to them or too obvious to me to need elaborating. Often these girls would come and talk about their appearance or their moods afterwards.

Again most of the quotations I give are not from pupils with serious problems. Their comments show already a degree of insight and sense of perspective which is healthy enough. More serious are the cases where the pupils cannot express their feelings at all or where the only feelings expressed are hostile and negative.

Group discussion of these points

Although I have taken this selection of comments from the autobiographical notes, they are typical of the kind of remark made in the group discussions. Thus many of the more obvious points of teenage conflict are dealt with there and then, spontaneously by the group. One of the purposes of the group discussion is for members to perceive and accept that it is normal to be different: for example not all girls of 13 or 14 want to go out in the evenings and certainly not with boys, yet many of them worry about this. Adults too are sometimes guilty of making similar sweeping statements about what girls of 14 should or should not do: 'A girl of your age shouldn't go out with boys, should be in by eight o'clock.' 'A girl of your age should get out a bit more, learn to mix a bit.' What we have to remember is that chronological age is not as important as developmental stage. Young people who mature later, or more slowly, need reassurance to gain the strength not to feel that they should be doing the same as their peers to prove that they are 'normal'. The group with its widely different views helps to provide this reassurance, more effectively than any single adult can. Young people who feel isolated from their contemporaries, who feel they are the odd one out, who have nowhere to go in the evenings or no friends in their neighbourhood may realize with a great sense of relief just how common these feelings are. They may come to understand and to accept that people develop in different ways and at different rates and gain some sense of their individual worth and values.

Sometimes it was easier for the pupils to discuss someone else's problem. The counsellor might make up a problem like this: 'Janet was nearly 14. She didn't have any boyfriends and the other girls sometimes laughed at her. But really she wasn't interested in boys; she much preferred to stay in or if she did go out, to be with her best girlfriend. All the same, she began to worry about being the odd one out. What should she do?' The counsellor did not say. The pupils themselves argued, suggested, discussed, at the same time gaining reassurance and developing a less narrow view of their friends. This was much more effective than a statement from the counsellor. It usually matters more to a young person what friends think than what adults think.

Another common dilemma is illustrated by this example: 'Pauline's mother would not let her go out with boys even though she was nearly 14. Pauline didn't think it was fair. She was however allowed to go to a youth club once a week provided she was in by nine o'clock. One day a boy she particularly liked asked her to go to the pictures. Her friend Anna suggested she pretended to her mother that she was going out with her. What should Pauline do?'

Again the counsellor did not give the answer. There wasn't an answer and it was far more valuable for the girls to argue this out among themselves. There were usually a few girls in each group who considered it quite logical to deceive one's parents in a case like this if the parents were not sufficiently confident to give permission and if the child felt that she could take full responsibility. Usually the problem was that the girls had not had the courage to discuss the issue with their parents and were assuming a negative reply. Or they asked permission for something unacceptable like going to see an X film, were firmly told 'No' and then took it that they would never be allowed to go anywhere. We might spend some time discussing how to set about this question of getting permission to go out for the first time. The more experienced girls helped the others; mostly it was a question of gaining enough confidence to bring the matter to a head. Some girls were not sufficiently secure in their relationship with their parents to take a stand on any issue yet eventually this is what they had to do to gain any measure of independence. Some asked for independence but were frightened of actually having any, which is why they asked hesitantly and then blamed their parents for the negative reply which had saved them from facing the dangers of freedom. Sometimes there *was* a genuine problem here: parents who would not let their daughters out of the house at all, sometimes non-whites, sometimes over-possessive parents who did not want their children to grow up. I came across several girls who pretended they did not *want* to go out rather than admit to their friends that their parents would not let them. These girls were guarded in the group but came afterwards to talk in private about their dilemma.

There is no doubt that parents sometimes are a real problem: too rigid parental control, or none, or inconsistencies. Sometimes the parents are insecure in their own relationships or their own social situation. Marital disharmony, financial worries, overcrowding, ill health, loss of job or status, mental breakdown—all these factors make for strain in a family. Sometimes a young person with the most difficult home situation manages to remain resilient and cheerful, indeed may grow in strength and understanding through this adverse experience. Sometimes a pupil may get the family situation out of perspective and blame herself for all the pain and anxiety that surround her. Such a pupil can be helped, sometimes through generalized group discussion, to see that the way other people treat us sometimes has nothing to do with our actual behaviour and response but is more a reflection of their own emotional needs. If a pupil can come to understand a difficult situation in the family she can often learn to tolerate it or even help to ease it.

We must not however expect young people to be too tolerant. A girl with a handicapped brother or an over-tired working mother or a physical disability of her own may appear to cope with an astonishing degree of forbearance and responsibility. Often these girls are under considerable strain and need help to gather for themselves the strength to communicate some consideration of their own point of view and needs to the rest of the family. In the group, individuals were not encouraged to express these sorts of personal problems at any length;

they might work out their own answer through group discussion or they might come later for individual counselling.

Questions about sex

This glimpse of the adolescent world would not be complete without some consideration of the girls' attitude towards sex. At least one of the group discussions was devoted to questions about sex and other sessions were devoted to discussions about allied social problems. Although there was not a syllabus to be covered we found from experience that the same topics inevitably arose. The girls had instruction about human reproduction in the first year and were well acquainted with the facts of life, though some had forgotten some things, perhaps because they were too young to take it all in at the time.

They therefore usually welcomed the chance to go over again the topics of menstruation, intercourse and childbirth and to have the opportunity to ask supplementary questions. They were still often worried about old wives' tales or confused about veiled allusions they had heard to such things as VD, the Pill, Durex, homosexuality, perversion. They could not escape reading about these matters in newspapers or hearing about them in television plays and discussions but it was sometimes hard for them to piece together what they heard and saw in such an oblique manner. The object of talking about it all was not to equip them with sophisticated know-how, but to remove from these topics any aura of furtive secrecy and provocative mystery, to replace worry with reassurance, fantasy with fact. It is doubtful whether the girls remembered what they were told in any detail.

The questions asked about sex varied tremendously in maturity, sophistication and purpose. Some were clearly asked simply to shock the counsellor and see if she was really trustworthy and permissive as she says. Many gave the impression of a degree of sexual experience way beyond the norm for such young girls: in most cases I am sure this was either because of bravado (which seems to exist among girls as well as boys) or unfortunate phrasing. However I think it is important for adults to realize the kind of questions young adolescents ask about sex. I also think it important that those who are training to answer these questions should experience something of the directness of the teenage approach. Children rarely ask textbook questions requiring textbook answers, as you will see from the examples of questions asked. When the questions are factual they are answered factually; when they were a matter of opinion or subjects for discussion they are put before the group. You might like to think about how you would answer them.

Questions about menstruation / puberty

Is it wise for girls of our age to use sanitary towels like Tampax? If not, why? If it is wise could you advise us a kind to use? What age should we start to use them at?

If a girl is worried about not starting her periods, at what age should she consult her doctor?

When you have got your period, why don't you feel well?

Why are some people flat, and some have a good figure?

If a girl misses her periods two or three months, what should she do? Should she worry although she wasn't playing about with boys?

How do you improve your bust?

Should you get your hair wet when having periods?

Is it safe to go swimming while your period is on?

Should your boyfriend know when you've started, and if he did, what do you think he would do?

Questions about boys

Explain masturbation and is it wrong?

Could you explain what circumcision is?

Why do boys get frustrated?

Is it true that every kiss takes three minutes off your life?

If a boy comes near you when you are undressed can you become pregnant?

Why does a boy like you holding his private?

What is the average age for a boy to have an erection?

Why do boys and men go on the horn?

Why is it that girls are raped a lot and boys are rarely raped?

Can you tell whether a man is clean or has got VD?

Virginity

Is is possible to lose your virginity without actually having sexual intercourse? Excluding riding etc.

Can you lose your virginity through horse riding etc? How can you tell if you have and what happens if you do?

Is it possible for a doctor to tell whether you are a virgin or not?

Why are people shocked when you say you're not a virgin? Because this is modern times and also why do boys take a nasty attitude and call you names when mostly they are boys of our own age?

What is breaking-in please?

Can your husband tell if you have had sexual intercourse before marriage?

If you've had sexual intercourse and you haven't had a baby are you still a virgin?

Why does it hurt when a boy breaks you in?

If a schoolboard or Welfare Officer found out she wasn't a virgin, would she be put in ball stalls *(sic)*?

Is it true about the medical you have in the fourth year that they look and see if you've been broken in? And do they do anything about it, eg inform parents?

Questions about behaviour with boys

Is petting wrong at our age?

What's the meaning of French kisses?

Why do boys have to break you in?

At what age do you think a girl should be broken in?

Does a boy go after you for what you have got or is it because he likes you or loves you?

Should you let boys do anything they want to? If not, what should you let them do and what shouldn't you let them do?

If you go out with a boy for the first time and he starts getting dirty and asks you to go steady, should you continue the relationship if you like him a lot?

Should you let a boy stroke your breasts?

Can love bites lead to trouble?

How do you control a boy with wandering hands?

Why does a boy lick your vagina?

Do you think it is right that a girl should suck a boy's prick?

If a boy is kissing you and he touches your body, should you walk off or let him do it?

Questions about childbirth

What is it like to be pregnant?

Is it dangerous to have sexual intercourse while you are pregnant?

What would happen if a girl became pregnant before she was 16 years old?

What is a miscarriage?

Can you explain a Caesarian operation?

Why do some women not know when they are pregnant?

Does it hurt very much when the baby comes out?

What do they mean by 'Oh, it was an accident' as if they didn't know she was pregnant?

How would you explain to your parents that you were having a baby?

Can you tell us about breaking the waters?

How are twins formed?

Is it dangerous to have an abortion?

Can you tell us about the afterbirth?

When a woman is sterilized does she still have periods?

If a girl is under 21 and is not married and is pregnant, and the mother of the girl wants her to get rid of the baby and the girl doesn't, can she still keep the child?

If a girl had a baby under 16 would the father of the baby go to court?

How are abortions performed? What are the dangers of such an operation?

Questions about intercourse

Is it right that newly-married couples have a sexual intercourse on their first night of marriage?

Do you have intercourse on your stomach or on your side?

Does it hurt to have intercourse?

How many positions can you have intercourse in?

Can you have intercourse while you are having your monthly period?

What happens to the semen that has not fertilized an egg but remains in the vagina?

How long does an intercourse last?

Would anything happen if you slept with your relation (eg brother)?

Can a man give a woman a baby at any age or time?

Is it true that when you have a sexual intercourse for the first time, that there is pain and loss of blood?

When you have intercourse do you have it on your periods or off?

When should you have intercourse, for how long and does it hurt?

How do you feel after you have had intercourse?

Is it safe to be intimate before marriage if you take precautions?

Questions about birth control

What is Durex?

How does the Pill work?

Are contraceptives dangerous?

Can you be sure not to have a baby when the boy uses Durex?

What is a diaphragm?

Questions about VD

Is it possible to catch VD by kissing if the boy is infected?

Do you only get VD when you have it away with other men, or when you just have it with one person? Because someone I know had VD and she only had it with one person?

What is VD really?

Why do we get discharge?

Can you get VD round the mouth through kissing many boys?

How do you get VD and how do you get rid of it?

Questions about homosexuality and perversion

Could you explain what is a pervert?

Why do homosexuals prefer men to the opposite sex as it is sickening and unnatural?

What does it mean when you read in the papers that a girl has been sexually assaulted?

What is a pansy?

What's the difference between being raped and being seduced?

What are homosexual practices?

Why are some women attracted to other women?

General questions asked

Is sex before marriage wrong?

Is it wrong to be a prostitute?

Why do mothers try to change the subject when their children ask them questions about boys, sex and the body?

Why do girls fall in love with pop stars and dream about them when they haven't the nearest chance of getting to know them?

Why do some parents have a favourite son or daughter if they have about three or four kids?

Why do some people make out sex to be wrong, even if you are married, when you have a baby?

Why do parents try to stop you growing up quicker (by wearing make-up and grown-up clothes) when at our age, 14, they were old enough to go out to work?

Do you think parents should open their daughters' letters or listen to their phone calls?

What is meant by trial marriage?

Should a girl go on holiday with a boy without parents?

I feel much more at home asking questions on sex and discussing it with my boyfriend than with anybody else as I can really face him and ask him at the same time. Is this right?

Comment

You may feel that some of these questions are possibly better not asked at all. But the point is that they *were* asked by young adolescents. They were not prompted; they arose spontaneously. Just a few were cooked up to shock or provoke, but most were genuine. I am assured by colleagues who work with boys that boys' questions are similar. Answering the questions, even questions of face, is a delicate and skilled task. If the counsellor was worried for example about shocking the unsophisticated for the sake of explaining to the sophisticated few, this very anxiety would be conveyed in the answers. The counsellor needs a calmness, a lightness of touch, a sense of humour, an ability to talk about intimate matters without making them provocative and salacious or sweeping them under the carpet. It is not easy and this is why it is important for teachers undertaking this work to be carefully selected, trained and supported. What is potentially damaging or distressing about this kind of work is not the content of the group discussion so much as the way the subjects are handled. The feelings and attitudes behind what is being said are what will make the discussion responsible and fruitful, or otherwise. The more the young people themselves, rather than the counsellor, lead the discussion, the more they are likely to think and to take responsibility for themselves.

In fact it is debatable whether it was a good idea to ask for written questions at all even though there were always a few questions which are important to ask but too difficult for the individual to voice. Writing down questions made for a degree of impersonality which might reduce embarrassment but does provoke more test questions. Wherever possible we got the girls to put their questions in person. This gave the counsellor an opportunity to check whether she understood the questions, and it often leads to more discussion (rather than just question and answer) and more responsible discussion at that.

In answering the questions about sex it was often more rewarding for the counsellor to group together questions say about menstruation and to review the whole topic, taking care to answer, not avoid, the original question. In fact the amount of time we spent talking about sex was very little — one session, two at most. Thus most subjects were touched on superficially. The girls enjoyed talking about marriage, how they were going to bring up their children, whether they wanted to plan their families or work when they have children. Sometimes the discussion turned to issues such as racial prejudice or social injustice, or to a group problem such as how to handle a troublemaker within the form.

What girls were most interested in discussing were the problems which come within their own range of experience. The main part of the discussion concerned the normal problems of adolescence: worries about menstruation and moodiness, conflicts with parents about going out and having boyfriends, anxieties over appearance or about the way to behave in a new situation, problems of having nowhere to go in the evenings and no friends in their neighbourhood. Through talking together the pupils realized with relief just how common these problems were. They realized that other people too had problem parents, terrible brothers and sisters, nagging grandparents. Through their common human predicament they were able to gain a sense of perspective, become more tolerant and take their problems less personally. If by the end of the group discussions they were still insecure or worried about anything they had the opportunity of talking further in an individual interview. Sometimes they had already indicated their problem in the group or in their autobiographical note. It is against this background of general comment from girls who did not have serious problems that I want now to discuss the comments made by those particular pupils who needed individual counselling.

Individuals

In this section I give examples of problems faced by adolescent girls and brought to the counsellor in school. Teachers often ask me whether boys' problems are any different, or whether it matters if the counsellor is a man or a woman. My discussions with counsellors who see boys confirm that the nature of adolescent boys' problems is similar to girls': to do with relationships with their nearest and dearest, with the search for identity and role and with the quest for independence and freedom without total loss of family support. Boys may be more overtly aggressive than girls, they may also seek to hide their tender feelings in the mistaken idea that these detract from their masculinity. But basically their problems will be similar to girls' with differences more in emphasis.

The sex of the counsellor seems to me not to matter, provided the counsellor is not exploiting the interview to satisfy his sexual needs (ie his need to be admired by the opposite sex, his need to be reassured that he is attractive, his need to form a dependent relationship). Even with counsellor and client of the same sex, similar problems may be encountered if the counsellor has not come to terms with his own needs or is not aware of the ways he and his client are interacting. The only time the sex of the counsellor might be important is when the client needs to relate to a father-figure rather than a mother-figure or vice versa. If a school has more than one counsellor it might well decide to have one male and one female counsellor and to let the students select which they prefer. But if there is no choice, no matter. Much more important than the sex of the counsellor are his counselling skills and the quality of the relationship he forms with his client.

The examples I give in this and the succeeding chapter are intended simply to illustrate the *types* of problems that a counsellor may come across and to indicate what I thought was the counsellor's role. I have grouped problems with a similar flavour together though no two problems are identical. I have commented briefly on each group of examples at the end of each section. But my intention, with the examples and with the comment, is to spell out 'the answer' as little as possible. Apart from the fact that interpretations vary and that there certainly isn't *an* answer, I prefer to leave room for my readers to think about each case. If in my efforts to make my points clear I have over-simplified or become dogmatic, I apologize. Were this book meant to teach counselling techniques, then my approach would be different. This book is meant as a statement of problems rather than a manual of answers.

I must also remind you that I have of course changed all the names and much of the detail in the examples I quote, though the nature of the problems remains as it was in real life.

Communication

Jennifer (14)

'I have parents and sisters with whom I do not get on. My mother often worries me and is extremely cross with me continually. I have few friends out of home as I do not make friends easily. My mother is strict about what I do and has a firm hand in what I wear. I am not allowed to wear make-up or short skirts. I help a lot in the house and have hardly any time for myself. I hardly ever have time to watch television or go out.'

Jennifer felt sufficiently strongly about her situation to write about her life in these terms. The first interview with her confirmed the impression given by her note — namely that she felt a lack of positive regard from her nearest and dearest, she lacked confidence herself, she was anxious, she bit her nails. At school she was no problem. Her work and behaviour gave no cause for complaint, though her form teacher observed that she had few friends. Her lack of self-confidence did in fact make her manner tense. Her negative attitudes undoubtedly detracted from her desirability as a companion. She needed to gain enough self-confidence to communicate her feelings to her mother, to assert her independence from her mother's rigid control at least in some small measure and to learn to relate better to her peers.

Her mother had a full-time job from which she returned tired and tense. Despite Jennifer's protestations it became clear that she really did enjoy the responsibility she took for preparing the evening meal and helping generally. What she could not tolerate was the fact that her efforts did not seem to be appreciated. True she was given pocket money in exchange for her help but frequently her efforts at cooking and cleaning would be criticized by both her parents. Mother in particular appeared to Jennifer to be moody and unjustifiably critical at times. Jennifer also felt jealous and resentful of an older sister who was seriously ill and therefore escaped household chores and received a lot of extra mothering.

It seemed to me that the problem was largely one of communication. Jennifer's mother was probably not aware of the effect her behaviour and attitudes were having on Jennifer, and Jennifer lacked sufficient confidence to air her grievances, simply storing them up into a grudge.

At various stages we discussed the possibility of my seeing the mother. This Jennifer decided against, I think not so much because she felt it was *her* job to do this, but because she was ambivalent towards her mother and afraid of the responsibility of replacing her mother's control with her own. Thus she allowed the unhappy home situation to continue for half a term before she felt sufficient confidence to bring matters to a head. She wanted to grow up, but not too quickly, and a small measure of autonomy was all that was needed to boost her self-esteem. Most important of all to her was to have her mother's affection and appreciation instead of her payment and criticism. It was interesting that despite the hostility expressed towards her mother initially she wanted to be a secretary like her mother.

One week Jennifer arrived very elated to report that she had had a 'big row' with her mother during which she had explained her feelings and stated that she was going out on certain evenings to do voluntary community work. She also decided to wear make-up. From this moment her attitude towards her mother changed: she expressed admiration for the way her mother coped with a job *and* a home. She also became more tolerant of her father and her sister. Her whole appearance began to alter: she stood well instead of hunched, her eyes sparkled beneath their make-up (worn even to school), she stopped biting her nails and her hair shone.

She came to see me for a few more weeks during which she reported that her mother now trusted her in the kitchen and had praised her cooking. She expressed sympathy for her sister's illness and need for attention. She began to talk of her career plans. She felt less tired and was enjoying life more. At this stage we decided to discontinue counselling with the understanding that Jennifer could always come back if this happier state of affairs did not continue. Jennifer did not expect to live happily ever after but she had made a good first step towards helping herself. Her form teacher confirmed that Jennifer had a more relaxed and confident approach to life.

Louise (16)

Louise came back to see me in the fifth year. She was an only child living in a household of adults who included not only her parents but also her maternal grandmother; her father's stepmother also visited frequently. Because of this environment Louise had taken on the attitudes and standards of an older generation. She was extremely conscientious and law-abiding. She felt her form mates regarded her as 'goody-goody' and old-fashioned. She did not have any boyfriends nor did she feel she had much hope of getting any.

But this was not her immediate problem. Her problem was rather that in spite of her 'goodness' she was not very well regarded by her peers; this began to throw doubts in her mind as to the virtues of being 'good'. Yet, at the same time she was frightened and horrified at facing the imperfections and 'bad thoughts' both within herself and her family.

She referred herself for counselling at this stage because she was beginning to realize that neither she nor her family was perfect. She began to feel the atmosphere at home claustrophobic. Although she did many good community deeds, she felt she was not getting any fun out of life. She asked for more independence at home but with so many adults to organize, discuss and control her life she found it difficult to gain any.

She began to ventilate her feelings, including her bad feelings, which I accepted without being shocked as normal reaction in her situation and at her age. One day she said she was going to let her hair down and when I looked at her I saw that she had done just this, literally. It was very important for her to begin to release her total self instead of only letting out the 'good' and controlling the 'bad'. Again she did not want me to see her parents, although it took a half term of counselling before she had gained sufficient freedom in herself to assert herself at home. The final straw came when she had to give up her room to yet another relative who was coming to stay. At last she had the courage to express herself to her family, who as a result accorded her the respect and adult status she desired and gave her back her room. She made only a small step forward; she was then happy to return to the security of the family network. But in terms of self-assertion and self-acceptance she had an important beginning.

Geraldine (13)

Geraldine's grandfather was getting her down. There was nothing anyone could do about it. The family doctor was already trying to find an old people's home for him though Geraldine's mother was resisting. Mother was clearly carrying a great deal of strain. It seemed to me that she was probably not aware how much Geraldine and her sister were suffering from the side effects of grandfather's nagging, and mother's preoccupation with his problems at the expense of everyone else's.

Geraldine decided to talk to her mother about how she felt instead of suffering and building up resentment. This seemed to improve communications between mother and daughter and help mother to weigh her various duties more rationally. For example, shortly after, mother at last took up the offer of the social services that they should look after grandfather while mother took a holiday. For the first time for years the parents and children took a holiday without grandfather in tow.

Betty (14)

'I have three sisters aged 3, 11 and 16 years. I argue a lot with the two eldest. My eldest sister goes out a lot to clubs and shows, which makes me quite jealous, of course, she won't let me go, so this causes arguments. My eldest sister is very modern and tries to help me a lot but being quite fat I can't get modern clothes to fit me. I get on with my parents alright now and again, although I don't think they like me as much as the others, because I get blamed for everything, I am quite unhappy at home and at school. I really hate school. I have no boyfriends though I would like one.'

Betty described herself as the family scapegoat, the odd one out, the only fat one, the one who took the blame for everything. It seemed unlikely to me that the actual situation was quite as bad as this but this was how it seemed to Betty, which is what mattered. Her dissatisfaction with school reflected the low opinion she had come to have of herself; she was becoming negative and apathetic and was also eating too much in spite of her intention to slim. Our objectives were therefore to increase her self-respect through the relationship with the counsellor, to help her to communicate with her family her needs and feelings and to help her understand better the pressures within the family as a whole.

The jealousy between the sisters and their rivalry for the parents' attention is both real and normal enough with children of these ages. But one factor that contributed a great deal to Betty's self-destructive attitude was the guilt she felt through having dropped her baby sister out of the pram when the baby was six months old. Thus her 11-year-old sister and her 16-year-old sister were able to curry parental favour by taking out the youngest child. Betty was not allowed to do this because she was not regarded as trustworthy and she did not trust herself.

Because of her self-deprecatory attitude, she brought upon herself the deprecation of the rest of the family and thus became a ready-made vehicle for many of their bad feelings. As a result she became resentful, sullen and fat. How to break the vicious circle?

Shortly after counselling began Betty decided to ask for some clothes. Apart from her school uniform she had no smart clothes. This was one reason she did not go out more; she often turned down invitations rather than have to appear in school uniform. To her surprise her mother supported the idea of more clothes. Betty had misjudged her mother's attitude towards her. Mother took a stand on this, which made Betty appreciate her mother more and feel that her mother did care about her after all.

Unfortunately there *was* no spare money in the family, as father was under considerable strain, financial and emotional, because he was having to support a relative of his. Thus Betty realized that her father *did* care about her and *did* want her to look pretty but that money was tight for other reasons. This increased her respect for her father. Two-way communication with her parents became re-established. They bought her a dress in spite of hard times, which provided just that bit of extra attention she needed to feel on the same footing as her sisters.

What happened in school? Betty became more cheerful and confident. She was elected form spokesman on a school matter, which increased her self-confidence enormously. She took a leading part in helping another girl in the form. She finally admitted to me that her older sister had serious problems, which is probably why she had so much attention from her parents.

Thus she realized that she was not, as she had thought, the weakest member of the family but one of the strongest. She continued to play a supportive role within her family but this time without being destroyed by her own self-doubts or being taken for granted by others.

Pamela (13)

Pamela was the oldest in a family of six children. Her mother had divorced when she was a baby, remarried when she was five. Pamela had adjusted reasonably well to all this. She said that her problem was simply that with so many younger brothers and sisters, she found it difficult to get on with her homework. One young brother (seven) in particular teased her and got on her nerves a great deal. She could not work in her room because there was no fire. The problem may in fact have been much deeper than this, but this is the level at which Pamela expressed it.

It seems incredible to me that she should not have discussed this with her parents or even with her form tutor. It is not a particularly confidential or sensitive matter. But she had not. After seeing me she did talk to her mother, who immediately got her an electric fire while her stepfather had a chat with the brother, who then became less of a nuisance. It was a simple matter, though it may have helped to serve complicated needs. It is not however untypical of the kind of problem which a girl of this age puts up with rather than dare to ask her parents about.

Comment

In these first examples there was nothing to be 'done'. It was far more constructive for the girls to communicate their needs to their parents than for me to step in on their behalf. The basic problem was internal rather than external; the actual situations in which these girls lived were not intolerable, and in any case there was no changing them. What had gone wrong, in each case, was the individual child's perception of the situation. Her inability to communicate her needs and feelings to her parents and siblings had turned them against her. At the same time she herself became a victim of destructive self-doubts and self-pity. Communicating with the counsellor was the first step towards communicating with her parents. Once she had done this, she began to see her life in better perspective.

Confidentiality

Brenda (13)

Brenda referred herself after third year groups with a secret she had shared with no one. Her note was ordinary enough; she herself was a pleasant and reliable child. She asked for an appointment and then in the first interview began to explain what was troubling her. As far as she could make out, her sister had had an illegitimate baby when Brenda was 11. The problem was that no one in the family had ever talked to her about this, presumably because they thought she was too young at the time to know about such things without getting upset.

Unfortunately *not* knowing was making her more upset. Her sister came to visit every few weeks but there was this taboo topic of conversation between them. Furthermore her own developing sexual feelings made her feel frightened and ambivalent both about what had happened to her sister and what might happen to her. She was very fond of her sister but always upset after seeing her. Her parents were strict, both over 50. Brenda found it difficult to talk to them about sex or indeed any of her feelings.

Her need to talk about her problem was great yet she could not talk to her form tutor about it because she did not want to let her family down. Through talking to the counsellor she began to express her feelings and gain sufficient confidence to get her family to tell her the whole story. This served the double function of relieving her worries and according her more adult status. Her case provides a clear example of a problem in which the counsellor's outside role and the confidential basis of the relationship with her were very important.

Josephine (14)

'I like going out in the evenings with my friend. I am shy when I'm with boys and have at present no boyfriend. I have an older brother. A couple of months he went through this stage of being very catty towards me. I think he went through this stage because before this he had tried petting me which I did not like and so I threatened to tell mum and dad. I would never have dreamed of doing this because I knew I would get into trouble as well. Also I did not think it right to tell them.'

She only came to see me once. She needed to tell someone 'safe' all about it. This helped her face her own guilty feelings. She seemed to have coped with the incident at the time; it was all over and there was nothing to be done about it that would have been constructive. She was not asking for help with her own sexual development and she did not want the matter to go any further. She knew she could come back later if she wanted. We left it at that.

Veronica (14)

'I have a boyfriend living some way away, so I only see him at weekends at the moment, though when he gets his motorbike I shall see him more frequently. He is studying for his A levels. My mother does not agree with my going out with him although she puts up with it. My father wants me to stay on for A levels.'

Veronica was a mature-looking girl who could pass for 16-17 years although she was only 14. She had been in love with her boyfriend for over a year. Every Saturday he came to spend the day at her house. On Sundays his parents would leave them alone in their house. What was worrying her was the strength of her own sexual feelings. She was sincere and steady in her love for him; she was reaching the point where she was finding heavy petting very frustrating and she was wanting to go on to have intercourse.

The fact that she wanted to talk to me about it first shows that in part at least she was worried and in doubt about what she should do. We talked it over for several weeks. I reminded her about the age of consent and answered several factual questions as well as discussing the possible psychological, social and legal results of her proposed action. During the discussion it emerged that she had a poor relationship with her parents who seemed to take little real interest or to realize remotely what she was doing: 'Had a good day, dear? Fine.'

Veronica herself had little time for girls of her own age; she did not seem to be able to widen her own interests. Thus all her need for love, affection and security was going into this one boy. He was not pressing her to go any further. Her battle was with her own desires. She left me very thoughtfully, a little more aware of the complicated forces which were driving her. The whole discussion had been confidential: without this safeguard I do not think she would have talked at all. She did not want me to communicate with her parents; I hope she began to do so herself. She knew she could get contraceptive advice and counselling, despite her youth, through a clinic nearby. She knew that she could come back to see me any time she wanted.

She came back six months later to tell me that after a lot of discussion she and her boyfriend had decided to break off their relationship as they felt it was getting too intense. During the holidays she had met someone else; though it had not lasted, it had made her think. By the next term the other girls in the form had grown up a bit and she found that she had more in common with them than she had thought.

Beth (13)

'I go swimming regularly in London. This causes concern at home. It is a long way away and my parents don't like me getting too involved with the attendants there as I do.'

She was worried about it too: she found the attendants devastatingly attractive, especially the one who was already engaged. Although basically she had a good relationship with her parents she found it difficult to discuss this problem with them as their attitude was tinged with disapproval from the start. She worked out her own answer through talking to someone who could allow her the freedom to express her own doubts without loss of face.

Comment

These girls all had problems which they needed to talk over with an adult, but which they could only share with an adult they could trust absolutely. Any precipitate action by the counsellor, any condemnation would have stopped them talking. Not that the counsellor condoned: we must not equate an accepting adult with a consenting adult. But if the counsellor cannot accept the 'bad' in each child the child will continue to cover over her real problem. For various reasons, these were problems that the girls found difficult to discuss with their parents or form tutor. The counsellor's role as an outsider who could be trusted with confidential information was important.

A friendly adult

Marion (13)

'When I was young my mother and I lived with my grandparents. I was sent to nursery school until I was five. At the age of six my mother married a man who adopted me as his daughter. He is now my father. He is very good and kind to me and I would not have anyone else in the world. My mother is happy with him also. I have no brothers or sisters.'

Nevertheless soon after she wrote this Marion came back to see me, filled with a desire to see her real father, from whom her mother had separated when Marion was very young. She realized that this might be an upsetting or disappointing experience, but her need to establish her true identity was great. She talked to her parents about it. They understood her very well; finally they told her the whole story of her early life; her grandmother also joined in and produced photos of her real father.

These revelations did in fact upset the happy balance of Marion's family for a while. She needed me to talk to about her sudden anger and resentment with her mother. She worked through her mixed feelings eventually. I'm not sure that she had been quite ready for the whole truth but the search for identity is certainly strong and overwhelming at this stage.

Donna (14)

Donna was worried about being fat. She *was* a little plump. Her current friends constantly teased her, particularly in mixed company, which completely undermined her confidence. She was interested in boys but had no hope of getting a boyfriend in these conditions. She told me all about it. She then decided to join a new youth club. She found her new friends accepted her as a lively and amusing companion. She found that boys did like her after all. She was able to withstand her old friends' criticisms, which began to fall off when they discovered they had little effect.

Frances (18)

Frances was referred to the counsellor by the staff in her seventh year. She was feeling very depressed and attributed this to her father's moodiness. She talked a lot about her father's moods, then went on to say why she thought he was like her. A week later she returned to say she had much greater sympathy for her father; they had begun to talk more and she felt generally less tense and worried.

It seemed too good to be true to me but there is no judging the effects of even one counselling session if it comes at an appropriate moment. Frances was intelligent and already showed insight. The counselling interview may have served to crystallize her thoughts and to focus them for once on her father's needs as opposed to her own. Having started on a new train of thought she may well have gone on following it throughout the week or she may have just covered over her difficulties again. Who knows?

Tao-Tao (13)

'I realy have a terrible time in here because of the language and no friends. I only learnt English less than two years.

'In my country I had a few friends but they are very nice so I didn't think that I wish more friends. I didn't know friends are most important thing in my life. I understand perfectly now why they are important. I want friends to invite to my house. But I can't because the way of living is completely different. Studying is no matter, language is no matter if I learnt it, but I am a lonely girl. I don't think I can make friend by myself, never. I am a terribly shy girl.'

Tao-Tao came from the Far East during the second year. She was highly intelligent but shy by nature — not just because of language difficulties. She was proud too and did not communicate her loneliness to her form tutor. To me she expressed, in her halting English, some of her worries. Going to boarding school back home would not help her, because she now preferred the freedom (eg to have boyfriends) of the Western culture. My role was simply to befriend her until she found herself.

By the end of the next term she had made several friends and was feeling much happier.

Audry (15)

Audry, an attractive, black girl, came back in the fourth year to complain that her father was too strict: he didn't trust her. I asked her whether she *was* trustworthy. It rather surprised her to realize that she was not. It dawned on her that this was perhaps why her father did not trust her. She decided to go straight with him.

She came back a month later to say he now let her go out to the Palais de

Danse once a week provided she was in by eleven o'clock. She had been doing this for ages, pretending she had been going to see a cousin. She said she felt much better now that her father knew where she really was; he had been much pleasanter once he realized she could cope with the young men she met.

Alethea (13)

Alethea had Greek-Cypriot parents who never gave her a chance to prove that she was trustworthy. It was really a cultural problem. 'I've got a feeling that my parents are going to choose my husband as most Cypriots do, but I despise this idea and want to find my own husband.'

When I saw her she was simply wanting to be allowed out occasionally. She did not want me to talk to her parents as 'that would only make them cross; they wouldn't change at all.' As she was still young at the time she decided to bear her problem a little longer. She felt better for having talked it over. The really testing time for someone caught in the cultural crossfire like this is when she is 16. If she does not want to marry someone of her father's choice or be relegated to the kitchen sink but prefers to complete her education, choose her own job and husband, then real conflict begins. We have a lot of girls with similar problems: some Greek-Cypriots, some Indians, some Pakistanis.

Comment

These girls were not really asking for me to do anything, not even help them communicate better with their parents. They just wanted to talk to an adult outside the family. What they had to say was not confidential in the sense of being an explosive secret but it was private and they wanted it to be treated with respect and privacy. They needed the relationship with the counsellor to help them through a difficult but transitory stage in their lives.

Support

Anita (14)

Anita is a good example of a girl whose problem was not what it seemed at first. She referred herself in the first place because her sister-in-law was about to have a baby and this was worrying her. But it was not as simple as this. She lived with her sister-in-law to help look after the first baby. This made her feel insecure about her mother, whom she only saw at weekends. Her mother worked all the week, so she reckoned she would not see much of her even if she were at home. But living with her brother and his wife in these particular circumstances made her aware of her own sexual feelings, which both fascinated and repulsed her. She felt that if she went out with boys she would get a bad reputation or become pregnant. She was particularly sensitive about what other people might say about her.

This feeling went back to an accident when she was eight when a friend of hers was killed. She felt in some way responsible and thought other people had held this against her. In fact it was not in any way her fault. When she had managed to talk about this she became less worried about her current reputation.

It took her several weeks to pluck up courage to tell me about this incident. At that stage I had begun to think that her problems were not all that serious. This shows the danger of the counsellor's judging that there are no 'real' problems and not allowing the client time to come to the point. It was not the only point in this case but it was important to Anita to come to it. Once she had expressed her guilty secret she became more secure generally.

Soon after this her sister-in-law's baby was born. Anita did not, as she imagined she would, have to cope with the two-year-old child during the confinement and she went to live back at home. Her father then went into hospital for an operation but this did not worry her unduly. She was already more confident, having regained her mother and survived the birth of her nephew. She then found a steady boyfriend, who despite her previous fears, behaved in a very non-threatening way. He was 16, but she reckoned young and small for his age. Her fears about sex were allayed; she had the security of a good friend without any complications. She was thus much more able to face the grown-up world realistically. Most of her problems had sorted themselves out through various turns of events but I think it was important for her to be able to express her worst fears about herself and about sex while she was in such an insecure developmental stage. Supportive counselling was in fact just what she needed.

Angela (15)

Angela had gone to live in a children's home at the age of four when her parents divorced. When she was eight her mother remarried and took her back. Angela liked her stepfather and new brother but clearly was ambivalent about her mother, who was often ill and irritable. She came to see me because she felt her parents were exploiting her by using her in their shop. However it became clear that this was not really the problem. In fact she enjoyed working in the shop. She came to see me to chat about life, her feelings, her fears. She came, sporadically and spontaneously, until she left school. There was nothing to be done about her; she was not in any dilemma about what she should do. She just needed more mothering than her real mother was able to provide at this stage. The relationship with the counsellor helped her to face the vicissitudes of her life more cheerfully and rationally.

Rachel (15)

Rachel had one older brother and three younger brothers. Her problem was in her relationship with her mother, who had just started a teacher training course. All the children were at school all day; father was co-operative and helpful with the domestic chores. Rachel, as the only girl, was expected to help a lot; the boys did relatively little.

Rachel resented being expected to help her mother, particularly as her mother was often cross and irritable. Rachel herself became touchy and sensitive with her friends, which was making her unpopular with the form. She was full of admiration for her father, though worried because her parents seemed to quarrel a lot.

She decided to sort the problem out for herself. She had a long chat with her father, who was able to explain that the parental arguments were not as serious as they sounded, simply part of the way marriage worked. She began to appreciate points about her mother: for example she began to talk about the clothes her mother made her, the fact that her mother was paying for her to go abroad. She showed more tolerance and understanding of her mother and she became more accepting of her female role.

Rachel was feeling much better. But it must have been too much of a strain for mother, who gave up the course the next term. 'Mother used to take it out on me, and I used to take it out on other people. Now we are all much happier.'

Jill (13)

'I get very involved emotionally with some boys, for example, when I was on holiday I went out with a 15-year-old boy who is much older than his age since his father died three years ago. I was very taken with him. When I went home he never wrote to me and ever since I have long depressed spells and get really fed up and miserable. My mother says I'll get over it, but with all her worries I have not told her how miserable I get.'

This illustrates a common dilemma: not that mum was not understanding but that she was too busy and worried about her own problems for her daughter to burden her further. Part of Jill wanted to be independent of her mother, of course. When she came to see me her depression about her boyfriend seemed to have completely lifted. What she needed to talk about was the family strains which were basically financial, to do with buying a new house. She took a pride in her parents' achievements but the move was making her feel insecure as well. She felt she did not want to add to her parents' strains but she *did* want to talk about it.

Elaine (15)

'My mother and stepfather entertain guests a lot. That leaves me, so every night I go in the back room and watch television. This is the drawback of moving at my age. I moved seven months ago and know no one at all where I am living. I go out three nights a week but to organizations where I used to live so it costs quite a lot of money to get there.'

Elaine had adapted well to growing up, with her church and youth club activities. But her mother's remarriage and the move to another district meant another period of adjustment. Elaine liked her stepfather particularly as he made her mother so much happier. But moving house at this stage is unsettling even with your own father. Elaine had to face the loss of her immediate friends and the loss of her mother's company all at once. Her mother had been widowed for the last six years; life had not been easy but the family had unity and a sense of purpose. Elaine felt lonely and slightly hurt at being excluded from her mother's new relationship, particularly as her mother was having so much gay social life. Again this is something many adolescents have to face, even with their own parents. But at least they are used to sharing.

After seeing the counsellor Elaine gained sufficient confidence to talk to her mother about her feelings. She decided to break with her old church and club and to join local ones. She began to build up her new life. Her mother, too, adjusted to her new married state and found more time for her family. Her stepfather insisted that Elaine have more pocket money and a dress allowance.

Carolyn (13)

'I have three younger sisters. I have a very strict father. He's the boss in everything. My family are very strict Catholics, that is why my dad won't let us have fireworks on Guy Fawkes night. I haven't any hobbies. I don't really do anything. I don't go out much at all.'

Carolyn was 13 when she wrote this. A year later her father was still being extremely strict and intolerant. By this time Carolyn could stand it no longer. She met a boy in the park, and they went out together for the afternoon. When evening came, she did not dare go home to face her father with the fact that she had been out with a boy, so she stayed out all night, huddled together with the boy on the stairs of a block of flats. The police picked her up next morning and examined her.

The only physical harm which befell her was the effect of cold and hunger. She was not a hard-bitten sexy delinquent doing this for kicks, but a rather shy and serious girl, who had responded to her father's extreme attitudes with extreme measures of her own. Fortunately her boyfriend was, like herself, not a sex addict but simply rather lonely.

She came to see me after the police incident. She had come for counselling in the third year to talk about her father's attitude, so our relationship was well founded. She had learnt her own lesson from the long, miserable, cold night vigil. But so had her father: he allowed her to go on seeing the boy, who became a regular visitor to Carolyn's house. The incident had achieved something, though I doubt whether Carolyn's objectives were as clearly worked out as this.

During counselling she expressed a great deal of anger towards her father for being too domineering and her mother for being too passive. Then it emerged gradually that her father was not at all well himself, had family worries back home in Ireland, whilst mother was also very tired and preoccupied with father's problems. She began to see the family situation in perspective. As her father had now given her permission to go out she realized it was up to her to take advantage of this. Half a term after the incident with the police, she gave up Colin, her boyfriend, who was beginning to bore her as well as restrict her activities with his evening visit. She went babysitting occasionally, to a youth club on other evenings, not in search of boyfriends but rather a more general widening of her experience. She stopped coming to see me at this stage.

A year later she turned up again. This time the problem was that her parents were thinking of going back to Ireland to live; this had the effect of making her want to leave school rather than do the CSE of which she was capable. Through telling me about it she began to realize what she was doing. She decided to stay on, whatever her parents did. That was the last I saw of her.

She had come to be because she felt I was the only person she could talk to freely. She had used me at a time of great need. It would have helped her more if she could have established closer communication with her parents. She said that they were unalterable and she was probably right. Through counselling and her own experience she had tried to make the best of a strained family situation.

Alison (13)

'I have not got any brothers and sisters. No pets. When I grow up I want to be a Repsenonist. My hobbies are collecting records, boys. I've no particular friends. I like everybody but everyone doesn't like me.'

Apart from a certain lack of ease with her contemporaries Alison's main and very real problem was the fact that her mother was in hospital, dying. Alison herself was worried and confused about what was happening particularly as she was not allowed to visit her mother. Father returned from his evening hospital visit exhausted, depressed and bad-tempered. Alison attempted to look after him but found him very uncommunicative. All this was of course very hard for her to bear. She really needed someone to talk to. I encouraged her to talk to her form tutor which she did to some extent, but rather self-consciously in the presence of other girls. Finally her mother died.

For a while her father became more possessive and difficult. He did not like her to go out because, he said, she was the only person he had left to depend on. She became moody, attention-seeking and difficult at school, and consequently even less popular with the other girls. She came to see me as often as possible for a friendly chat: to tell me her thoughts and plans in the way a girl might talk to her mother. After the first terrible shock both she and her father began to go out more and thus to feel less resentful towards each other. Once Alison felt more secure in her home situation she felt more secure with her friends and had less need to show off. She would probably have recovered without counselling but the counselling gave her a chance to grieve, to assuage her need to talk about her mixed feelings and get some of the individual attention that she now missed so much. I think this helped a lot.

Catherine (14)

Catherine's mother had left her and her father, who was out of work and under a psychiatrist. There were no nearby female relatives or friends to take on a supportive female role with Catherine. My role was just this: Catherine came

113

for a friendly chat from time to time. Mostly she managed on her own; just occasionally her father's moods, unreasonableness and possessiveness got her down. As she grew up she was able to handle him herself with greater firmness.

Jane (15)

When Jane came in the third year groups it was clear that she had had an unsettling and difficult life but that she was making the best of it. When she was four her parents had separated and she had gone into a children's home. When she was eight she had gone to live with an aunt whom she loved and respected. However when Jane was 15 her mother remarried and took her back.

Jane was then faced with a real mother whom she hardly knew, a stepfather for whom she did not care and a little sister of eight whose existence came as a complete surprise to her. Not surprisingly she found great difficulty in accepting this new situation. Her work at school began to suffer and she became defiant. At the year mistress's suggestion she was glad to come for counselling. She was a girl of great spirit, courage and determination and all she needed to get back on course during this period of readjustment was a safe place to express her bewilderment, resentment and anger. She was confused by this sudden turn of events, resentful of not knowing what had happened to her mother in their years apart and angry with her sister who was a nuisance, stopped her getting on with her homework and had prior claim to mother's affection and attention. Her mother was stricter and less understanding than the aunt had been about such matters as going out. On one occasion, when Jane did not go straight home from school, her mother called the police and there was a big family row. After that Jane was able to go out more as she wished, and felt less resentful of her sister. For various reasons her mother became more critical of her stepfather and this made Jane feel closer to her mother, though it did not help the family situation as a whole. However Jane's school work remained uneven while she was still sensitive and vulnerable to the pressures within the family and too overwhelmed to take a stand, for example about being given enough time and privacy to do her homework properly. Her own resilience and determination came to the rescue when she decided she wanted to work in a bank and to get the promotions she wanted. She worked with renewed vigour, achieved the necessary results and was accepted for the job. The motivation came from within her, which is why she was successful. But I am sure that expressing her mixed feelings about her family situation helped her to regain her sense of perspective. What she had to say was essentially personal and private to her family and it took time for her to work through her feelings. Thus the counsellor's role fitted her needs very well.

She did not dwell on her problems but used supportive counselling wholeheartedly until she felt strong enough to do without it.

Comment

In these examples it seems to me that I was a kind of supplementary mother-figure. Mother was too busy, too tired, too emotionally exhausted, too close to the girls or too distant, too active or too passive to fulfil their needs just then. My role varied of course according to the problem. But I was in the fortunate position of being able to give my full attention to the girl concerned without the constant interruptions which befall a busy mother. In the cases where there was no mother my role was even more vital. Non-possessive warmth, genuine concern and empathic understanding: this is what these girls needed and this is what I tried to provide.

Conclusion

Counselling is perhaps too grand a word to describe what happened in some of these cases. Applied commonsense based on respect for the individual concerned, perhaps even a simple practical suggestion, was often all that was needed. In other cases the counselling relationship, rather than anything that was said or done by the counsellor, was what helped these individuals face up to their problems. The girls worked out their own answers or took constructive action on their own behalf or decided to leave things as they were. They did not want anyone else to be brought into it. There is no real telling whether they were helped in the long term, or how long the effects of counselling lasted. Halmos[3] says that counselling is an act of faith. It is one which I feel is worth making.

References

1. Hemming, J (1967) *Problems of Adolescent Girls* Heinemann
2. Veness, T (1962) *School Leavers: Their Aspirations and Expectations* Methuen
3. Halmos, P (1965) *The Faith of the Counsellor* Constable

Chapter 6

Action

In this section I want to give examples of pupils who *did* want other people to be involved in helping them to solve their problems. Sometimes an interview with the parents was all that was needed; sometimes a referral to social services or the child guidance clinic was the next step. I prefer for the moment to let the individual examples speak for themselves. It rapidly becomes clear that there is no set formula for getting a child the help she needs. To serve her clients to the best of her ability a counsellor has to learn to work in a flexible way. What works in one case may be completely inappropriate in the next.

Deidre (13)

Deidre was referred to me by her form tutor, who was very concerned about her uncontrollable emotional outbursts. Deidre was rather an aggressive tomboy. She had few friends in school; at home, she kept out of the house as much as possible, doing a paper round in the morning and going swimming at night. She was very independent, rarely admitting her emotional needs. She hardly ever talked about her parents; she certainly did not want *me* to see them.

I saw her once a fortnight for about two terms. She gradually peeled off layers of defensiveness like skins of an onion, until we reached her feelings. She began to talk a little about her family. She expressed her anger towards the school which she claimed had unjustly accused her of stealing. At this stage her form came for group discussions. This was useful to her for it gave her more confidence in me. I was pleased to find her quite well integrated in the group, despite her claim that she had no mates. Interestingly she did not swear at all in the groups though this was something staff frequently complained about. After the discussions I found her much less defensive.

Her relationship with her form tutor was the next problem to be faced. She was very antagonistic towards the tutor and provocative beyond the point of endurance. I was wondering what, if anything, to do about this when fortunately the form tutor came to discuss with me the angry feelings that Deidre provoked in her and the effects this relationship was having on the rest of the form. The tutor and the school seemed to be taking a lot of the anger which Deidre really felt about her mother and her home. Soon after, the tutor and Deidre had an argument in which they both aired their feelings. After that they felt much more kindly and positive about each other.

116

The next time Deidre came to see me she was a new girl. She thanked me for all I had done, something totally uncharacteristic of her 'old self'. She suddenly revealed a whole host of relations living near her whom she had never mentioned before. She had fallen in love, which helped her tremendously to admit her emotional needs! She decided to stay on and do a typing course instead of leaving early.

I saw her a little more, just in case this was a passing phase only. We had had stages before when she had become happier but it had never lasted. It was not until she had worked through her angry feelings that she could live more peaceably. She told her mother about her boyfriend which at last brought her closer to her mother. Her tutor reported that she settled down after that.

Marjorie (13)

Marjorie and her best friend came together because they said that everybody in the form laughed at them. They were rather sensitive girls—a ready target for the form's high spirits. Even their form tutor appeared to them to side with the rest of the form against them. There seemed to be only two ways out of this: to develop a thicker skin, or to talk it over with the form tutor and the form. They tried both. I did nothing except make myself available should they want to talk it over again.

Jessica (14)

Jessica said her form tutor was alway picking on her. Very often this simply means that the girl concerned is insecure for some other reason, perhaps in her relationships at home. In this case there *seemed* to be no reason for Jessica to be extra sensitive. I felt sure that even if the form tutor *were* picking on her this was something unconscious or irrational. Jessica decided to make her feelings known to her tutor. Her tutor had not realized the effect she was having on Jessica. After that Jessica felt she was no longer victimized. I said nothing to the form tutor about the incident.

Annette (14)

Annette did not refer herself to me. A member of her form came on behalf of the others because the whole form was worried about her. She was large, rather pasty and lethargic. The girls in her form alleged that she smelt and was also a lesbian. They deduced this from the fact that she often took girls' arms or put her hand round their waists. The form was beginning to find her unacceptable and wanted no more to do with her.

I said that there was nothing *I* could do as this girl had not come to me for help. As the girls in her form were worried about her, there was probably plenty *they* could do themselves to make Annette feel more lovable and acceptable. Was this Lesbianism or was it simply a great need for affection? Was there anything in her home situation which might account for her behaviour? What effect did it have on Annette for the form to reject her just now? Was the form tutor worried too? There were in fact many good reasons why Annette should have felt unhappy and starved of affection. The girls and their form tutor worked out their own practical solution. Annette did come to me in the end but already much helped by the support instead of the rejection of her form.

Comment

These girls' personal problems were affecting their relationships with the staff and pupils. I did not act as intermediary but left them to work out their difficulties for themselves. It was only when a member of staff approached me to discuss her side of the problem that I felt able to help without undermining her position or appearing to tell her what to do.

Susan (13)

'My name is Susan. I am 13. I have two sisters and one brother aged 14, 11 and 12. I live in a house.'

When I saw her in the group she was quiet and well behaved. A year later her mother came up to school to say that she was impossible at home. This surprised everyone because she had suddenly blossomed at school into a most responsible school citizen. When she came for counselling, her main feeling was that her two sisters were favoured, while she herself did a lot to help but was never appreciated by anybody. Her older sister was by now out at work, which meant that Susan had been ascribed the role of chief mother's help, formerly her sister's job. What is more her sister expected to be waited on when she returned from work, which enraged Susan's jealous feelings further. Although she was paid for her help Susan felt that no one appreciated her efforts (which indeed were probably loaded with resentment). She hardly ever went out. Home life became a grudging prison house; school was in the equally unreal state of seeing all the 'good' side of Susan's character.

Susan agreed that it might help for me to see her mother. Her mother, slightly suspicious of what I was up to and anxious to put her side of the case, was glad to come up to school.

Her mother talked a great deal. At the end of the interview she had begun to question her own attitudes. She was proud to find Susan so well regarded in school: this aroused a wave of positive feeling in her. She recognized that Susan might need to let off steam at home. She sympathized with Susan's position as the second of four because she remembered how she had felt in the same family position: jealous, overlooked, unappreciated. She thought of various activities Susan could take up to get her out of the house more. She decided to confide in her more.

The effect on Susan was that she began to communicate better with her mother; going out helped her to relax more and brood less. She began to make Christmas presents for her family: stuffed toys, clothes. These were warmly and fondly received. Her older sister sometimes set her hair and lent her clothes. Her mother took her out during the holidays and together they chose a dress.

If this had been a really deep and long-term problem of family relationships, one interview between the mother and myself would have had no effect. The problem was one of adjustment to a new stage of development and status within the family. The interview with the mother helped the family as a whole to pay more heed to Susan's needs, which helped Susan in turn to appreciate her home in more realistic terms.

Rose (15)

Rose was a West Indian. Her problem was basically that her mother was ambitious for her and worried that she might become pregnant which would stop her completing her education. As a result she never allowed Rose to go out, told her off if she ever saw her in the street with a boy and constantly checked the dates of her periods to make sure she was not pregnant.

Rose herself was an attractive and hard-working girl who, in the absence of any other outlet, began to fantasize about the only men in her life, her stepfather and the lodger. In the third year she had talked to me about the attraction she felt for her stepfather, though it seemed to be no more than a twinkle in her eye. She came back in the fourth year because, she said, the lodger had tried to make love to her. It was hard to assess what had actually happened, though intercourse did not take place. Rose had told her mother about it and was also willing for me to see her mother. This supported my view that she had provoked this dramatic crisis in order to bring home to her mother how desperate she felt about being cooped up all the time. She was also using me to help her make this point to her mother.

Rose's mother was concerned about her but she was more worried about her educational progress than about what had happened with the lodger. She wanted her daughter to complete her education and get a good job before getting married. She said that Jamaican boys were not trustworthy; this was why she did not let Rose out more. Her main complaint about her daughter was the total lack of communication at home: Rose did not tell her anything about what she was thinking or what she wanted to do when she left school.

Mother also needed practical help about Rose's future career. To this end I put her in touch with the form tutor and careers teacher. She left saying that it might help Rose to grow up more if she went to evening classes, as long as she knew where Rose was. Rose herself was confused about her career: she needed the interview which we arranged with the careers officer.

Rose and her mother began to communicate better, by discussing her career and by talking a little more about boys in realistic terms. Rose was allowed to go out. She went on to be a nurse and as far as I know her mother's fears proved unfounded. But without counselling and help in communicating with her mother at a critical stage she might have been forced to more extreme measures.

Margaret (12)

Margaret was referred to me by her tutor in the second year because she was rather withdrawn and shy in school, yet her parents had complained that she wore make-up and was boy-mad. She certainly looked rather shy, frightened and tired and did not talk easily. Sometimes she would remain silent, sometimes she would talk, sometimes she would write me a story or draw.

She gave permission for me to see her mother early on. Her mother explained to me the significant fact that she herself was seriously depressed and had been receiving psychiatric treatment for some years. Margaret had expressed some of her anger towards her mother by putting on make-up and provoking a big row. More normally she cut herself off from the family when at home and escaped into a world of fantasy largely stimulated by her addiction to television. She had considerable creative ability which allowed her to express her feelings in her writings and drawings, in a rather macabre and powerful way.

I wondered at this stage whether Margaret herself needed psychiatric help; however one of her worst fears was of being like her mother, so she was completely against the idea and her parents only reluctantly for it. The interview with the mother had helped to clarify this for me, though I certainly also discussed the case with the educational psychologist.

Part of Margaret's problem was to *accept* her mother's condition instead of hiding from it. Another part of it was her own guilt in thinking it was her fault that her mother had repeated attacks: after her outburst with make-up, mother had become ill again; the same thing happened the next time Margaret had a row with her mother, except that this time mother went back into hospital for a while. When Margaret first came to see me she could not talk about her mother at all. When she spoke she would avert her gaze, never smile, as if this helped her to hide her guilty family secret. After I knew about her mother she was able to look at me directly.

When her mother went into hospital during the school holidays Margaret was able for the first time to take over the running of the house, with father's assistance. At last she could do something for her mother. This helped to assuage her guilty feelings and awakened pride and mutual respect between herself and her mother. Margaret found she could take on the feminine role without breaking down or becoming just like her mother. Indeed she became stronger and more positive through the experience. When her mother came out of hospital she and Margaret were able to communicate in a way which had hitherto been impossible, partly because previously Margaret was afraid to say much in case she triggered off another attack.

Because Margaret was more confident and less defensive her father was able to talk to her in an adult way about her mother's illness, which helped her to understand her mother better. In school her form tutor observed that she was still rather shy but that she did communicate well with her two best friends; she also laughed more and answered in class more.

Comment

In these cases I saw the mother once only. The interview served two purposes: it helped me in deciding whether a referral was necessary; it also increased the parents' awareness of their daughter's needs and possibly helped them to rethink their own attitudes. This is hard to judge: all we can say is that, as far as the girls were concerned, their problems worried them less from that point on.

Social services

Bridget (13)

'My Mother and Father are divorced. I don't see my Father much. I don't particularly want to, he's no good. We had a difficult time at first then my Mum met this man, Sid. He's nasty, not cruel or wicked, just deceitfully nasty. He nags a lot and watches me so that at the slightest fault he can call me selfish and lazy. Well, I'm not. Him and my Mum have terrible rows. I've witnessed some awful scenes. She's always telling me what she's done for me. I'm tired of it.'

At this stage Bridget was so tired of it that she wanted to leave home, be taken into care, anything. With Bridget's permission I consulted the social services, who also saw Bridget. There were no legal grounds for taking Bridget away from her mother and indeed it soom emerged that Bridget did not really want to leave her mother, only to escape from Sid, whose attempts to take on her father's role as disciplinarian thoroughly irked her. In consultation with the social services it was decided that as I had easy access to Bridget and more time than the social worker for preventive work, I should give Bridget the supportive counselling she needed to work through her problems.

I saw Bridget's mother early on; this helped a little in giving mother and daughter more awareness of each other's needs. I tried to get social casework help for the mother too but she resisted. In the end there was nothing to be done except for me to provide for Bridget a secure and steadfast adult relationship while she grew up and out of her difficulties. In school she was no cause for concern except for a general feeling that she could do better. Once she came to accept her difficult home situation and mature in spite of it her work began to improve too. 'I know it's up to me now and so there's some point in working.' Previously she had hidden behind her problems and taken no initiative in helping herself make the best of it.

Faith (15)

In the third year groups, Faith was ordinary, not precocious or conspicious in any way, a Girl Guide and member of the St John's Ambulance Brigade. A year later she came back spontaneously. She looked completely different: eye make-up, modish hair style, fully developed figure. She had been going out with a boy with her parents' permission. He had recently gone to prison on a drugs charge. Her parents had suddenly clamped down completely on all out-of-home activities. Relationships between Faith and her parents had completely broken down. Father had sent for social services, threatening to get rid of her and put her in a home. There was no case for removal from home but father said she could set up on her own just as soon as she was legally old enough.

Unfortunately as part of her general rebellion Faith decided to leave school early, particularly as school too had had to punish her. I contacted social services who undertook to keep an eye on her and offered support to the family should they ever need it. What interested me in this case was the fact that Faith regarded social services as an arm of the law, brought in against her as a weapon on her parents' side. She kept from them her feelings about being apparently rejected by her parents. Underneath her tough and defiant exterior she felt vulnerable and hurt. She found a job she wanted, as a punch-card operator, and she left.

Maria (15)

'I don't like being with a lot of people because I feel too shy. I prefer to be with one or two friends that I know. I find it a great problem because I am foreign and am a different colour from other people to mix with them. I find it hard to mix at home because I'm always being compared with my sisters at home and I am always in the wrong. I don't get on at home very well. My mother and I are always rowing and because our father does not live with us, I can never get a second opinion on any matter and many times I have wanted to leave home but never have. When I am old enough I think I would prefer to live in a flat with a friend or by myself. I lead a very jumbled-up life really which I have not yet sorted out.'

Maria's rebellion against her mother, her assertion of the contradictory aims of wanting to be independent and live alone, at the same time as feeling shy and in need of more support—all this is typical enough of her age group. But the extra complication of being coloured and having separated parents made Maria feel, at this stage, more than normally insecure and sensitive even though she usually cloaked this with an air of defiant confidence.

When she first came to see me Maria kept out of her mother's way as much as possible with the result that they hardly spoke. It seemed to me that mother was having to take all the blame for the colour problem (father was white) and also for the broken marriage.

Maria came to see me on and off for about a year during which time she gradually became more sympathetic towards her mother. There were many factors which helped this: she had gained in maturity; her father had come to live near by, which had given her an opportunity to test out what he was really like; she had come and talked to me about her feelings when she felt the need.

At the end of the next academic year she came back to say that she and her mother were terribly worried about the way her younger sister was behaving. She had re-identified with her mother to the extent not only of understanding her mother's problems but of sharing her worries, not just about the sister but also about health and finance. The mother telephoned me and I was able to put her in touch with the most appropriate welfare agency, in this case social services.

Christine (14)

Christine referred herself after the third year group discussions. It became clear from what she said that several welfare agencies were working with her family, which had many problems. Christine herself was the one member of the family dubbed sufficiently normal not to have a caseworker of her own at that time. She was obviously carrying and covering over a lot of strain and glad to come across someone in whom she could confide.

With her permission I got in touch with social services, who were the agency principally concerned with this family. It was important for me not to disturb this child by increasing her anxieties; it was also important for me to work with, not against, the other agencies involved, to minimize contradiction and duplication.

It seemed to me that my role was to keep our discussion to the normal, the positive and the good. If Christine should need to talk more deeply it seemed better for her to return to the therapist she had seen as a young girl. So for example I took care to praise Christine for the role she took within the family of supporting her mother physically and emotionally. My consultation with social services had served to clarify the limits of my role in relation to this particular child.

Comment

In these cases the counsellor worked with social services in various different ways. Each time it was important for the counsellor to consult social services as early as possible in order to work out their respective roles, which varied according to circumstances. In several instances not quoted social services referred to the counsellor for preventive supportive counselling girls whose problems were potentially serious but about which no legal action could be taken. The counsellor had easier access to these children and more time for this kind of preventive work, provided the girls themselves accepted the idea of counselling. If not there was nothing the counsellor could do to help.

Helping the parents

Irene (11)

In the first year Irene was often late or absent. Her mother wrote one day to say that the reason for this was that parental squabbles were making Irene ill. The staff referred the matter to me.

When I saw Irene she said that her parents were talking of separation. She often went to stay with her grandmother. Irene agreed that I should see her mother but the mother resisted this by saying that her husband had come back and everything was better. Later however the mother requested help from me and I made a home visit. Mother told me something of her troubles but it was clear to me that I could not take her on as a client and that one interview would make no impact on her many real problems. I suggested that the family welfare association might be able to help her. Mother phoned for an appointment and social casework began. After that I saw Irene only occasionally. In this case helping the mother was the key. Luckily the mother was prepared to accept help which is not always the case.

Monica (15)

Monica was in a form which happened to be predominantly bright and middle class. She herself was intelligent but from a completely different social background. She was the youngest daughter of a large family, with older brothers and sisters in their thirties. Her father was out of work and in fact had left home. When Monica came after the group discussions she told me of the family's circumstances but on no account wanted the school to know of the hard times facing her family.

At this stage she did not even receive free school dinners. I explained that these could be arranged and possibly a grant too, for clothing and maintenance. The school would naturally have to know that she was eligible for free dinners but the details of her family circumstances would be regarded as confidential if this was what she really wanted.

I wrote to the mother telling her where she could get help if she wanted it. The mother was extremely relieved and immediately went for help. Up to that point she had not known where to go and she had felt too ill, desperate and worried to find out.

The education welfare service which organized financial help on her behalf also arranged a case conference, during which it was decided that the mother would be helped by the family welfare association and I would continue to see Monica.

Unfortunately in this case social pressures were too great for Monica to get the education she deserved. Although her mother got a part-time job and some social security benefit through the help of the family welfare association, money was still short and Monica felt that she should be making a financial contribution instead of staying on at school. There was more to it than this. She already felt different from the other girls in her form; her progress had been impaired by various illnesses and absences and a general lack of motivation. Her mother wanted her to stay on to get qualifications but Monica did not like the thought of struggling on, studying every evening, having no clothes to go out in and no time for boys like all her mates.

The careers teacher arranged an interview with the careers officer; with Monica's permission I also sent in a report. She went to work in a computer firm. The family welfare association kept in touch with the mother.

Comment

Getting real help to the parents is sometimes difficult and often unacceptable to them. These are two examples where through the counsellor the parents themselves were put in touch with a casework agency and began to get to the root of their problems. The second example shows the importance of having a problem case discussion when more than one agency becomes involved. Our respective roles were defined to avoid undue overlap and duplication. The family welfare association caseworker and I were able to work closely together which had advantages for our clients too.

Judy (13)

'My hobbies are reading and writing plays. I love visiting historical buildings. I loved school but now it is different as I seem to take things more seriously. I would like to be a history teacher. I would like to teach 11-year-olds who have to try hard to keep with the rest of the class. The one setback is that I am not so good at written work so teaching is out of the question.'

She was an only child, serious, conscientious and somewhat anxious. Her desire to teach children with learning difficulties stemmed from her own experience at junior school where a particularly skilled teacher had inspired her confidence. Her work had been going quite well but suddenly it had got harder and she was having to face her limitations. To some extent her tenseness and moodiness seemed to be related to her monthly periods which had recently started. She was reassured to realize this. It was difficult to assess at this stage her ultimate academic level; she talked about this to her form tutor who was able to say that she might be capable of O levels, though not without a lot of determined work. In the meantime we discussed various alternative jobs which might fulfil her aim of helping others with learning difficulties, yet require fewer academic qualifications. I put her in touch with the careers teacher and the careers literature. She finally came to say she thought she worried too much about her work, which only made it worse. She had decided to concentrate on doing as well as possible but not to worry any more about which job she finally did because after all there were many ways of helping people.

Comment

I give this one example, though I can think of several others, of a careers problem which was really a personal problem. The careers teacher could have handled it from the start if it had reached her at this early stage. I was lucky in coming across Judy *before* her ambitions became too rigid and in having the time at my disposal to support Judy while she readjusted her sights.

Linda (13)

Many of the girls I see have problems which are not apparent in the classroom situation but this was not the case with Linda. From the moment she arrived at the school she was persistently aggressive, rude and violent. She hit other girls; she swore. The school attempted at the outset to refer to the child guidance clinic but their every contact with the family was greeted with hostility.

When Linda met the counsellor in the third year discussions she decided she needed help. She wrote in her autobiographical note: 'Lots of children call me names, but it upsets me, and I squabble and fight them, then I lose my friends. I do not get on with teachers, I don't know why, but I don't.' The fact that she wanted to know why showed that there was some possibility of helping her. But the help had to be gentle and at Linda's pace; otherwise the opportunity of helping her would be lost. She resisted, as was hardly surprising, any suggestion that her parents should be brought in with a view to attempting yet again a psychiatric referral. She said they would be angry and refuse to co-operate. As this was borne out by the previous experience of the school it was accepted. But Linda herself could have some help from the counsellor and it was felt that some help was better than none. Many of the staff had tried at various stages to help Linda but she was particularly difficult to help in the authoritarian setting.

Linda used the counsellor very well at first, expressing considerable hostility and anger to the world in general and becoming as a result less aggressive in the classroom situation. But she did not come for counselling consistently; she used the counsellor as she wished, staying away for half a term, then coming back, spontaneously, when the situation got out of hand.

In the fourth year, she gained immensely in poise and maturity yet was still subject to outbursts beyond her control. Her parents began to express concern that her work was not going as well as they had hoped. This was the moment for the counsellor to press for psychiatric help. Linda herself now accepted the need for this and the parents realized that the school was genuinely concerned about Linda's welfare and that this was not a question of a passing phase in Linda or mismanagement on the part of the staff.

The counsellor's role had been to support Linda in so far as she was able and prepare her for specialist help when the time came. It is to be added that the staff generally were working to this end.

Joy (16)

In the third year groups, Joy had been quiet, sensible, without problems. In the fifth year she became aware that she was lacking in confidence in her relationships with other people, that she was frightened of boys and never mixed with them and that she was turning more and more to her studies to avoid facing her problems. She hardly ever went out, nor did she want to. It was not apparent that she felt like this; she was sensitive, industrious, perhaps a little shy. She kept her worries very much to herself.

In talking to the counsellor she began to reveal her fears and anxieties which appeared to go deep and to have origins in her infancy. She was pleased for the counsellor to see her mother; both accepted the counsellor's recommendation that it would be wise to ask for a diagnostic interview at the child guidance clinic. This meant that if necessary (as in fact it was) she could be helped by therapy to work through her difficulties at a stage when she was flexible and easier to help. This was indeed preventive rather than remedial work. Without the counselling service and the trust Joy showed in it it seems to me that Joy's problems might have gone unnoticed until they caused her to break down. This way she never reached breaking point. She went to the child guidance clinic for therapy for two years. I discovered later that she had then read sociology at university and herself became a social worker.

Mandy (14)

'I have a half-sister and half-brother, ages three and four years. My father lives quite near. I often go and see him. I miss him terribly. As he is engaged I hope he will soon get married so I could live with him. I have a stepfather and I don't like him as much as my real father but I suppose he's alright.'

She did go to live with her father. It did not work out and she was soon back with her mother. She came occasionally for counselling but only when she was fed up. She may have recognized that her life was basically insecure and that this fact was unalterable, but that it cheered her up to have an occasional chat. She was also ambivalent about me. On one occasion her mother had forbidden her to talk about family matters to me. Mother had later rescinded this but after that I felt Mandy was always slightly inhibited in what she said.

When it became clear that I was not going to be able to refer Mandy for psychiatric help (for she was extremely unsettled and insecure) because I had no powers to do this unless Mandy herself wished it, the school made more direct attempts to bring in help. A home visit was made by the education welfare officer to seek parental consent for a referral to the child guidance clinic.

This home visit illustrates vividly the difference between a parent's view of life and the way the child herself feels. The EWO concerned is not to be blamed for getting a completely different picture of the family from the school's. The EWO came back with reports of a splendid home, sensible mother, very concerned about the welfare of her child but sure that Mandy was just going through a passing phase. The school and I knew that the mother was defensive and did not really want to face the family's problems and that Mandy was insecure, emotional, unsettled and unable to work, living in a world of make-believe.

The breakthrough came in a strange way. Mandy stopped coming to see me. She went to live with an aunt for a while but that did not work either. Then one of her best friends was referred to the child guidance clinic. On the basis of her friend's recommendation, Mandy decided this might help her. Her mother agreed; the referral went through. Mandy may have done this partly as a dramatic gesture but it does not really matter. We had all been working as a team to get Mandy the help she needed. The delay was of no importance for Mandy had not been mature enough to face her problems before. When she reached the clinic she was ready to be helped which made the clinic's task easier though by no means easy.

Diana (14)

'I do not get on with people very well. At weekends I usually watch television. I have only been abroad once but I did not like it. All the girls went with the boys and I just slept most of the time. I am not interested in sex or boys or fashion. I have always been fat or big built. I don't like cooking or needlework because I cannot do any of those things.'

Diana had worried the school for some time. Before she came for group discussion in the third year she had already been referred to the school doctor twice because the school was concerned about her size, her lethargy and her lack of friends. Diana had reacted in an extremely hostile way to the doctor, which meant that it was difficult for the doctor to help her. Diana was clearly defensive and sensitive about her problems at this stage.

When she reached the counsellor after the group discussions, she was ready to admit for the first time that she had serious problems: she had cut herself off almost completely from the society in which she lived and was beginning to wonder if life was worth living. She was seriously thinking of killing herself. With her agreement I saw her mother, who first took the view that this was a passing phase but who a week later agreed, as did her daughter, that Diana needed psychiatric help. A referral was made.

The counsellor was fortunate in coming across this case at a critical stage when there seemed a real danger that Diana might continue to resist the treatment she needed and break down completely. In this case the way we have structured our counselling service gave Diana the opportunity of revealing how she really felt. It was not obvious in school how near breakdown Diana was.

Vivienne (14)

In Vivienne's case it was the school doctor who was instrumental in getting her the psychiatric help she needed. Vivienne had been seeing me for two terms. She had a lot of deep problems, mostly to do with the emotional and financial insecurity of her background and her own inability to accept her female sexual role. She went around with gangs of boys who looked upon her as one of them. When she matured physically she was sometimes deeply hurt, sometimes very relieved to find that they did not recognize her femininity. She did not get on well with girls at school; she was often absent. Her one passion in life was horse riding.

She talked to me a great deal, hardly ever missing an appointment despite her general absenteeism. She resisted any suggestion of mine that she should go for child guidance or even that I should see her mother. Because of the permissive way in which we work there was nothing I could do to force this upon her. However the school was very concerned about her too; because she complained frequently of pains in the stomach she was given a special medical. The school doctor, in her more authoritarian position, was able to set a psychiatric referral in motion. In fact, Vivienne was well prepared for this by then and accepted the referral without difficulty. She continued to come to see me, which indicated there was something in our relationship which met her many needs.

Comment

These girls all reached the child guidance clinic eventually. Sometimes the counsellor was able to get them the help they needed quickly. Sometimes she was only able to support them until some other turn of events brought matters to a head. There is no one formula for making a referral.

These next examples illustrate non-action rather than action. This is something the counsellor has to face; for various reasons, she cannot always take action or continue counselling even when it seems appropriate. I have put these examples here to show that counselling is quite often a waiting game, hedged by frustrations and sometimes even blank walls.

Mavis (14)

'At school I am quite popular as I am a different person because I must not be selfish to the people around me in being moody, so I put on a happy face, but this is not me. As I say, I like to be alone, but this is difficult sometimes as people keep interrupting me, but I do need to be alone in a way I cannot explain. I cannot understand phonies who go around in a crowd just to be in. My mother asks me why I don't confide in her, but she thought I was being funny one time when I tried to explain myself so I never tried again. She is nice in her own way but she will never understand me. My father thinks that everyone should be happy at all times and if you are not smiling you are called miserable, but he doesn't seem to realize that he himself gets miserable sometimes but no one can say a word against him. Later on in my life I would like to live on my own.'

These comments sound typical enough of an articulate adolescent but in fact Mavis's sense of isolation and of being different was exceptional. She never quite succeeded in breaking through the communication barrier with her parents. She felt so different from her parents and her peers that she left school before she found her real self. She needed psychiatric help.

I tried very hard to get her parents' agreement for this, making several home visits. Mother eventually agreed but father remained adamantly opposed to the idea of her seeing a psychiatrist, which meant that her case could not be accepted by the local clinic. I continued to see her myself, taking care to discuss her case with the local psychiatrist at intervals. Finally Mavis took an overdose of aspirins, fortunately without fatal effects. She told me about it the next day; together we told her mother, who upon my advice put the whole matter in the hands of the family doctor. He was fortunate in having a psychiatric social worker attached to his practice; she was able to continue work with Mavis and keep a close watch on her after she left school. In fact leaving school seemed to help her to find herself.

I had been in a difficult position with this case, certainly carrying more than I was qualified to do and needing the case discussion which mercifully the clinic provided. Both the school doctor and I had advised the parents of the need for child guidance; when the parents refused, we could have left it at that. Yet at the time I felt some help was better than none.

Georgina (14)

'I'm 14 years old. In some ways I'm still rather tomboyish. I'm always laughing and talking. I love food and I'm always eating. I also love dreaming and imagine I'm in some kind of adventure. At the moment, I'm rather bored with life and would love to get involved in some kind of adventure.

'I'm an only child so I'm used to being on my own. I am very independent and could manage well on my own. I think this is because I've never got on with my parents. I look after myself really. My big problem is that I hate my father and have not spoken to him for a year. I don't like my mother much either. When I am old enough I have to leave home, but this does not bother me.'

She may well have approached me more in a spirit of adventure than in a quest for the truth, for although she talked a lot about her feelings she did not *really* want to alter the situation in any way. She was out every evening at the house of a friend whose parents she liked; in school she appeared cheerful and extrovert and, like many of her contemporaries, was crazy about pop groups. She had found an acceptable *modus vivendi*. She never told me what was at the root of her hatred for her father; she did not want to go into it any deeper (for example by being referred to the child guidance clinic), so we left it at that with an invitation for her to come back at any time. She had simply wanted to talk about what she normally kept to herself but for the time being that was all.

Jeanette (13)

All Jeanette wrote in her note was this: 'I have three brothers and two sisters. They are 14, 11, 10, 8 and 5. In my spare time I like to go swimming with my friends.'

This note is a clear statement at this stage that she did not want the counsellor to know anything about her. In fact she had serious problems in her relationships with her siblings. It is easy to interpret the note in retrospect. Anyone of 13 with so many brothers and sisters so close is likely to have problems. She doesn't mention her parents which is significant and her only positive statement is about her friends. She seems to be disassociating herself from her family and keeping herself very much to herself.

As it happens this was the case but the counsellor could not have assumed this from the note, indeed would not have presumed to assume this without further indications from the girl herself.

In fact Jeanette did not turn to the counsellor for help until about a term after writing this note. By then she was feeling totally alienated from home and school and talking to the counsellor was for her the first step towards restoring her relationships with her world. In fact such was her need to be independent of all adults that she chose not to come for any more counselling. In the end she got into serious trouble and was referred by social services to the child guidance clinic. In her case our permissive approach made it difficult to help her for she wanted help from no one. She provides an example of the limitations of the counsellor's role.

Stella (14)

'I do not talk to my father much as I am not over-fond of him and have lost my respect for him over the last few years because of family trouble. Through this a lot of my love goes to my grand-parents, though mostly to my mother.'

There was a genuine marital problem here which Stella kept very much to herself in school. The parents had been to the Marriage Guidance Council for counselling and the mother was also seen regularly by the family doctor for her nerves. I didn't see Stella many times for she seemed to have adjusted well to the family situation, to accept it, and to be unaffected by it. She did in fact show considerable dramatic talent, which helped her to remain confident and outgoing. The note itself shows dramatic flair though it is also surprisingly detached and matter of fact in tone. What was interesting about this case was that when Stella's parents began to get on a great deal better, Stella herself was very put out by having to share her mother with her father. She over-idealized her mother and normally made great allowances for her shortcomings. These became less tolerable to her when she had only a part-share of her mother's affection and when she was forced to admit that her father was not entirely 'bad'. She was beginning to see this when she stopped coming for counselling. It was too uncomfortable to face reality. In any case in all probability the basic marital situation would remain the same. Stella had already worked out a way of existing alongside it and it might only unsettle her to probe further at this stage. Self-insight is not always in the client's best interests; she wasn't ready for it then and so stopped coming.

Jonquil (14)

'I like my father and mother very much, but sometimes after I have been told off and shouted at, I think in my heart that I hate them, and when I'm old enough I would leave them and get a flat of my own. I don't always accept the fact that 'tellings-off' are for my own good and sometimes think they *definitely* aren't. My parents sometimes cannot see why young people do silly things, like taking drugs etc. They think it is their own silly fault for taking them at their age, but my parents do not realize it is the older people that started giving the drugs to young people and making money out of it.

'I don't rightly know what I want to be or do when I leave school. I think I would like to be a secretary or a punch operator as long as I could work in an office. If this were not possible I would like to work with small children as I like children.

'I don't go out a lot, but my sister does and brings her friends home and I am quite happy to listen and talk to them. My mother and father wonder why I don't go out and get boyfriends but I just like to stay indoors and watch the television and read girls' comics or books. I suppose really I will start to go out and about more when I really want to, but not yet and they find it difficult to understand. I suppose I find them difficult to understand sometimes, but we will all just have to put up with it.'

There is a negative tone underlying these wise but sad comments on the generation gap. Jonquil was not in fact as happy staying at home as she makes out here but the relatively unusual situation of having parents urging her to go out did not help her to summon the courage to venture forth. Her basic problem was insecurity about her parents' love so that their exhortations seemed to her in many ways a kind of rejection of her. She needed to feel much more confident about them before she was ready to leave them.

Her brother and sister on the other hand appeared to her to be the parental favourites. What is more she regarded them as attractive outgoing people, and considered herself shy and felt that her appearance was hampered by glasses. Another factor that contributed to her feeling of being different from her family was that she was intelligent, certainly A level standard, if not more, and was therefore able to argue with her parents with a degree of logic which made them feel insecure and resentful that she should win arguments. The other children were much more in their parents' mould, though Jonquil's relatively low job aspirations may well reflect a desire to remain acceptable to the family.

As far as Jonquil was concerned she found it very depressing to have her parents mock or block her every attempt to hold an intelligent adult conversation. She interpreted this as meaning that they did not accord any adult status to her, the recognition as a young adult which she needed to feel confident enough to go out.

We never worked right through this. Like many of my clients Jonquil only came three times. It is impossible to know whether she did in fact rethink her own attitudes to her family and realize her own strength sufficiently for her to become more tolerant and relaxed in her attitude to her parents. Three sessions might have done something with such a perceptive child. Perhaps not—her family relationship might have simply remained in her eyes an unsatisfactory one which in her own words she would just have to put up with until she was truly adult. I do know that her mother had in fact been suffering from nervous strain and when she went to the doctor about this and also changed to a part-time job, the atmosphere became more relaxed. I also know that Jonquil already had one sympathetic adult to talk to about her feelings, namely a young married woman for whom she baby-sat sometimes. So we did not prolong our counselling sessions.

If the clients seem happy to cease counselling for a while as Jonquil did, then we hope that they will come back later if the situation again becomes intolerable. But we do not *encourage* girls to have problems. If they appear to be coping reasonably well with their own problems without us, then we are able to concentrate more on the girls who really need our help.

Comment

These are all examples of cases where counselling had only a limited value. In some cases the individuals concerned did not really want help and within the permissive framework of our particular scheme the counsellor had no powers to see them unless they wanted to come. In other cases their problems were too deep or complex for the counsellor to handle alone, yet offers of more specialized help were refused. In cases of deadlock I always take care to ask the staff whether they are at all worried about the individual child. If they are, they are able to press for action in the ways they did before counsellors existed.

Conclusion

These last examples are for you to think about and discuss. They are typical of the sort of problem a counsellor may have to face — or a form teacher, for that matter.

Ann (14)

'Ever since I was nine I have lived with my great-aunt because my mother died and my father was separated from her when I was two. Because my Auntie is old (76) she doesn't understand or approve very much of the younger generation and when I wish to go to a quite normal place she will say no. When this situation arises I usually act deceitfully and go regardless of what she says, and I don't enjoy doing this for I would rather tell her. I am not allowed to have boyfriends but I do usually without her finding out and when I want any advice about them, instead of going to her I go and talk them over with an older woman I know. My Aunt expects me in at 9.30 every night of the week, but I never keep to these times. She never trusts me to go out and says before I leave that if I become pregnant I will go into a home. This proves that she don't really know what sort of a person I am.

'When I leave school I don't really know what I want to be, but I am going to carry my education a little further.

'I like to wear fashionable clothes and usually make my own, whch works out much cheaper. Sometimes I see people along the street wearing way-out clothes, then when I have the time and the money I make something of what I have seen. I have many moods and sometimes I feel that I want to be noticed so I wear my way-out clothes but at other times I am shy and wear ordinary clothes.'

Gwen (14)

'I live with my nan and grandad, not with my mother and father. My mum left my dad when I was about two and my little brother was one. Because my dad could not look after us, my nan took us over. Then my dad went to live with another woman, taking my brother with him. He did not take me as my nan would be upset to lose both of us. They had another four children and come to live near us. Recently, my dad kicked my step mum out, so then, although I live with my nan, I looked after the children every night after school till he came home from work and of a Saturday. Then my dad and my nan had a row and I'm not allowed to go near my dad's house any more. It worries me to think of those children not being looked after properly. Nan is ever so nice, I like living with her but she's ever so strict and won't let me go out much of a night. She worries. It upsets me not to speak to dad but he doesn't want to know: I get really hurt when the other children aren't allowed to talk to me.

'I've gone all moody and even the girls at school have noticed how grumpy I am. I used to go out with boys quite a bit but I'm so fed up at the moment, what with nan worrying about me, and me worrying about my brothers and sisters, I don't seem to care any more.

'When I leave school, I don't know what I want to do, but it must not be a boring job. I would like to get married and have at least four children. I do not think it' a bad idea to get married young, but I don't think I will get married young. About 20-21 years old. I would like to have quite a bit of money to buy what I did not have, especially a good modern house. Although my house with my nan is very nice, my dad's house is not very nice.'

Wendy (13)

'I have two sisters and one brother. We all live in a flat. My dad has a bad temper but that's better than a clip round the earhole. My mun is a bit overworked and has just had a check-up at the hospital. When I leave school I want to be a nurse, the qualify to be a midwife. Can you help me about this? My brother and sisters sometimes drive me up the bend. What can I do about it? I love all dogs and cats, but the trouble is I have asthma, although it's going I hope. My mun at times gets me very angry and depressed.'

Lesley (14)

'Both my parents work. I have two older sisters. My mother is always going on at me, but doesn't at my sisters. My father is always telling me off for the slightest little thing. If I have a fight with my sisters I get blamed for it and called all sorts of names like slut etc. My sisters never get told off but I always do. My sister is nearly 18 and Dad said going out once a week is too much of a girl her age. I'm not aloud to go out either. It's rotten. Just because I live and hour away from school, my parents won't trust me to go anywhere in case anything happens. They don't like my friends — they say they're not good enough and will only get me into trouble. I'm fed up with it. They never think about *me*. How can I learn to be grown-up?

Hetty (13)

'I have one brother of 14 and a sister who's 10. I get on well with my brother and not with my sister. I get on well with my dad who is strict but doesn't keep me chained up. I *hate* my mum and don't get on well with her. We don't talk and never want to. My sister gets me into trouble all the time (that's partly why my mother hates me). My dads away a lot on business. I miss him then. When he comes back, he and mum go out a lot, to parties and that. They often leave us alone in the evenings. The other night they got back before I did and there was a terrible row. They said I must have been having it off with a boy, but I never. They hit me and said I couldn't go out for a fortnight.'

Outside bodies

Who are the people outside the school itself who are concerned with young people and who can help? Can the counsellor really do anything to help communications within and between the school, the home, the community and its resources? Should he attempt to do this or should he limit his role to work with individuals?

These questions are easier to ask than to answer; indeed there is no real answer, for so much depends upon the circumstances of each particular case and the age of the young person. It does however seem to me that the counsellor who confines himself rigidly to the four walls of his counselling room is only doing part of his job. Counselling must remain the counsellor's main function; in the majority of cases it is neither appropriate nor necessary to bring in other people. When it is, the counsellor's skill lies in choosing the right moment for action, in knowing the different strengths and qualities of the local community resources and in having already established with them a working relationship based on mutual respect and personal contact. Like the relationship between the counsellor and the pupils or the counsellor and the staff, this relationship is not something which springs up overnight in response to the information that the counselling service exists. It grows gradually as a result of careful preparation and constant renewal. With young people over the age of 16, the counsellor is less likely to take any action at all, but to leave the responsibility for action with the young person.

Parents

Of all the counsellor's extramural relationships, the most important is with the parents. These are the people whose attitudes and attributes most influence his clients for better or for worse. Furthermore without the parents' agreement the counsellor is powerless to bring in the specialist help of experts when necessary. It is therefore essential that the parent/counsellor relationship should be well prepared and carefully handled. We have to remember that like teachers and unlike certain social workers the counsellor is in the delicate position of being able to ask children to talk about their private lives without parental knowledge. What are the parents' rights in this? What do they think of the idea of a counselling service? How much do they really know about it? Do they object to having their private lives and habits discussed with a stranger without the opportunity of putting their side of the case? What can the school and the counsellor do to reassure them, to help to perceive the counsellor not as a usurper of their rights and a meddler in other people's affairs but as someone whose work may ultimately benefit the family as a whole?

In our experience we found very little parental opposition to our scheme. When it came to individual counselling, some half-dozen parents over the years have telephoned or written to say they object. One mother complained to the head that she did not like her daughter to talk about her marital problems, then proceeded to tell the head rather more than the child had told the counsellor. Other parents were invited to come and see the counsellor. As soon as they realized the way the counsellor worked and the vital fact that the counsellor kept confidential information confidential (a safeguard which does not automatically apply to what children tell their teachers) most parents felt greatly reassured and began to work *with* the counsellor. In one case a child was so inhibited with her counsellor because she had to report everything back to her mother that the counsellor gave up working with the child and took on the mother, whom she saw about once a term.

Group work with parents, through the PTA, proved to be a very valuable exercise. The parents were divided into small groups and given various problems to consider. They were asked first to discuss the situations, then say what they thought the parents should do. Most of the groups never got further than the first problem, which stimulated an amazing amount of controversy and disagreement. Here are a few of the examples:

Janice is 14. She has a boyfriend, Michael (16), whom her parents have met. She is allowed out with him until 9 pm. Last Saturday then went to a party and did not return until 10.30 pm.

Sally is a mature 15-year-old who goes round with some girls of 17 who are already working. Her friends invite her to come to a holiday camp with them for a week.

Julie is 15 and came home from her club one night looking very pale. She burst into tears and after much persuasion told her mother that a man had molested her on the common.

Sue and her parents have always wanted her to be a doctor. She is shattered one day to learn from her favourite mistress that she has no chance of achieving her ambition since her academic work is not good enough. She confides all this to her mother.

Maureen's parents had really wanted a boy first. Maureen herself (14) is rather a tomboy, always scrapping with her younger brother (10) whom her parents idolize. She resents helping her mother with the housework since her younger sister (eight) gets off scot free. She keeps out of the house as much as possible. As

136

far as her parents are concerned she seems helpful and reliable enough when she is in. Her parents are very surprised to learn from the school that Maureen is restless and noisy in class, aggressive in the form and that she has been truanting.

The parents found it hard to agree (which is healthy enough) about what age a girl should be allowed out at all, let alone with a boy or older girls or alone. Some parents were relieved to find that when their daughter said 'but everybody else goes to parties except me' this was not exactly true. Other parents were left wondering whether they were not a little too strict—or too lax.

We hope they thought and talked afterwards both to each other and to their children about the difficulties of balancing their duty to protect their daughters against their daughters' need to grow gradually into independent and responsible adults.

Interviews with parents

In chapter 7 I gave examples in which it was not possible or advisable to see the parents. Although one of our general objectives is to improve communications between parents and their children it is usually better for the pupils to tackle this themselves without the intervention of a third party. In families where the atmosphere is already tense and explosive it seems unlikely that parents would give permission for their daughters to let off steam in confidence. So the counsellor leaves it to the individual child to tell her parents that she is seeing the counsellor.

In some cases I am sure the girls were right *not* to tell their parents. In others they judged astutely what is a good moment to explain, often using it as a way of introducing a discussion with their parents about their own problems. In other cases they told their parents from the beginning: but these were the parents most able to tolerate the idea of not knowing everything about their daughters. After one girl told her parents she had confided that she was worried about their arguments they stopped arguing in front of her. I remember feeling that this was probably not the solution to their marital problems. But it would have been impertinent and out of place for me to have suggested marriage guidance counselling, particularly as it might not even have been necessary. Sometimes in an interview with the parents it is possible to suggest that they might be able to get help of this nature and to be more specific if they ask for details. But for the counsellor to tell the parents to go for marital counselling is rather like telling a teacher she needs a refresher course; it is not the counsellor's business unless her advice is specifically sought by the individuals concerned.

Sometimes a girl will ask the counsellor to see her parents. Sometimes the counsellor takes the initiative in making the suggestion. When the counsellor does decide that it would be helpful to see the parents she first gets the child's permission to do this. Some children are apprehensive about what may be said, particularly when what they have been telling the counsellor is a distortion of the truth. The child's trust in the counsellor may be shaken by a parental interview, even when the interview has been entirely as expected. If a child has been twisting the truth to get sympathy, the parental interview can help her to face what she has been doing. As long as the counsellor has not brought the parent in too soon, as long as the counsellor/client relationship is well established, this may be the turning point in the child's understanding the dynamics of her family situation. In one case for example Sylvia had given the impression that her mother (who was divorced) and her mother's boyfriend shared the same bedroom as herself. In fact the mother was very careful about where and when she made love and her boyfriend did not normally stay the night. What Sylvia was really trying to get across was the fact that her mother had not realized how sexually aware she was nor how much she needed mothering and guiding in her own sexual behaviour. I don't think this was clear until after the counsellor had seen the mother and the true picture had emerged. The interview with the mother helped Sylvia to communicate to her mother that she needed more of her attention.

The counsellor will see parents for a variety of reasons but only ever if the young person requests it. Sometimes it is to help the counsellor assess the extent of the problem and decide whether a referral need be made; sometimes it is to get the parents' agreement for a referral to the child guidance clinic or the parents' permission for a discussion of the case with the child guidance staff to see whether they advise a referral. Sometimes the interview with the parents is enough in itself for it may increase their awareness of their daughter's feelings or help them to rethink their attitudes towards her. Sometimes the interview with the parents reveals problems in them so great that they themselves ask for help and can be referred to an appropriate agency.

What happened when the parents refused to co-operate, particularly in giving permission for psychiatric diagnosis or treatment? If this kind of referral was indicated one of the counsellor's tasks was to reassure the parents that going to the child guidance clinic did not mean their child is a 'nut case'. She will show her own confidence in the clinic and describe in realistic terms what the parents may expect to happen if they agree to diagnosis. Even then parents often take a distorted and sceptical view that a psychiatrist is, as someone once put it, a 'cross between a witch doctor and a lavatory attendant'. The children themselves and the younger parents are less resistant to the idea of preventive psychiatric treatment, accepting that a psychiatric illness, like TB, is easier to cure in the early stages. The children who go for guidance have not usually reached the stage of being mentally sick. Even so it is sometimes hard to get across what it *is* all about: as one mother said to my colleague, 'She doesn't need to go to that clinic. She's not sick you know—it's all in her mind.'

It was not always necessary or helpful for the counsellor herself to see the parents. Sometimes it was better for the head or deputy head to do this, because the referral was being based on the way the girl had been behaving in school, which was something they knew about and the counsellor had only heard about. With certain parents the authority of the head or deputy head added weight to the recommendation, which made the parents more likely to accept. Sometimes their authoritarian and judgemental role had the reverse effect—the parents were on the defensive and were not going to admit there was anything wrong with their daughter or the way they've brought her up; it must be the school's fault. 'She's no trouble at home, she never bleeding-well swears in front of us.' This kind of hostile parental reaction may come about when the head or deputy has not in fact been the least authoritarian or judgemental but when the parents have expected them to be so and have attacked even before battle has commenced.

With this sort of parent (and the school may well know from previous encounters which parents these are) the counsellor could usefully present herself as someone outside the authority structure who was in no way criticizing or complaining about their daughter, simply as someone who is concerned about her general well-being and progress. If the reason for the child's disturbed behaviour in school lay in the family circumstances at home, and this was something the counsellor already knew in confidence, then the parents were more likely to break down their defences and talk about the real problem, rather than cover it up; furthermore if they realized that the counsellor knew something of the truth they were less likely to gloss over their fundamental problem and slide away. But there was no guarantee of this either: why should parents tell the counsellor everything?

Take the case of Antonia: she appeared very disturbed yet the mother's account of the home situation gave no indication of why this should be. The counsellor said that she was nevertheless still very concerned about Antonia but that her mother was in a better position than she to know what it really was that was worrying her and how serious it was. The mother must have weighed this carefully; soon after she asked for a child guidance appointment. It transpired that the marriage was on the point of breaking up, something both mother and daughter had concealed in talking to the counsellor.

I know, especially now, that many heads find themselves burdened with parents' problems: marital, financial, social and psychological. Yet there are again certain parents who never quite overcome the feeling of awe a head teacher inspired in them when they were young. This has nothing to do with the actual attributes of the head: she may be the most approachable of persons, yet some parents will only ever approach her wearing, metaphorically speaking, their best hat and putting on their best front. I have found this type of parent, once assured of the counsellor's trustworthiness, willing to confide some family secret which they would never on any account wish the school to know, yet which does have an important bearing on their daughter's problem.

In our experiment, when the counsellor first began to see the parents, the year mistresses or form tutors would naturally enough ask if they might also see the parent while she was at school, particularly if it was a parent who was hard to catch. We soon stopped this arrangement by mutual agreement. It was confusing for the parents and generally made them more defensive when they saw the counsellor, because in their minds she was mixed up with the 'powers that be'.

Yet even here we have learnt to be flexible according to the needs of the situation. For example in one case the counsellor saw the mother to express her general concern about her daughter and explain about the child guidance clinic; then the year mistress was invited to join the discussion to explain the exact way the daughter was behaving in school. The mother accepted the need for referral. This did not happen by chance: the year mistress and the counsellor had worked out their respective roles very carefully.

Other agencies

When we began our experiment, our position in relation to the existing services for the welfare of children was ambiguous to say the least. Although our local education authority obviously knew we were there and why, had agreed to our appointment as an experiment and indeed paid us our salaries as off-quota teachers on a temporary terminal basis, our establishment as counsellors was not officially recognized. We were regarded as an experiment, but one for which the school rather than the local education authority was to take responsibility. There was no reason why any of the local community services for the welfare of children should take any notice of our existence at all let alone take referrals from use, make referrals back to us, engage in joint case discussions or work closely with us.

When we first began our work the head took care to introduce us to various key people in the children's services. It is fair to say that our relationships were not very fruitful at first, for reasons which are wholly understandable. For our part we were too busy trying to work out our relationship with the girls and the staff and to establish our identity within the school to have much time or energy for community work. For their part the social workers in the community bided their time, wisely waiting to see whether we were useful and remaining possibly somewhat ambivalent towards us. Why were we needed when their services existed? Did we really know what we were doing? Weren't we going to cause even more duplication and confusion than already existed in the social welfare services? Nobody actually confronted us with these questions. If they had they would have found us equally unsure about the validity of what we were doing. As in our relationship with the teachers, the onus of proof as to what a counsellor was lay with the counsellors. In a sense we needed to be left alone for a time while we worked out what we could do. Then when we felt stronger and a little more clear-headed we took the initiative in contacting the social welfare agencies again. We visited each agency in turn, feeling sufficiently confident by then to express some of our own doubts and being in a position to raise some practical problems requiring mutual co-operation. It was from this moment that our working relationship with the community services really began.

It seems incredible in retrospect that this obvious stage should have taken such a long time to reach. It is extraordinary how much *knowing* the people in a particular agency facilitates contacts with them. For example after we had visited each agency we would for a while find it much easier to pick up the phone and seek their advice on a particular legal point or their help on what procedure would best ensure a smooth referral if this was indicated. If we did not renew our contact at regular intervals, we would hesitate a little more to bother them and only ask for help in cases where we were *absolutely* sure we were not wasting their time. This is not healthy. It puts far too much responsibility for diagnosis and assessment on the counsellor and risks her sitting upon borderline problems until they are too far gone to be helped. In short it puts upon the counsellor the same limitation that teachers have when they do not have the opportunity to air their doubts in discussion.

So again as in our relationship with the staff it soon became clear that to be effective, community contacts had to be structured and they had to be structured on a regular basis. On the other hand there were so *many* social welfare agencies, statutory and voluntary, in the area to to keep up with them all would in fact involve the counsellors in an endless social work merry-go-round which would take them away from their clients and only be marginally useful to them. So we went for a deep relationship with a few agencies, confident that they would advise us who else to contact if necessary. Our work compliments most of all the work of the education welfare officer, the social services and the child guidance units. It is with these three agencies that we had the most regular and constructive contact.

The education welfare service

Under our local authority we had a well-established education welfare service. It acted as a clearing-house for all social problems concerning schoolchildren, thus helping to avoid overlap and confusion; it provided home visitors, many of them voluntary workers guided and supervised by professional social workers.

Although we often saw parents we have also found that in certain cases the welfare worker is better placed than we are for making a visit. The establishment of a friendly relationship between a family and a welfare worker enables the worker to keep an eye on the problems of the family as a whole so that when the time is ripe she may well be able to advise them on what to do. Sometimes this approach is useful for getting parental permission for a referral to the child guidance clinic though in an equal number of cases it is more appropriate for us to do this ourselves: it depends upon the nature of the case.

When a family appeared to have multiple problems the education welfare service also organized a problem-case conference to which the counsellor could make a valuable contribution, provided again she had cleared this with her client. When a family's problems were severe enough to warrant a case conference, the client was usually glad for the counsellor to add her viewpoint to a conference which will take place in any case. At the conference were representatives of the education, school medical and education welfare services.

The social services

We were less closely involved with the social services, though we often sought their legal advice. We saw them about once a term, sometimes less, but our relationship became sufficiently well established for us not to hesitate to phone them. Whenever it seemed that a case was potentially one which social services would have to take on eventually (eg care and protection, removal from home) we developed the practice of seeking advice—either with our client's permission or without naming names—in the early stages. A social worker was then assigned to the case. He could be kept informed of the progress of the case and advise us on when or whether action was appropriate.

Cases of suspected cruelty or neglect, moral welfare and sexual danger put us in a difficult position legally. The advice of our education officer was that all such cases should be instantly reported to the education welfare service. Were we teachers we should not hesitate to do this. When teachers voiced their suspicions to us we advised them to report the matter. When we were told about such instances by the children themselves we first made sure of the facts of the case, then discussed with the child whether it was in her best interests for something more to be done.

But it was not *always* in the child's best interests for something more to be done and often there was nothing more to be done. We might know that a child was unhappy or worried yet all we could do was to support her until the danger was averted or the evidence was strong enough to bring in the law. Our first aim was obviously to prevent and avert a crisis. Our responsibility here, for good or for ill, was great and worrying at times. Yet for us to be simply secret agents of the welfare service or automatic referring and forwarding machines was not in accordance with our principles.

Sometimes a social worker would phone us and ask us to take on an individual child for preventive and supportive work. If the counsellor already had a relationship with a particular child, referrals like this could work extremely well. On the other hand because coming for counselling was voluntary we could not help unless we happened to have the confidence and respect of the child concerned. For example Sarah was in moral danger but not sufficient for a court action to be taken. The social worker responsible asked the counsellor to undertake preventive counselling with her. The counsellor had to make it quite clear that although she was aware of Sarah's problems and had tried to help her, she did not want help. The counsellor was out of touch with her; even if she had still had Sarah's confidence, she could not have guaranteed that Sarah would not henceforth get into trouble. Our method is entirely dependent on the co-operation of the client. Sarah did not accept the need for self-help. She needed firm guidance and strict control; the counsellor was not in a position to provide this secure framework. The person officially assigned to take responsibility for Sarah's general welfare was in fact a professional worker within the welfare service, known as the children's worker. She contacted the counsellor for a case discussion; the counsellor was able to put her in direct contact with the form tutor, who had already established with Sarah exactly the kind of strict but friendly relationship she needed. The children's worker and the form tutor worked closely together. Sarah eventually reached the child guidance clinic.

In this case the counsellor had recognized and defined the limitations of her role. She still had a useful function in co-ordinating what was happening in school and putting the people who could most help Sarah in touch with each other. There is no reason why social workers or children's workers should not telephone school staff direct. Yet the counsellors found increasingly that they were telephoned by social workers from outside the school and asked either to take on a case or to help in some way. The counsellor acted as a useful link-man and sieve.

This co-ordinating and communicating role could often save time both for the staff and for the social workers. The social workers knew that the counsellor understood and shared their ethic, whereas they might not be sure about the teaching staff unless they knew them personally. The differences between the professional ethics of the teaching and the social worker professions might not be as great as many social workers imagine but they had to be recognized nevertheless.

Our work with social services was two-way: we benefitted from their specialized knowledge, their experience and sometimes their unofficial casework supervision; we helped them sometimes by taking on individuals for preventive work, sometimes by putting them in touch with the member of staff who could most help, sometimes by telling parents about their service so that parents might refer themselves for advice, sometimes by discussing with them a particular child in order to define our respective roles clearly.

Child guidance

Our work was closely allied to the work of the school psychological services. It is with this service that we worked the most closely and to which we made most of our referrals. In order to ensure that appropriate referrals were made we established a system of regular case discussion with the two clinics that served our area. One of the greatest difficulties for counsellors in an unofficial unstructured experiment is getting their work supervised to make sure that they do not keep cases beyond their capabilities, or perpetuate their own errors of approach. We were extremely lucky in getting constructive help and guidance from our clinics, in particular from the educational psychologists. We had case discussion with one or the other every three weeks; we could also telephone at any time with complete assurance. Sometimes we went into the guidance units in which case the psychiatric social worker might join us; sometimes we met in school. Apart from this the psychiatrist might convene a special case discussion for a new case, a joint case or a psychiatric case which the counsellor was having to keep because of lack of parental co-operation.

In the general case discussion with the educational psychologist we raised first of all the borderline cases where we were not sure whether child guidance treatment was appropriate, and then cases which were undoubtedly counselling cases, but about which we felt unsure, worried or dissatisfied ourselves. The educational psychologist did testing for us if it seemed appropriate, which was not often; usually she simply passed on the benefit of her much wider experience. When there was any doubt about whether a child needed treatment we asked the psychiatrist for a diagnostic interview: this after all is what he is qualified to do, and what we are *not* qualified to do. The counsellor is neither trained nor paid to take the kind of responsibility a psychiatrist will take for recognizing a psychotic or carrying a potential suicide. A wise counsellor takes medical cover in good time, recognizing (with some sense of relief) that it is not her job for example to decide what to do about a suicide threat and that this must be put in a doctor's hands, even if initially this has to be the family doctor rather than a child psychiatrist.

There is no doubt that the question of deciding what is normal and what is abnormal for a child of a certain age is very difficult. I am sure that if teachers took any definition of disturbed or maladjusted children literally, they would refer a large proportion of their pupils. (See for example the definitions given in the Underwood Report.[1])

The problem is in defining the degree of maladjustment, granted that many children show certain symptoms of disturbance at certain stages in their development. The Underwood Report says that 'a child may be regarded as maladjusted who is developing in ways that have a bad effect on himself or his teachers and cannot without help be remedied by his parents, teachers, and other adults in ordinary contact with him.' The symptoms do not in themselves indicate maladjustment. 'It is only when they are excessive or abnormal, when they prevent a child from living a normal life that investigation is needed.'

Defining what is excessive and abnormal is what is difficult, especially when we consider that there are bound to be a number of somewhat maladjusted children in any normal school, particularly since Warnock.[2]

The counsellor has to have a flexible approach. Rather like a good general practitioner he may through his experience of a sample of the raw population come to recognize which cases may need specialist help and which are within his sphere. But he does not do this alone; he recognizes that he is neither omniscient nor omnipotent. He asks the opinion of the form tutor and the advice of the educational psychologist and thus avoids either sitting on cases which ought to be referred or passing on every case which is in the least disturbing. In our scheme, the educational psychologists helped to ensure that we made sensible referrals. When educational psychologists are so highly trained and in such short supply[3] this seems to me to be an effective and efficient way of using their expertise.

Referrals

When the counsellor did make a referral to the child guidance clinic she naturally first had to get the consent and the co-operation of the child and her parents; next she informed the head and the education welfare service, so that they would collect a school report plus any other facts already known about this child's background; she then wrote her own confidential report to the psychiatrist and awaited an appointment. In the meantime she continued to see the child. After the diagnostic interview the psychiatrist wrote to the counsellor (among others) to give his considered opinion and advice on treatment. He might convene a special case discussion to which the counsellor was invited and at which it was decided whether the counsellor should go on seeing the girl as well as or instead of the psychiatrist or therapist. Either way the counsellor kept in close touch with the psychiatric social worker and with the child's form tutor so that two-way feedback (on how the girl is behaving in school and how she is responding to treatment) was maintained. Occasionally when a child was being particularly disruptive in class the psychiatrist would come into school with his whole team of workers in order to hear at first hand what the staff felt about this particular child. This not only helped the psychiatrist in his understanding of the child's behaviour, but had the very valuable side effect of improving the relationship between the clinic and the school.

It was important to note that this simple mechanism for counsellor referrals took some time to establish. The counsellors could not make referrals at first because their position was not recognized. We finally established with the welfare service the principle that the counsellor would make clinic referrals direct, provided she also informed the welfare service so that it could retain its co-ordinating function. The child guidance units would not of course accept referrals from counsellors unless they recognized their existence and their value. We found it both encouraging and reassuring that the clinics took some note of what we said: for example we might be asked whether we thought a case was urgent. If we said it was urgent then the growing waiting list was waived. Clearly this is something we could not afford to abuse or misjudge but it resulted in the kind of *flexible* arrangement which should exist between a school and a clinic. More than anything else the idea of a rigid inflexible waiting list stops schools from using the child guidance clinic. If the problem is urgent, staff may feel that in six months' time it will be too late to help the child at all. In our case we have a hot line to the clinic.

The counsellor as go-between

I have already mentioned the important role the counsellor had in explaining to parents what child guidance is all about. The counsellor had an equally important role *vis-à-vis* the staff. Parents were not the only people to feel ambivalent about psychiatrists. Teachers too are often wary or sceptical of them. This attitude has been described as the 'magic wand syndrome': the teacher keeps a difficult child until he becomes absolutely impossible, then refers him as a last desperate measure. The psychiatrist is expected to wave a magic wand and 'cure' the child in a matter of months. If the child remains as difficult as ever, this is taken as proof that child guidance is ineffectual.

On the other hand child guidance units sometimes suffer from the 'closed shop' syndrome. So anxious are they to retain confidentiality and divorce themselves from the authority setting of the school that they omit to feed back to the teachers any comments or guidance. Teachers whose pupils have gone for guidance often feel insecure about how to handle these pupils in future. Should they be punished or will this make them worse? Should teachers turn a blind eye? What should they do if a child has a tantrum? It is usually neither desirable nor possible for the clinic to provide a straightforward answer. Clinic staff may modestly feel that they should not interfere with a teacher's professional techniques. In my view what the teacher is after is not a blueprint for helping Johnny but just some communication back to help increase her own insight. The counsellor can help both the school and the child guidance staff in this.

The careers service

Of the remaining community services for young people, the most important is the careers service. We knew our careers officers and we did not hesitate to contact them if our clients felt this would help them. We ran group discussions for early leavers during the few weeks before they left school but these were not to do with job choice, but with helping to bridge the emotional and social gap between school and work. The help we gave the careers officers was indirect, early and probably unknown to them. We always asked the pupils in the group discussions what they wanted to do when they left. In the groups we tried to get the girls to think a little about what sort of people they were but we did not administer a self-searching questionnaire such as is used by many careers officers/teachers. But what we did pick up among the 'don't knows' was a certain proportion either of unsuitable job choices, or of job choices dictated through social pressures rather than by any consideration of the girl's qualities and qualifications.

We have already considered the girl who wanted to teach children with learning difficulties although she was unlikely to achieve college entrance requirements. There were many other such examples: *Hyacinth*, who was a West Indian, wanted to be a ballet dancer, although at 14 she had not yet begun lessons. *Amina* from Pakistan wanted to be a doctor even though she had been put in a non O level form. Helping these individuals to face their limitations without losing self-confidence or becoming defensive, so that they might begin to think realistically about alternatives, was a skilled task and took time. If together with the form tutor we could help a child work through these difficulties and face the moment of truth well before the careers interview, then we had really helped that young person.

We could also sometimes help when there were emotional or social problems stemming from the home situation. *Dorothy* was capable of O level but her father had just deserted her and her mother, leaving them virtually destitute. She wanted to leave early to earn money. *Alice* was very bright but from a working-class home, which saw no virtue in staying on. Instead of doing her homework she read extensively but without purpose. If she was leaving at Easter, why work for GCE? *Helena*, a Cypriot, wanted to do A levels but her parents insisted that she leave early to help in their shop. *Carol* on the other hand shared her parents' negative attitudes towards education. Her only ambition was to marry as young as possible. *Colette* was leaving school early to spite her parents whom she detested.

Children with this sort of problem need much more than information about job qualifications and much more than exhortations to do better if they are to begin to do themselves justice. They may be helped by individual or group counselling to make a more rational decision about their future, though sometimes the social pressures of their backgrounds make it impossible for them to fulfil their academic potential. If the counsellor can work on the irrational and emotional factors involved in vocational choice early enough, this may again save the careers officer from the unsatisfactory process of eleventh-hour crisis vocational guidance. But the counsellor's influence in this sphere will be minimal unless the policy of the school as a whole is directed not just towards careers information and job selection but includes experience throughout the curriculum and throughout the school career of self-analysis and decision-making, with more consideration of how to motivate the individual child. Schools should heed also the parents who, if they lack aspirations for their child, may be the most obstinate and influential blockage to their child's progress.

The head, the counsellor and the community

In many schools the head or deputy takes on the role of co-ordinator of work with the social welfare services. This is an important job. Well done it may take up an undue proportion of a head's time. Inadequately done it may, through omission, fail to bring in help at the right time, which may indirectly hinder a child's progress. It seems to me that whilst retaining his power and responsibility as general overseer of what is happening in a school, a head could usually delegate some of the daily tasks of contacting the welfare services to the counsellor. The counsellor for his part must be trusted to keep the head informed of important developments but not bother him with detailed accounts of every phone call.

Similarly the head who finds himself burdened with large numbers of social problems brought to him by parents may be tempted to take them on for himself at the expense of his other duties, or he may fail to bring in the service which exists to help just this situation. A head with a counsellor on his staff could save himself a lot of time and worry by giving the counsellor the time-consuming task of contacting the appropriate agency and arranging the first interview.

These communicating, co-ordinating and contacting functions of the counsellor are not of course counselling, but they are functions which could be aptly assigned to the counsellor, provided they in turn do not take up so much of his time that his work with individuals suffers.

Another role the counsellor may usefully fulfil within the staffroom is to keep the staff as a whole well informed about local welfare resources. The counsellor can also take an in-service planning role with the staff. Ideally the counsellor in the staffroom should be available and able to give information to any member of staff on any incipient social welfare problem. If he does not know the answer he should know where to find it and have the time to follow it up. On the other hand the counsellor also needs support and help and must recognize his limitations during counselling.

Comment

In working with parents and social workers as well as with staff and pupils, the counsellor has many different roles. Sometimes he is a communicator, sometimes an activating agent, sometimes a go-between, sometimes a public relations agent, sometimes a co-ordinator, sometimes a consultant. The counsellor has to learn to be flexible, to develop a good sense of timing, to wear two hats without becoming two-faced. Above all the counsellor has to remain genuine and loyal towards his client and to remember that, in many cases, involving other people may not only be unnecessary but also positively unhelpful or even harmful to his clients' best interests.

In most cases the counselling relationship is all the pupils want and all they need.

The counsellor's problem

During counsellor training it is not all that difficult to accept intellectually and academically the concepts and precepts of the counselling literature. Counselling practice, tape-recorded and properly supervised is certainly, like teaching practice, better than no practice at all. But, as any trained teacher knows, the difference between the cushioned leisure of teaching practice and the cut and thrust of a full timetable is enormous. In the counselling situation the contrast is even greater, partly because the job is more emotionally demanding than teaching and partly because the job itself is ill defined and arouses ambiguity and ambivalence on all sides. When the counsellor actually begins the job he really comes up against the problems of his own limitations. He may find that his actual behaviour is quite different from the behaviour his academic self would describe; for example he knows the sort of question he should not ask but he asks it because he is feeling insecure. Furthermore he may find himself a prey to strong feelings which may interfere with his professional competence: anger, jealousy, anxiety, self-doubts, hatred. He may become over-involved with one pupil, dependent on another; he may collude with one client, or he may be totally manipulated or deceived by another. It would be a very abnormal counsellor who did not succumb, at least in part, to these sorts of feeling and pressures. What is important is to recognize, not to deny, that these feelings exist, and to improve one's counselling techniques through coming to terms with them. For a counsellor to deny the emotional repercussions a counselling interview may cause within him may block any growth and development in his work and possibly indirectly in his client. To face and accept his limitations and to make the best of them, the counsellor needs help—systematic, structured and specific help.

The counsellor needs help particularly in his first probationary year at work. But it is important to note that the need for counselling supervision does not disappear as the counsellor becomes more experienced, though it will not be needed as much. Counsellors need to be supervised weekly, fortnightly or monthly, according to experience, by someone appointed for this specific purpose. Local authorities could arrange casework supervisions for groups of counsellors, for individual counsellors or for both; in some areas this is already done. There is bound to be debate as to whether this person should be employed as part of the psychological, welfare or education service, whether he should be a psychiatrist, educational psychologist or psychiatric social worker or a counsellor. No matter: what is important is that the counsellor's work should be supervised. In an area with very few counsellors this could be a part-time appointment; it could be undertaken—as indeed it is undertaken in some areas—by the staff of the child guidance clinics. To appoint supervisory personnel specifically for counsellors is not an extravagance but an essential. If counselling is worth doing, it is worth doing well; bad counselling may be worse than no counselling at all. All counsellors have potential for good or bad; without supervision they may do as much harm as good, which may not only be distressing to individuals, but also a waste of time and money.

References

1. *Report of the Committee on Maladjusted Children* the Underwood Report (1956) HMSO
2. Warnock Report (1981)
3. *Psychologists in Education Services* the Summerfield Report (1968) HMSO

Chapter 7

The counsellor as educator

In 1971 I changed jobs. I became deputy head of Thomas Calton School, London. My belief in the value of pupil counselling remained unchanged, but I recognized more and more the need for similar work to be done with parents, staff, community and syllabus. My conviction was, and is, that counselling, far from being a frill, is an integral part of the education process. The more this unity is recognized, the more effective will be the education we provide. The pastoral care system of a school is not separate from the organization and curriculum, but is expressed through it. There is little point in adding a counsellor to a school where the pastoral care system is poorly conceived and barely executed; it is no good devising a brilliant pastoral care system if this in itself is separate from and contradictory to the academic system. In education, we need to spend time looking at the *total* message conveyed by the institutions we create. If we do this, we will find that the basic principles underlying both the counselling and the educational process are very similar. If they are not, then we may well have problems.

In recent years, the importance of good 'pastoral care' has been increasingly recognized.[1] So far so good. But in some cases, the unfortunate corollary of this welcome development has been for 'pastoral care' to be tacked on to a system, rather than integrated with it. Delegation of responsibility to a senior member of staff seems a wise step: but how often does delegation become relegation? Unless there is unity between the teaching and caring aspects of a school, as expressed through the organization, then there may result an unhealthy 'splitting', rather as children sometimes split parents into the 'kind loving' one and the 'harsh rejecting' one. In this situation, not only is there the risk of children playing one side off against the other. One section of adults may, wittingly or no, undermine what the other section is about, with resulting confusion and deadlock. Elizabeth Richardson's work[2] analyses this split in terms of task/sentient groups. She makes the point most emphatically.

It is vital that the same principles of pastoral care permeate the whole system, not be regarded as some kind of 'extra' to please those teachers who like to play at nymphs and shepherds. 'Caring' will of course include setting limits, and not allowing pupils to do as they like when they like, but the motive will not be to control, or to make the school easier for the administrators to run. Rather the aim will be to provide sufficient security to stimulate growth. Pupils need structure but not stricture. They will soon tell you the difference.

Unless the academic and pastoral are integrated there is a risk that the system itself will negate, undo, confuse or make impossible the work of the 'pastoral care' department. By the system, I mean not simply the overall organization, but also the timetable, the syllabus and the approaches to learning. There is for example no greater dictator of pupils' or teachers' lives than the timetable. The timetable can *prevent* form 1 teachers being with their forms; they can *create* instability by moving pupils and staff round all the time; they can order our lives to the point where we can no longer exercise initiative. *Il faut manger pour vivre et non pas vivre pour manger.* The system is not there to make life easier for *itself*, but to serve the objectives of the school.

Underlying this discussion are several important counselling concepts, concepts which are in my view equally important to education: genuineness, trust and congruence. It is too easy in education to ignore the emotional implications of our intellectual decisions. In teaching we often fail to realize how many 'non-verbal' messages our institution will convey to its users. Nor do we always realize to what extent our users may be sensitive to contradictions between our stated objectives and what actually happens. For example a school may claim to like and respect its pupils, to value them, to wish to encourage their full development. Yet the organization of the school may spell out mistrust, the curriculum may stifle any active learning or any real growth and development in the individual, the relationships between staff and pupils may be based on fear or indifference, rather than love or commitment. We trust you; but we lock the doors between lessons. We value you; but we can't allow you to do anything for yourself in case you get it wrong. We want to prepare you for an adult role; in the meantime you must do as we say when we say it. We welcome parents; but only by appointment and preferably at our command.

This kind of *double entendre*, exaggerated as it may seem, is more common than most of us would admit. If the 'hidden curriculum' of the school belies its stated objectives, then the institution may appear not to be genuine. It may be difficult for pupils or parents to trust something which contradicts itself, yet trust is as fundamental to the learning process as it is to the counselling process.

If the discrepancy grows too great between what a school *thinks* it is doing for the pupils, what the pupils *feel* the school is doing, and what the pupils' actual needs are, then we have another counselling and educational malfunction: incongruence. If the administration is out of touch with the way pupils and their parents see the school, then misunderstanding and stalemate may ensue. In other words, for a school to function effectively there needs to be a large area of *congruence between pupils, parents, staff and community.*

Counselling and teaching

If we turn now to the teaching relationship itself, we find that at an expressive level, the basic requirements of an effective teaching relationship and an effective counselling relationship are one and the same: respect for each other, acceptance, trust, empathy, genuineness, non-possessive warmth and congruence. When we teach, we inevitably communicate our feelings about that class to the pupils, and vice versa. Any experienced teacher will know that if he is fed up with a certain class on a certain day, that class will immediately pick up these negative feelings and react accordingly. If we are frightened, our pupils become frightening; if we despise our pupils they become despicable; if we are not sure what we want from the lesson, our pupils will be confused and confusing; if we mean what we say, our pupils will take us seriously. In both a counselling and a teaching relationship (and indeed in relationships with colleagues and friends) we will inevitably communicate at a non-verbal level what we feel, whatever we say. Whatever their IQs, our pupils are not fools, neither are they easily fooled. If our message is false, then little learning will take place. Our pupils will not learn much unless there is trust between us, mutual respect, genuine caring, which will include not allowing ourselves to be duped, manipulated or unduly baited. In both teaching and counselling these are important factors.

Similarly the counselling process, which puts its emphasis on enabling an individual to face his own conflicts and problems for *himself* and to grow through them, is at one with the kind of teaching process where the pupil is enabled to learn for himself. Indeed, the trends in curriculum development and teaching methods which burgeoned in the early 70s seem more and more to confirm this unity. There is a growing tendency for 'personal development' to be included, either explicitly or implicitly in the curriculum.[3] Humanities projects, moral education, careers lessons, integrated studies, community education, thinking lessons, tutorial work, these all put the emphasis on helping the individual learn for himself.

They seek to give experience in taking responsibility for one's own actions, in making decisions; they aim to help individuals realize their potential and value their own experience and judgement. They should help to make pupils more self-aware, more confident, more sensitive to the needs of others, more able to choose a job when the time comes. As a result of these methods our pupils should be more articulate and questioning, active pursuers of learning rather than passive receivers of knowledge. For counselling and for teaching, the objectives are very similar indeed.

Counsellors and teachers

There are some tangible gains for teaching in schools where there are counsellors. Denis Lawrence's book[4] shows that in his school pupils who were counselled made substantially greater advances in reading than those who were not. Teachers have become more interested in the use of the small group as a teaching unit, particularly in mixed ability teaching.[5] In this the counsellor has experience and expertise to share, though it is vital that he himself can distinguish between group teaching, group discussion and group counselling.[6] It is inappropriate for a counsellor to indulge in some technique which he may have found beneficial in training but which may be inappropriate in the classroom situation.[7]

At all times the counsellor offers to the teacher a 'model' of behaviour: this in the sense of 'example' rather than perfect example. From this the teacher will learn indirectly, even unconsciously. In an article in *Trends in Education*[8] I have described in detail the kind of support and training a counsellor can provide for the teacher, making the significant point that the process is reciprocal and the counsellor will also learn from and be supported by the teacher.

Once a counsellor has established a position of being accepted and respected in the staffroom, he can then fulfil a more specific training role, by acting as group leader or consultant to various kinds of staff group, eg year or house teams, integrated studies teams, probationer staff or staff who are interested in developing further their counselling skills. None of this will work however unless the staff want his active support and unless he can define realistically what each group can and cannot do. He may be able to share with staff (and they with him) skills in interviewing, in writing letters to parents, writing reports for social workers, though most of what he teaches will be through practice rather than theory.

Like Leona Tyler[9] I define a counsellor as someone who spends his time counselling. It may be difficult for a counsellor to spend a major part of his time on in-service training of staff, but there will be by now many ex-counsellors taking a senior teacher role with a large training element. Such a person may fulfil an important role in helping staff work through their feelings about policy developments and innovations. Elizabeth Richardson's work[2] has highlighted the importance of the dynamics within and between staff groups in the implementation of policy decisions.

The welfare team

There are many ways in which a counsellor's work can develop. Is he to concentrate on counselling pupils, or group work with pupils, work with parents, or family casework, work with staff, work with other agencies, or work with the environment of learning? In an article on community schools[10] I made the point that 'In the community school, whilst we need maximum contact and co-operation between the various workers serving that school, and a shared philosophy, we still need specialists and specialist skills. It is unrealistic for every worker to do everything. It is important to build a team.' Within the school the team must include a senior member of staff if the work is to remain integrated with the work of the school as a whole. In the second part of this chapter I shall describe how I took on such a role, as deputy head, no longer counselling but working with the environment of learning and leading a team which included a counsellor and a social worker.

Authority, role diffusion and boundaries: some dangers

Counselling and teaching methods are much intertwined: so in teaching the terms of 'non-directive', 'non-authoritarian', 'child-centred' are much in vogue, and sometimes used inappropriately. The skill in teaching and counselling is knowing *when* and *how* to be *what*! These concepts *rigidly* applied can make a nonsense, and more so in teaching than in counselling. A completely non-directive approach in the classroom can leave pupils totally baffled. A teacher has authority whether he likes it or not: he does not have to use it in an authoritarian fashion; when he has it but does not recognize it or use it, he leaves his pupils in the air. A teacher also has expertise, experience and knowledge: yet he appears at times to try to do anything but actually teach. He is a friend, social worker, confidant, enabler, facilitator, but not a teacher. Do our children really feel so put down if we put our knowledge and experience at their disposal? Do they really want our roles to be so blurred and confused? Ethel Venables's study of teachers and youth workers shows this is not so.[11]

Further there has come into play what I call the 'law of diminishing expectations'—'He can't help it, he's only a child', 'It isn't her fault, her family's got problems', 'Officer Krupke I'm really a slob' as the song in *West Side Story* puts it. This I see as a way of handicapping further the have nots, for he who expecteth nothing shall not be disappointed. Children are adept at playing up their weaknesses. Rewarded for this skill they only become weaker.

There is considerable evidence that young people thrive neither in authoritarian nor in *laissez-faire* climates.[12] Neither *extreme* is helpful to their development. To achieve a genuinely responsible atmosphere in which young people may grow, adults must neither dictate, nor simply leave young people to get on with it. They must provide support and an adult model which can be accepted, modified or rejected as appropriate. Adults cannot do this if they themselves are pretending to be adolescents. John Bazalgette sums this up very clearly in the conclusion to his book *Freedom, Authority and the Young Adult*.[13]

By 1972 I was sufficiently disturbed by this lack of adult leadership to add a note of warning. 'Some of the most distressed girls I saw as counsellor were those whose parents or teachers set no limits at all.'[14] For the adolescent in search of an identity, this kind of freedom can be paralysing, paralysing because the adolescent cannot grow in such insecurity, only search wildly for someone to show concern, for someone to assert an adult identity against which they can measure themselves.

The net result of this 'permissiveness' in adults was to push anyone in a counselling role into a position where they were under pressure to do what other adults were failing to do. This I regarded as a curious and undesirable role reversal. I am not saying that the counsellor should never set limits: he will do so, consciously and unconsciously, simply by his adult presence. But he cannot function if this becomes his main responsibility, for this is not his prime task. In 1971 I summarized the kinds of problems current at that time.[8] I found more and more that my role was to help individuals express the terrifying 'freedom' they were exercising, and to help them get sufficient confidence to tell their parents how they felt. It amazed me that so many parents failed to see what was happening under their eyes. I could only assume that they really didn't want to know, partly because they didn't know what to do.

Theory into practice

Much of what I have said so far is reflected in the work I went on to do as deputy head. In my new position, I quickly discovered what I had already suspected, that I could not effectively combine the roles of deputy head and counsellor, though there was inevitably a counselling component in my work. In this I differ from Alick Holden[15] who claims to combine successfully the roles of deputy head, counsellor and teacher. My job as deputy head was not to do the counselling, but to see that it was done; to support those who were doing it; to ensure as great a harmony as possible between the academic and the pastoral. My principal clients were the staff, not the pupils or their parents. My methods had to be more direct, even directive. My skills were still there (and very useful in interviewing) but I had no unpressurized time at my disposal. The only individual pupils I attempted to counsel were those referred to me by counselling staff, usually at a remedial rather than a preventive stage. In other words, I was a prey to the usual pressures which beset a teaching member of the hierarchy: pressures of role, of time, and of organization.

Integration of pastoral and academic

Fortunately the head and staff had already perceived the need for integration of academic and pastoral: this is reflected through a timetable which favoured block timetabling, and the teaching of most children in their own form rooms and in form groups. It was particularly reflected in the integrated studies programme for the first and second years, and the community education programme for the fourth years. The teachers themselves were well supported through the team teaching methods used.

Through integrated studies, the first and second year teachers spent two and a half days a week teaching their own forms, thus ensuring continuity of care, security of tenure and stability of relationships. Contact with parents was particularly encouraged through report days: reports were not sent home but handed over personally and discussed by form teachers, who were able to talk confidently both about academic progress and personal development. The teaching methods used were designed to encourage initiative, decision-making, and the taking of responsibility by individual pupils. The community education programme, a whole morning a week for all fourth years, was designed specifically to help prepare the pupils for their adult role. None of these innovations was easy to put into practice: indeed a school based training programme to evaluate the integrated studies teaching was set up. But the fundamental philosophy recognized the link between the form teacher's pastoral and academic role, a link which primary schools have long since fully exploited.

Preventive work in lower school

The counselling/welfare team itself was built up over a period of three and a half years. It began with the appointment of a teacher/social worker in lower school. Her job was divided into three parts: to teach, to work with parents and to support staff, particularly heads of year. Her brief did not include counselling as such. The pupils in this school, and their parents, needed a great deal of practical help and encouragement. The counselling orientation was there, but the approach was largely action orientated, bridging the gap between home and school, between home, school and social welfare agencies, reinforcing and encouraging attendance, pressing, where necessary and when parents wished, for financial help or even rehousing. Until these practical fundamentals were dealt with, counselling for these particular pupils seemed inappropriate, particularly since on the whole they were pupils who act out rather than internalize their problems.

Our next step was to undertake systematic screening of the first year intake, with a group reading/comprehension test, a maths test, a non-verbal reasoning test and finally a social adjustment scale filled in by the form teacher. The tests were done towards the end of the first term, after the children had settled in. The aim was to help us ascertain which individuals needed extra help and of what kind. The most valuable part of the testing programme was not so much the actual statistical scores (though occasionally interesting discrepancies of score and opinion arose) as the discussion between the form teacher, the social worker and myself which, though ostensibly about the pupil, did a great deal to develop and encourage the staff concerned. It also helped to counteract the crude labelling and stereotyping which might have come from a study of figures without facts. The next move was to decide upon strategies for helping each child in need. Not every child who appeared from these tests to be 'at risk' could be referred to the child guidance clinic nor did they need to be. Those children categorized as 'antisocial' rather than neurotic often responded well to firmer handling. Our educational psychologist was always ready to discuss individuals and advise on action where appropriate.

Alternative provision in lower school

After we did this research (and probably before it!) it was clear that there were some children who needed more help in the teaching situation than could be offered by the mixed ability form unit. Remedial teaching was already done by withdrawal of small groups (*not* by having a remedial stream). But some of the children's problems were not remedial so much as behavioural and psychological. A few of these children already went out of school for 'tutorial' classes, on certain sessions each week. We decided to start our own school based tutorial unit as well, hoping thus that it would be easier to keep pupils integrated with the main stream; and that we should thereby help more of the children needing special help: a kind of Warnock approach ahead of its time.[16] It took a long time for the staff as a whole to agree that this was needed and even longer to find the right teacher, capable of drawing up a frame of reference.

Included in our thinking was the concept of the 'nurture group' which was an idea developed in primary schools at that time. The theory was that some children needed 'nurturing' before they were ready to begin learning effectively; this nurturing would include feeding, playing with sand and water, learning, through adults, internal controls and strategies for coping. Many of the children at the secondary stage were as much in need of this fundamental 'family group' experience. The aim of the unit was not to separate the child from his peers, but rather to help him to integrate better with them and to benefit from the education provided. There were 10 sessions a week with children attending for a minimum of two sessions and a maximum of five. Entry and exit procedures had to be carefully monitored. But the unit (fundamentally a 'teaching' unit) did something which was *not* counselling yet which was more appropriate to the needs of those children.

The appointment of counsellors

The success of the teacher/social worker in lower school eventually created a demand for a similar worker in upper school. We were well served by the social services and had an education welfare officer who worked exclusively for our school. Nevertheless we found having our own worker so beneficial, specially in terms of work with parents, that staff were unanimous in creating yet another scale post from the teaching quota. For upper school, we deliberately chose someone more counselling-orientated, who was also capable of undertaking family casework and careers guidance where appropriate. Shortly after her arrival we also found a part-time counsellor for lower school, since by this time staff accepted the need for counselling as well as all the other provision. She worked mainly with third years on the model I had used previously.

Next there came in upper school a demand for another special unit. This we called a 'compensatory unit', or C group, but its function was mainly to provide a home base for childen who could not cope with the more academic rigours of upper school. All pupils were encouraged to attend their options, but some frankly could not cope with them, and needed a secure base from which to set off when they felt stronger. Truants returning, particularly those who were school phobic, also found this group a welcoming place to gain confidence to return fully. Disruptive and unmanageable pupils seemed to divide into two types—those who behaved badly because they would not do the work, and those who just behaved badly. Only the first kind were given refuge. The others were dealt with in the usual manner.

The welfare team

By the time the special unit was set up in upper school, the welfare department had grown enormously, with myself acting in effect as head of department. The link with the remedial department was very close. By then we had two full-time teacher/social workers, one part-time counsellor, one teacher in charge of the tutorial unit (lower school) and one in charge of the compensatory unit upper school. All of us worked closely with heads of years, their deputies and form teachers, also with the educational psychologist, education welfare officer and social workers in our area.

Group work for staff: in-service training

Our sense of identity was greatly increased by another notable development. Through links we already had with a nearby psychiatric teaching hospital, we were able to establish a monthly 'group discussion' for staff. This group went on for some two years, meeting each month. The dividend was not obvious immediately, but gradually we realized that, though the group itself did not take any action, we were able to ventilate our feelings in the group, to begin to say what we really thought, to trust each other because we were more honest with each other, and to take action outside the group.

The group was always 'open'. Initially a wide range of staff came, including some heads of years. Gradually the group consolidated into simply those staff directly concerned with social welfare, counselling and remedial work. Although it was not our original purpose to form a group for these particular staff, it was nevertheless just what we needed to supplement our more action-orientated departmental meetings.

We had foreseen the original purpose of the group as being to work on the school environment of the child. We were working on the theory that it was not enough to counsel the child, or the child and his parents. We had to look hard too at what the school was doing. We had no doubt that schools exacerbate, consciously or unconsciously, many of the problems about which they complain so loudly. We did not imagine that our school would be any exception. Some of these problems come from organization, some from curriculum, some from the kind of corporate ethos which grows up in a school, some from staff's own particular personality problems; all this apart from what the child is like. In any school, all these aspects need looking at, however painful the process may be. Our group did not purport to do away with the problems miraculously, but it did increase our understanding of them. Sometimes organizational changes could be made, sometimes we realized that our fears were just fantasies, feeding our own insecurities.

We could not have run this group ourselves. I was a participant member. The group was led by a psychiatrist, who brought with him a psychiatric social worker, a clinical psychologist (all from the children's department of our nearest hospital), together with our own educational psychologist.

Support from the psychiatric services

Through our increasing link with the hospital we not only took part in various pieces of research, thus getting additional preventive help for our pupils, but also got support for our counselling staff, a 'hot line' for emergency cases. A further development was a weekly group for adolescents held in upper school, and run jointly by a psychiatrist from the hospital and our teacher/social worker. For some time we had the idea of establishing a group for deviants or for phobics. Neither came to fruition since the deviants deviated and the phobics never came! This group was carefully selected to make a balance between extroverts/introverts, conformists/non-conformists, fearless/fearful. From all accounts it went very explosively and certainly needed the expertise of the psychiatrist.

The in-service training role of the deputy head

It is clear from what I have said that much of my time as deputy was taken up in supporting the developments I have so far described. But my brief as deputy was not simply to be 'head of guidance and welfare'; apart from the usual administrative and teaching duties which befall a deputy, I also had specific responsibility for students and probationers. In this role I used my experience as a counsellor as much as my experience as a teacher.

Students and probationers

For students I ran a weekly discussion group and gave occasional individual help to supplement the work of heads of department if necessary. Social work or counselling students had a regular individual supervision period either from myself or one of the teacher/social workers. I wondered whether *non*-social work students receive generally as much support? In many cases we do not make time for this in school, yet teaching students need as much if not more help.

For probationers I ran a special induction programme, which lasted three days and was followed by regular fortnightly working lunch hour meetings. I was an official probationer tutor for the area I served which meant I could offer further courses through the nearby teachers' centre. These included 'role play' and invaluable visits to primary schools. I often felt in individual discussion with probationers that they were reluctant to reveal their difficulties to me— the 'judgemental' role of the deputy was not to be escaped. Because of this, I appointed a more junior member of staff to act as a less formidable father confessor. But his job was impossible for a different reason, not so much because of role, but time. In other words, looking after probationers is a *proper* job and needs time allocated to it. It must be added that on the whole staff, like adolescents, get a great deal of help from their own peer group and not from the person officially labelled 'probationer tutor' or 'counsellor'. But this does not mean that there is no need for either of the latter! My own support as a probationer tutor came from the monthly lunch with the other tutors in the area, most of whom were primary head teachers. Not only was I sustained by this group but I was able to start a two-way process of communication between our school and the primary school feeding it. This process was ostensibly at a factual level but in fact was to do with the building of trust, mutual respect and genuine co-operation.

Links with nearby schools

I was fortunate in having an existing link with yet another group of primary heads in the area. Within this group we planned and executed various in-service training activities, including two residential weekends. The inter-mingling of staff from various schools was always productive. But the most interesting of the activities we undertook was a further weekend run on our behalf by the Grubb Institute. Our aim was to study 'schools in their communities'. Seven schools participated, two secondary and five primary. Each secondary school sent seven representatives and each primary five. To record what happened would take another book! But as a result of this weekend, the amount of genuine co-operation between neighbouring schools increased enormously. The staff group who attended became revitalized and saw much more clearly where best to put their energy. There was set up between ourselves and our nearest feeder junior and infants school a monthly working lunch. For each meeting a different topic was taken, such as reading, integrated studies, transition from primary to secondary. Apart from the heads and myself, different staff were invited each time, a maximum of two per school. The plan was that a network of interrelationships between schools would be built up between those staff most intimately concerned with each topic. We planned eventually to do the same kind of work with other neighbourhood schools. With our neighbouring secondary school, we began an exchange and sharing of staff and facilities which seem so obvious now, yet would never have happened without the shared experience of the weekend.

Counselling and administration

It is interesting to note that all the developments which took place while I was deputy head were the result of teamwork, consensus and co-operation. They came with staff agreement, sometimes in fact at their request. This in itself is a counselling approach to management. My aim was, as in counselling, to give staff sufficient support for them to activate and use their own resources; not to 'take over' the work myself but rather to build strength in others, and to build a team. It was a difficult role with few immediate satisfactions. Yet after three and a half years it began to fall into place. The welfare team emerged strong and confident; one social worker began to organize her own weekly working lunch, the other undertook student supervision and intensive group work. The staff as a whole no longer sniped surreptitiously at the 'fancy work' done by the new team members. Heads of year began to be less threatened by new personnel and vice versa. Each member of the team began to work more effectively, each fulfilling his specific role, but in harmony with the others.

Like any system, this one was far from perfect and continued to develop and evolve according to changes in needs. There were some incipient dangers, notably that of beginning to function more like a social welfare agency than a school. The prime function of a school is to educate, not to take over the functions of other agencies; to get other agencies to do their job, not to take on all the failures of other agencies. The social welfare agencies in the school are there to *back up* the academic aims, to enable the pupils to benefit from the education provided. We include in the education provided the development of the total individual, but in doing this we must not neglect his academic development. We have had to draw firm boundaries. Our reputation in the neighbourhood for dealing miraculously with impossible children meant that we were constantly asked to take children that no one else could, apparently, deal with. We did not believe this to be so, nor did we feel it healthy that we should do so. This was like being the counsellor who must take on everything himself. Our first duty was to the children we had, many of whom need more help than we can ever provide.

The message is clear. Schools must not expect to perform miracles, but we must never give up trying. The more clearly we understand the *limits* of the job we are supposed to be doing, the more we understand and work at the irrational as well as the rational aspects of our task, the more likely we are to succeed. In this section I have talked as much about education as about counselling. I have not been trying to make too many claims for counselling. Understanding of counselling principles can enhance the educational work of the school but it is not a substitute for education. The best of our teachers will instinctively incorporate counselling principles into their teaching. The best of our counsellors will instinctively contribute to a particular kind of learning. Yet the two jobs are different. It is only by understanding in which ways they are the same and in which ways they are different that each will be able to do his job properly.

A counselling approach to headship

At this point I left Thomas Calton to become the Head of Vauxhall Manor School, Lambeth, London. I took with me and developed further many of the ideas and structures we had established at this school. Vauxhall Manor was fertile ground for much of this work. My article from *Concern:* **20**[17] sums up what happened there:

The single-parent child in the inner-city school

How can a school compensate for an unstable home background, and provide the essential support to a child from a one-parent family, without at the same time 'labelling' and stigmatising? Vauxhall Manor, a girls' comprehensive school in South London, has organized its structure to meet this challenge.

Imagine a typical inner-city school: nineteenth century buildings, holding out bastion-like in a visibly crumbling area, gradually losing its indigenous population to the outer-city ring or beyond, taking under its wing a more immigrant population, a complex mix of nationalities, customs and creeds, serving a populace which scores above average on any statistician's index of social deprivation. This is a pattern we see in any large inner-city conurbation. The problem for those of us who work in schools in such areas, is to recognize and cater for the nature of our intake without pandering to its problems, without labelling and without lowering our expectations: blessed is he who expecteth nothing for he shall not be disappointed. At Vauxhall Manor we do not single out

161

one-parent pupils for special attention: we accept the one-parent family as a feature of society which is normal in some cultures (eg West Indian) and increasingly normal in Britain as a whole, with one in five marriages ending in divorce and a growing acceptance of unmarried motherhood by society. We also recognize that two-parent pupils can be deprived and stressed, as indeed can pupils from affluent homes. We notice that many pupils cope admirably with seemingly 'difficult' home circumstances, developing tremendous qualities of character and practical skills. So we do not label, either by background or by ability. We teach our pupils in mixed ability classes and we expect them to do their best.

All our pupils need to feel loved, valued and respected; they also need to work within a secure framework, a structure rather than a stricture, which gives them sufficient freedom to be able to develop their own particular strengths and talents. In seeking to provide this, we clearly supplement and complement their home lives. We make special efforts to help new pupils settle into the school and to identify with it to help them get maximum benefit from the education provided. We try to do this in a number of ways.

Easing the transition from primary to secondary school
We recognize that the transition from primary to secondary school can come as a rude shock to any pupil, insecure or otherwise: a crisis point which merits extra attention. So we have appointed a teacher in charge of 'primary links', who works closely with neighbouring primary schools, arranging for both pupils and teachers two-way visits, shared projects and even joint lessons. As a result, communication, interaction and understanding between us and our neighbours have greatly improved. More importantly, many of our new 11-year-old pupils already know the school and some of its teachers before they come; further, their primary teachers are able to be more reassuring and confident about the transfer because they, too, have a clearer idea of what we are about.

Continuity and stability in teacher/pupil relationships
Most junior schools work on a system in which the pupils spend the greater part of their day in their own classroom, taught a variety of subjects by their own teacher: a strong feeling of 'home' can build up in the classroom. On transfer to secondary school, the pupil may have suddenly to adjust to a number of different teachers, and changes of subject/classroom and teacher at regular intervals: a kind of musical chairs dictated by the tyranny of the bell. We have tried to cut down this movement. As far as possible 'first years' (ie 11-year-olds) are taught in their own form room for several subjects, if possible by their own form teacher. It is therefore easier for them to take a pride in their form rooms—in which they may be for up to half the week—and to put their work and pictures on display.

We also offer double lessons (1 hour 10 minutes) or even 'halfdays' with the same teacher when the subject allows. All this has done a great deal to help the pupils feel more secure and to develop in their work in greater depth. We give the 'first years' special priority in this, but throughout the lower school the basic teaching unit is the form; thus girls are not constantly having to readjust to a new peer group. Continuity of subject teacher is given priority where possible, so that at the beginning of the academic year the class does not waste time and energy readjusting to a new teacher. The 'heads of year' who are responsible for the 240 pupils in each school year move up with their pupils for several years so that they can build up their knowledge of the girls and their families. All this is designed not only to increase learning opportunities, but to give pupils consistency in their relationships with adults and continuity of care. This is always important, but particularly so if pupils lack this at home.

Curriculum and teaching methods

Our teaching methods, based on mixed ability classes, use the small group within the classroom situation, as a further way of integrating academic and pastoral objectives, and developing the total resources of the pupil. The groups provide opportunites for learning how to co-operate, how to share, how to help others, how to solve a group task, how to take and share leadership and responsibility, how to discuss and reach a group decision. We aim to give the pupils as much responsibility as possible for the management of their own learning, either in groups or as individuals. We teach them where to find out, how to study, evaluate, assess, organize, and make decisions or judgements. We do not always succeed, but our methods do help to increase their self-confidence and resourcefulness.

Preventive work

We recognize that though teachers can do a great deal to help pupils 'at risk' by the way they teach, by providing a 'model' of adult behaviour, by listening to and supporting the pupil, there is a need for specialist help to be brought in at the earliest opportunity if an effective *preventive* (rather than remedial) service is to be provided. Attached to the first year (age 11-12) we have a school-based social worker seconded full-time from social services, working closely with the head of year, form tutor and education welfare officer. For the rest of the school, we have appointed our own part-time counsellor and social worker. Not only are the pupils helped directly through these services, but the teachers too can get 'instant' advice and support. Teachers are less tempted to get out of role, yet their skills are not lost, rather enhanced. The boundaries between the professions are not blurred, yet the amount of direct help to the pupil is increased, and referrals to specialists can be made early enough to be effective. We also have two 'compensatory' units, one in lower school to help pupils with learning difficulties, particularly immigrants needing extra help with English; the other in upper school to provide a secure base for truants returning who need a 'half-way house' between home and school, or for pupils going through a particularly unsettled phase. Both these are organized on a sessional basis with the aim of getting the pupil back into normal lessons as soon as possible. Our provision here is minimal, and on-site because we believe that to proliferate off-site centres eventually undermines the main stream work of the school. All this extra provision of support *in school* has required back up from extra secretarial staff and extra interviewing rooms, made from converting under-used cloakrooms. The counselling and social work services are already working to full capacity. The benefit to the pupils is obvious.

Enriched facilities

Luckily the school has recently been redecorated and refurnished; we have more wall displays, and a garden; the girls have also started to paint the walls with murals. But what about that arid time of day between school and when parents come in from work? We have set up an 'End-on Club' which meets three evenings a week from 3.30—5.30 pm. in lower school. This provides a wide range of educational and recreational activities from drama to gymnastics; attendance is voluntary and the club is well supported.

Many of our pupils have never been away from their parents for a holiday, some have never travelled much, not even in London. We build in to our normal lessons a full programme of visits, excursions and school journeys; the half-day session is particularly useful for this. Visiting a museum or gallery not only expands intellectual horizons, it also gives the girls the confidence to go again, or to try others. We now as a matter of policy offer all first years a full week's residential course, for which they obtain a grant if necessary. Half this year's first year accepted the invitation; the other half were given a special week's programme of outings and excursions based on London.

Increasing contacts with parents

We make a great deal of effort to get to know whoever is responsible for our pupils at home, because we know how important it is to get maximum co-operation, understanding and support between home and school. In junior schools, parents have easy access to the class teacher. In secondary schools it can be more difficult for parents to gain informal access. We try to get round this by offering an interview before the pupils come, by making it clear that parents are welcome at any time and particularly by our system of giving out reports: we do not send out reports, but instead invite parents up to read and discuss what the teachers have said.

In lower school some 80 per cent of parents come up. The benefits of this are enormous. It is too easy for parents to be sent for only when their children are in trouble. This method provides an opportunity for a positive interchange. When parents come, particularly parents on their own, they often confide in us their own personal difficulties. We listen and then put them in touch with the agency that can most help them. Our social work staff follow-up this liaison work. When a girl seems to be unsettled and disturbed, we ask the parents to come up, as early as possible. We find our parents relieved to know that we care, and that we will not tolerate antisocial behaviour. Together we discuss what best might be done to help the pupil benefit from her education.

A small minority of our girls are absent from school, sometimes permanently. We do what we can, through the education welfare and social services, to get these girls into school. Sometimes they are away because they are needed to look after a sick parent or child. Sometimes they are chronically ill. Sometimes they are overdependent on their parents and cannot leave home and sometimes they are just bored or antisocial and do not like school. The attendance in our lower school, particularly in the first year, has improved greatly since we set in motion the measures I have outlined. This gives great hope for what schools *can* do, though some pupils will never come *whatever* the school is like.

In the last few years many schools have felt overwhelmed by the social problems surrounding them. It is easy in these circumstances either to give up teaching and concentrate on trying to solve social problems—in fact, to become a kind of social work agency—or alternatively to cling Canute-like to teaching methods and standards which worked in the past but do not work now. It is clear to us at Vauxhall Manor that we have to be sensitive and adapt to the changing needs of our pupils, but that the best way of helping them is to do the very best job we can as a *school*.

However, we became more and more aware that we had *too* much of a social problem approach to our work, and that in spite of everything there was still a split between the pastoral and the academic. At Easter 1979 I delivered the following paper to the staff at a staff meeting.

Pastoral care: myth, mystique, mistake or misunderstanding?

For some time now I have wanted to say something about pastoral care: the way the concept has developed and been interpreted has been causing me—and many of you, I know—great concern. I mean, specifically the splitting that has been going on, not just in this school, but nationwide between the pastoral and the academic. I'd like to elaborate my thoughts which reflect what I see and hear; and I'd like to check out whether this analysis makes sense to you.

I never have liked the term pastoral care. To me it smacks of nymphs and shepherds, Fragonard and Watteau, noble idylls while the peasants are revolting; it smacks of sheep following blindly, being herded; it smacks of do-goodery, missionary deeds among the less-fortunate-than-ourselves; it smacks of smother-love, rather than mother-love. It doesn't have to be any of these things, and very often it isn't, but sometimes this is how it turns out, particularly when it becomes a *separate* thing in its own right.

To be honest, I don't altogether like the term academic either, which has equal limitations: it smacks of the grammar school, pre-1870 tradition, elitism, graduate staff, intellectual pretension, exam snobbery and cramming. Again it doesn't *have* to be any of these and neither do these terms *have* to be negative or judgemental. Nevertheless it is an *inappropriate* term to polarize against 'pastoral'. Both words beg questions and they beg the *wrong* questions. We need to change the questions and the vocabulary.

Before I attempt this, I'd like to sketch out briefly how it seems to me that we got into this state of affairs. In the last 15 years or so there has been a tremendous boom in the pastoral care industry: this boom, with its attendant creation of pastoral care posts of responsibility, has made the 'academic' side of the staff and the 'academic' hierarchy feel put out and devalued. David Hargreaves even goes so far as to say that these two ladders reflect the historical split in the teaching profession between the 'sec mod' and the 'grammar', the teacher of pupils and the teacher of subjects. Really I don't think that applies here, but I see what he means.

The original reasons for setting up, making specific and institutionalizing pastoral care systems were extremely positive and responded to a real need. When we teach it is nonsense to ignore the emotional needs or the developmental stage of our pupils, it is nonsense to teach *at* people, it is nonsense to ignore the child's background circumstances if they are having a devastating effect on him. This is of course a caricature, yet with enough truth in it for us to recognize that at the time some 15 to 20 years ago, there was a balance to be redressed. But alas, the pendulum swung so far, and what began as compensatory became overcompensatory, what started as loving became suffocating, what started as helping and strengthening became weakening: instead of promoting healthy growth and independence it began to stunt growth and promote an unhealthy kind of overdependence. Again, a caricature and an injustice to many: but with enough recognizable truth.

Even more devastating, the influence of the pastoral 'caring' spread to the (separate concept of) 'learning'. And so there seems to have developed the 'do-it-for-you' rather than the 'do-it-yourself' syndrome, epitomized by the ubiquitous worksheet, so often pathetically thin and undemanding even on those occasions when it was well reproduced. Further to this already unchallenging situation, we have to add socio-economic-psychological excuse making: 'Officer Krupke I'm really a slob'. O.K. so you can't help it. We can't expect anything. It's all predestined, give up. Fortunately Rutter's key work on secondary schools and their effects on children (*15 Thousand Hours*[18], available Open Books, copies for staff available) has shown that this is just not true. Schools really do make a difference to what happens to pupils. Schools with pupils of comparable backgrounds have completely different effects on the pupils: in other words the *ethos* of a particular school and the nature of the educational process in that school *will* change a pupil's life. I find that message challenging and hopeful.

However we are still left with a split which is reflected in most schools in dual academic and pastoral systems epitomized by the way the points are allocated. When a teacher applies for a post, especially a scale post, he is usually by implication being asked to declare himself either 'academic' or 'pastoral'. There's an implied assumption: are you about social learning or about intellectual learning?—as if the two were incompatible goals. And mixed ability teaching which clearly has as part of its original rationale a desire *not* to split learning in this way, often in practice appears to put *social* goals before *intellectual* goals. When this happens it too is unwittingly subscribing to this often consciously unacknowledged chasm in aims and objectives.

When we look at the Scale 1 teacher who is also a form teacher and so hasn't been forced to declare his hand upon entry, we often see even here a terrible conflict within the same person. The same teacher can be seen to behave quite differently according to whether he is in his form teacher role or his subject teacher role. 'I will not have this pupil in my class,' he says as subject teacher. 'How can you reject this pupil who has so many problems and needs', he says as form teacher. It's one aspect of teacher stress: a kind of 'pastoracademic schizophrenia'.

When we look at the form teacher—who is still in my opinion the most important teacher for the individual pupil—we find him simultaneously asking for *more* time with his form, then not sure what to do with it and asking for *less* time. We find him wanting to get to know his pupils 'individually', but realistically not able to do this, and indeed very unsure *how* to do it, or what to do if he did! We find the form teacher able perhaps to make a series of relationships with particular individuals or even particular groups (within the class) but often unable to work with the class as *a whole* except in a rather negative, nagging, punitive way. It seems to me that when this happens it is because he is holding back from his teaching/learning role as form teacher and only trying either to 'care' or to 'shepherd'. On the other hand the subject teacher is trying to 'teach' so he doesn't necessarily see himself as an 'instrument of pastoral care', neither does he always realize to what extent the pupils model their behaviour on his. And on the whole few of us look very hard at the general overall messages given out by us as a staff in for example between lessons, lunch and break behaviour, corridors etc.

So how do schools get out of this syndrome? I've already indicated that I think this is a nationwide disease and in many ways this school is not as deeply into it as some, partly because of mixed ability teaching and partly because we've always prided ourselves on our *general* tone, quality of relationships, and we've always *said* we *don't* support the split. But I know a lot of you are conscious that it exists to some extent, and when I examine carefully various statements of policy and role definition I see the split unconsciously accepted in a way I cannot now condone. For example, the definition of the role of the head of year says 'to support the academic function', 'to see that girls are in a fit state to learn', as if the head of year were simply a snapper up of unconsidered trifles, a picker up of the pieces so that the class teacher can 'get on'. For example, the constant tension about whether the problem in the lesson is a head of department problem or a head of year problem, with a great deal of passing the parcel going on. And for example in the question of assessment, which, is seen as an 'academic matter', with unconsciously a revealing split, and a missing link with the form teacher. And the pupil is hardly let in on this at all.

So we need to stop and reconceptualize the whole thing. The whole thing is based on a mistaken assumption. It isn't a question of either/or, nor even a question of both. Everything is total—neither academic nor pastoral but much more than that, and certainly much more than the mechanical sum of the parts. We are really talking about whole school behaviour, whole staff, whole pupils, whole people.

So how did we get to this point?
Stage 1. To recap—in the beginning school was about academic learning to which you added a bit of pastoral care if necessary:

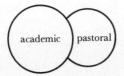

Stage 2. Then social learning became recognized as very important, a kind of implied final goal, for which academic learning was a means:

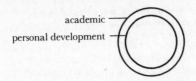

Not all schools have been through Stage 2—some are still in Stage 1
Stage 3. *Total learning process*
I am postulating that we are really talking about something like this.

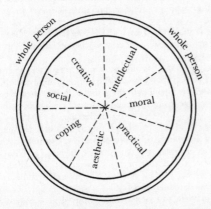

No doubt we could argue about the categories I have outlined, but the point I am trying to make is:
a)   the process is a total one, and much more complex than academic/pastoral
b)   all the parts are interdependent
c)   all the parts are being worked on at once whether we want them to be or not
So in the subject lesson the pupil is learning social skills as well as the subject—but he is also learning everything else as well; he is learning from the content of the lesson but most of all from the *total process* within the classroom. So the class teacher is not only teaching his subject but also study skills, decision making, coping skills etc.
In the form room it also follows that the form teacher's role is not confined to loving or disciplining, he is part of the total learning process. Once we internalize

this concept the form teacher is liberated to take a more specific teaching role, eg study skills, making sense of what is happening, moral education, decision making, even teaching a subject like 'health education'. And indeed we've already had considerable discussion about all this in this school.

So if we return to a basic question about what school is for, the answer is that it is about learning. The *purpose* of school is *not* 'to be a caring community' though we would hope to be one. The *purpose* of school is not 'to love the pupils' in the sense of being all forgiving and all embracing, though we would hope to love them and not be afraid to be angry and sometimes set limits as part of that love. The *purpose* of school is not to see each pupil as an *individual* with problems we have to solve for him, nor as solely a member of a peer group which may be more of a prison than a support or stimulus. We need somehow to see the pupils more flexibly, not trapped in an individual, group, or even a class, stereotype. And we need to look at the total process not just the separate bits.

As far as the methods go, I am certain that the process at present is often too undemanding of the pupil's energy. This happens when the teacher does all the work for the pupil; when the teacher rushes round all the time handing out things, when the teacher pleads for co-operation, waits on the pupil hand and foot: in short when the teacher behaves like a slave, the pupil becomes a bored tyrant. When the teacher is slave, the teacher also becomes stressed and exhausted.

Nobody originally meant the teacher to be a slave and when it happens it is part of the reaction against the other extreme, the teacher as tyrant. But it is also part of a well-meant but often misplaced desire on the part of the teacher to stop the pupil from facing problems or having difficulties—a desire to smooth his path so that he can learn more easily. Yet it is precisely the challenge of learning to cope with transitions, with problems, with changes and with difficulties that our pupils need if they are to cope with life after school and indeed if they are going to cope with school itself.

Engaging actively with the learning process includes learning gradually, step by step, how to take responsibility for oneself. Concentrating on pupil comfort, at teacher expense, does not really help the pupil, it merely stresses the teachers.

A lot of our strain comes from our desire to protect the pupils, eg the question of assessment. But maybe they'd feel better (and so would we) if they knew where they stood. In a way this is a part of respecting and valuing the pupils, in being genuine, accepting and emphatic. Honesty doesn't have to be destructive; half truth can be. Besides pupils are not fools nor are they easily fooled. Further, the pupils infinitely prefer it, and learn more if we are able to take adult roles and use our authority. And especially if we can be secure enough to recognize our pupils' adulthood as well as their childishness.

In this paper I am trying to articulate something which is not altogether clear, but which is emerging from within us. I regard this year as a very important year for the school: there is less overt change, but a lot of growth and development in us as a staff. I feel the energy of the whole staff coming together in a more coherent and constructive way. I feel an atmosphere of trust, of openness, and a corporate moving forward which is quite profound. I hope we can continue to share our experiences and keep working on this issue. If we can really break through, then we shall really be doing something significant towards meeting the real needs of the adolescent age group in transition to adulthood.

The ideas were not mine exclusively—I saw it as part of the role of the head to speak for the staff as a whole, ie to gather up feelings and ideas, to assess them within the context of reality and to try to integrate them and restate them in a meaningful way. It seems to me that after a few years of unease it was about 1978-9 that we stopped talking about pastoral care and social problems and moved our attention to the curriculum of the school. By curriculum we meant everything that happened to a pupil in the school. We began by looking at the careers programme.

In Lambeth we were in an area of high unemployment and falling rolls: because we were on the edge of the precipice, we began to work on some issues earlier than many other schools. So, the question of the transition from school to work was one which we took up specifically from 1977. We had found that in the fifth year pupils' main difficulties in getting work stemmed from their inability to fill in an application form adequately, to make the best of the qualities and experience they had and to interview well. Thus we began in the Summer term of the fourth year a programme of mock interviews with the staff of Oval House, a nearby voluntary community agency. We had done a certain amount of practice with letter writing, form filling and interviewing skills in normal lessons, particularly in English. However, we found that our pupils were insufficiently nervous with staff they knew, and therefore did quite well, whereas with a stranger they were nearly paralysed with anxiety. Furthermore, the staff were so keen to please and help pupils that they tended to correct their spelling mistakes for them, or even not to see or to hear the gaps and inadequacies in what was written or said. There was a halo effect which made us see our pupils over-kindly because we knew and liked them. The careers teacher had the excellent idea of developing the Oval House link. The whole process was done very formally, with application forms, a choice of jobs, and a stranger to do the interviewing in a crisp and professional way. The pupils had a real jolt just at the stage they needed it: soon enough to effect their work and attitude to work in the fifth year, and to get them to perceive more of a relationship between school and work. We also incorporated into this work as much as we could to overcome the effects of sexual stereotyping. A few years later the scheme was adopted as an inner-urban project and offered to all North Lambeth comprehensives.

The fourth year programme was followed up in the fifth year with further careers education work, both individually, in groups, in lessons, and across the curriculum. Many of the pupils did work experience, but many regretted 'missing' normal lessons for this. One most helpful factor at this point was the appointment of a careers officer to the school who saw his job as working with the whole staff as well as individual pupils. He came in for the whole day every Thursday, and was one of us. The fact that he was West Indian also helped the pupils, 80 per cent of whom were from the Caribbean in origin. Interestingly enough, in a period when the unemployment rate among young people was over $33\frac{1}{3}$ per cent in our area (Brixton), we had among our school leavers very few who did not get jobs (eg only 2.5 per cent in 1979).

However, the careers work did not stop here. In 1978, we also began to develop the idea of a school-to-work course for pupils in the lower sixth. I was at the time a member of three important groups: the TASK group, a sub-group set up by the MSC which wrote a document called *Making Experience Work*[19]; another MSC working group which produced a paper on women and girls' opportunities[20]; and the panel of the Engineering Industry Training

Board's girls Technician Scheme. These all helped to develop and confirm our ideas at Vauxhall Manor. In other words, I could learn from these committees as well as put forward our ideas which we were trying out at Vauxhall Manor and find whether or not they were appropriate.

The course we set up for the lower sixth offered pupils three different kinds of work experience when they went on for three weeks at a time, a job-tasting scheme. The MSC helped us to find the work placements, though we had no financial support for the project or for the pupils. Nevertheless, the pupils gained a great deal from the course and all got jobs at the end of the year.

So far so good. In retrospect, what was not good about this particular course was that we thought of it as 'remedial'. It was for pupils who had 'failed' so far, that is, those who not only had not done very well in exams, but who also were still having difficulties with reading, writing and numbers, despite the best efforts of our compensatory department over five years. They were very late developers. Significantly, the course was run by the head of the compensatory department who had considerable skills in what is now called 'social and life skills' work. What was remarkable was that we ran the course very modestly without realizing that it was a genuine precursor of both YTS and the City and Guilds 356 prevocational certificate. The girls who got into work from the course did so relatively easily, in spite of their continuing lack of academic qualifications and considerable personality problems, particularly in relationship to adults in authority. Very often, the very best trends in education are pioneered in 'remedial' education; it takes time and experience for it to dawn on people that methods which work well for the deprived and the 'difficult' are actually appropriate for, and much needed by, the whole ability range.

Two other traditions at Vauxhall Manor were started in the mid-1970s by one careers teacher and kept up and extended by the next. One was the idea of a 'school-to-work' conference, held for all fifth years (not just leavers) at the end of the Easter term. To this conference we invited some adults but mostly young people—at work, at colleges of further education, at universities—to talk about their experiences and to answer questions in small groups. In the first year we invited some 'big noises' from industry, but the platform speech and questions in a large assembly were not the best ways to meet students' needs. The following year, the greatest success was with the many young workers who came (some of them ex-pupils) and who answered endless questions in a small group setting. The fifth years really took notice of their peers or near peers.

The second noticeable development was the way in which we kept up with pupils who had left. We always found out what happened to our ex-pupils and analysed the results statistically and personally most carefully. In 1978 the new careers master did a personal questionnaire plus (if possible) an interview of ex-pupils who were at work. He not only found out how they were getting on, but also what they thought of their experience of school. The message was nearly always the same: if only they had listened more, learnt more, worked harder, taken more notice of what the teachers said. Having been 'at work' they suddenly realized that school was relevant after all, that there were connections between what they had experienced at school and what they experienced at work. Obviously we shared this information with our current pupils, but they were not going to take it from us, the teachers, as much as from their peers.

This realization had two effects on us. One was to question the way we talked 'at' our pupils. Teachers so easily develop what may seem to pupils a 'hectoring' and nagging tone, that pupils almost visibly put their ear flaps down as the teacher begins to talk. The question was: how to change our teaching methods so that they actively involved the pupils, so that they took more responsibility for themselves and worked out for themselves what they needed to do. I think we were groping towards the concept of the 'negotiated curriculum', certainly one where the pupils had more say. However, at the time we did not have a word for it!

We began to realize more and more that the connections between what went on inside school and what went on outside school needed to be made more explicit, and made sooner. It was not too early to begin at the age of 11. Further, the more direct experience we could provide for pupils of all ability of the world outside school, and particularly at first hand, the more the pupils would be able to make and to use these connections.

We therefore undertook a curriculum review: in general, and specifically in relation to careers education and health education. Later, the school went on to do the same work in relation to equal opportunities, multi-culturalism and community. What we did at that stage was to look at the whole curriculum and to examine ways in which the content and methods used developed pupils' readiness for adult life, for coping with an uncertain future and, in particular, for working life. We were amazed and encouraged to find that we had already gone a long way down that path except that we had not made the necessary connections in our heads, so we were not helping the pupils to connect the two as much as we might. The work continued. Much to my delight I discovered recently that this work went from strength to strength after I left! This I interpret (I hope not wrongly) as meaning that the staff as a whole had really internalized the ideas we were working on and that they were not simply the rather way out ideas of a head who was (after seven years) about to move to another headship!

What I have been describing about the work at Vauxhall Manor was something of far-reaching importance. During those years (approximately 1977-81) we had moved from a social problem/ pastoral care orientation of when we 'looked after' the pupils too much (because they all had problems) to one where we knew they had problems but that was what life was like, both then and in the future. We would help the pupils if possible, but the most important way in which we could help was by getting them to help themselves. The ethos of the school—built on mutual trust, respect and help—was not one which maintained that the teachers have the power and you, the pupils, are powerless. It was one in which we tried to mobilize everybody's power—skill, strength, love, potential—and harness it for the good of all of us. 'Everybody' meant pupils and staff alike. Obviously we did not succeed 100 per cent—but we had gone from being over-protective, with an emphasis on problems, to being more demanding and with the emphasis on the whole curriculum. I do not think we realized at the time what an important shift that was. It is certainly a shift which is at the root of the present 16-19 developments, and which has its roots in the very best of counselling practice. Thus counselling skills shifted from the individual in need, to the system, and finally to the teaching and learning processes.

References

1. Marland, M (1974) *Pastoral Care* Heinemann
2. Richardson, E (1973) *The Teacher, the School and the Task of Management* Heinemann
3. For example, Schools Council: Integrated Studies Project
   Living Decisions (BBC)
   McPhail, P *Moral Education*
   de Bono, E *CORT thinking lessons*
   Various exercises in decision-making (CRAC) eg:
   Hopson, B and Hough, P *Exercises in Personal and Career Development*
   Law, W *Decide for Yourself*
   Jones, A Marsh, J and Watts, A G (1974, 1977, 1980) *Male and Female, Living Decisions, Time to Spare*, The Life-style Series. Hobsons Press
4. Lawrence, D (1973) *Improved Reading through Counselling* Ward Lock Educational
5. Kaye, B and Rogers, I (1968) *Group Work in Secondary Schools and the Training of Teachers in its Methods*, Oxford University Press
6. Thompson, S and Kahn, J H (1970) *The Group Process as a Helping Technique* Pergamon
7. Grainger, A J (1970) *The Bullring: A Classroom Experiment in Moral Education* Pergamon
8. Jones, A (1971) School Counselling *Trends in Education* Department of Education and Science no 23 July
9. Tyler, L (1961) *The Work of the Counselor* Appleton Century Crofts
10. Jones, A (1972) 'The All-purpose, All-Age Community School' *The Youth and Community Review* no 22 Spring
11. Venables, E (1971) *Teachers and Youth Workers: A Study of Their Roles* Evans Methuen Educational
12. White, R K and Lippitt, R (1960) *Autocracy and Democracy: An Experimental Inquiry* Harper
13. Bazalgette, J (1971) *Freedom, Authority and the Young Adult* Pitman
14. Jones, A (1972) 'The School Counsellor' Home and School Council
15. Holden, A (1972) *Counselling in Secondary Schools (with special reference to authority and referral)* Constable
16. The Warnock Report (1981)
17. *Focus on One Parent Families* Concern: **20** National Children's Bureau
18. Rutber *et al* (1979) *15 Thousand Hours* Open Books
19. *Making Experience Work* (1979) MSC
20. *Opportunities for Women and Girls in the MSC Programmes for the Unemployed* (1979) MSC

Chapter 8

New training initiatives

It should not come as a surprise to anyone that, when I moved to Cranford Community School in Easter 1981, the first things I did were:

(a) To ask the staff what skills, knowledge and values they thought the pupils should have when they left school.
(b) To ask the pupils what they thought of the school now, and what they thought it should be doing next.
(c) To set up a school-to-work course in the lower sixth.

What I did not necessarily expect, and was overjoyed to find, was that the staff and pupils appeared to be on the same wavelength as myself, and that therefore we had common agreement as to the basis on which we should try to move forward. This did not make the tasks we had set ourselves any easier, but at least our energy went largely into moving forward instead of arguing with and obstructing each other, as so often happens in staffrooms. This is what the staff said at a staff meeting in June 1981.

What are the aims of the school

We divided into groups and asked ourselves what knowledge, skills and values we would like our pupils to have when they left. We came up with the following lists which overlap in some ways.

1. Areas of knowledge

a. Numeracy
b. Literacy
c. Linguistic skills
   — fluency and confidence
   — presentation of argument
   — selection and organization of materials
   — sensitivity to 'tone', listening skills
   — ability to communicate orally as well as in writing
d. Logic
   — how to question, criticize
   — how to make rational decisions based on information
   — how to use resources/environment/facts in this
   — how to make choices
   — how to learn by discovery and how to solve problems

e. Creativity
   — artistic sensitivity
   — divergent thinking
   — imagination
   — aesthetic appreciation
f. Scientific literacy
   — including manual dexterity and technological competence
g. Physical
   — how to take care of selves and others
   — exercise, diet, health, sex etc.
h. Political and Social
   — knowledge of current affairs
   — ability to accept change but also to participate and contribute to changes in society
   — how to be good citizens, politically aware
i. Moral and Spiritual
   — awareness of different cultures and beliefs
   — ability to tolerate/respect differences
   — sense of social responsibility
   — not restricted by sexual differences

2. Social and personal skills

a. To be able to communicate
b. To be able to develop relationships
c. To be able to work with other individuals
   — in groups
   — in an authority/work setting
d. To be able to cope with the demands of life
e. To be able to present self well
   — self confidence
   — self awareness—awareness of own potential
   — interviewing skills
f. Independence and personal autonomy
g. Independence and mutuality
h. Reliability
i. Tolerance of differences and respect for others
j. To accept and adapt to change
   — to be willing to broaden horizons
   — to be willing to take risks—adaptability
   — to be able to work on own initiative
k. To relate to adults/those in authority as well as peers
l. Balanced persons, co-ordinated

3. Life after school

a. Awareness of relevance of school life to working life
b. Awareness that education/learning is a life long process
c. Awareness that learning continues at work
d. Appreciation of the value and possibilities of leisure
e. Aware of career opportunities
f. Prepared for life, leisure, unemployment, parenthood, citizenship

Comment

No doubt we could refine or add to these categories. The next question is: If this is what we are trying to do (and we might want to check that out, add/subtract a few more things) then *how* can we do it within the framework of our curriculum?

Our answers had nothing much to do with subjects, exams or content. They formed a framework which went across the whole curriculum. The puzzle then was how to reconcile these aims and objectives with existing subjects and how to adapt our styles of teaching to methods which placed less emphasis on content and product, and more emphasis on processes, skills and recorded experiences.

Since then we have been working very systematically to develop along these lines. Not only have we embarked on a massive staff development programme, we have also undertaken two serious reviews of the curriculum, moving forward at a pace we can cope with. The comment of the first curriculum working part which reported in December 1981 was that 'what we needed to change was not the content of the curriculum so much as the processes and methods'.

The sixth-form 'school-to-work' course (described in detail later) turned out to be a revolution in the sixth-form. We now have a totally comprehensive sixth-form, double its original size, which offers to *all* pupils (including the most able) social and life skills, expressive arts and general studies. *All* the fifth years undertake work experience for three weeks and all the fourth years do voluntary service in the community for half a day a week for a term. What we have taken on board here is the idea that what is valuable for the less able, remedial, and problem pupil is just as much needed by all pupils; namely experiences which extend young people's confidence and capacity to cope with life, take initiatives, take risks and go on learning. It is of considerable significance that the staff have also demonstrated their capacity to do these things.

The school-to-work course

This course, when began in September 1981, proved to be the catalyst for action. First, as it was a new course, not dominated by a subject or (initially) an exam, we could and did use a curriculum framework (*A Basis for Choice*[1] in fact), rather than existing subjects to devise the course. Second, as the course involved only a small team of staff, we could build a practical working model of successful practice. Not that any of us found the changes in style required easy, but it was better and more effective to move forward step by step. The method of curriculum change was, in fact, remarkably similar to the teaching styles we were adopting: learning by doing, being given support and guidance in relation to a task, an idea in action rather than simply an idea, reflecting on experiences, evaluating and redesigning as we went along, negotiating, and working as a team. The course had to be modified constantly in the light of changing external and internal circumstances and the students' needs. We quickly realized that if we had spent a year planning all the course in detail, we would have been wasting our time. The course consisted of 12 weeks' work experience, one week's residential experience, all punctuated by our in-school curriculum consisting of communication skills, numeracy, economic, social and environmental studies, social and life skills, vocational studies/simulated work experience, and individual and group counselling. The students took the City and Guilds 365 (prevocational studies) at the end of the year. We soon learnt that it was impossible to keep even to these 'subjects'—all parts of the course fed into each other. Thus it was important for the course to be integrated and for the teachers to work as a team. This took a lot of time but we found it to be well worth it in terms of our job satisfaction and motivation. The most effective agents of staff change were the pupils themselves. We learnt from them as well as they from us. The following detailed account of the course is taken from a school's council publication[2], part of which was written by Mrs Caroline Gallup who is the course co-ordinator.

The rationale

In September 1981, in line with the proposals for the 'new training initiative', Cranford Community School (initially in conjunction with the Air Transport and Traffic Industry Training Board) embarked on a pilot action research scheme to find ways of developing skills for working life within the secondary-school curriculum. The motivation was not simply the problem of youth unemployment or helping young people to increase their chances of finding and keeping a job or extending the range of employment opportunities open to them. It was also to enable the students to make a successful transition from school to adult life. Behind this aim was a fundamental belief in the importance of relating the curriculum in school to life outside school, of making the school curriculum less content-based and more process-based, and of developing teaching methods which do more to develop in students skills for living and self-confidence. It was hoped that ultimately this would extend throughout the school curriculum.

Overall aim: meeting students' needs

The basic aim of the 16-19 prevocational course was to provide learning experiences which enabled our students to cope with the transition to adult and working life. These experiences were designed not to be narrowly vocational or job-specific but to help our students:

(a) to cope with the demands of a job;
(b) to realize that their skills are useful in a variety of settings;
(c) to become more self-confident and autonomous;
(d) to be able to make decisions and cope with change;
(e) to take responsibility for themselves and others.

We were concerned about adult and working life, not simply work.

The aims and objectives of *A Basis for Choice* provided a framework for the courses. We therefore put great emphasis on developing in our students the following skills, competencies and concepts: career and personal decision-making; problem-solving; communication and study skills; numerical/ graphical/computer competence; political, economic and environmental understanding; coping skills, including the ability to transfer or use skills in different contexts. We included some aesthetic, creative, physical, practical and expressive work in the course as important vehicles for learning the above skills. The course was made up of 12 weeks' work experience (two blocks of six weeks), one week's residential experience and the rest in school, though this included further simulated work experience.

Integration, support, negotiation and progression

The principles of integration, support, negotiation and progression were also important in making the course really useful to the students.

(a) *Integration.* The course was integrated, a set of experiences which all subscribed to the same overall framework of aims and objectives, not simply a collection of individual subjects. The common core went throughout the whole course.

(b) *Support.* The students themselves needed considerable support and time to reflect on their experiences in order to make full use of the courses, and so too did staff. Time and resources were needed for team-building, team meetings, staff development and mutual support. This was essential to avoid uncertainty and fragmentation of the course.

(c) *Negotiation.* The concept of the negotiated curriculum was also regarded as very important. The idea was that, within a clearly defined framework, students and staff together took decisions about what they would do and how they would do it. Obvious examples where this operated included the planning of work experience, visits to firms, law courts, etc, mock interviews, presentations and publications. This style of learning was crucial in helping the students to become more self-reliant and self-directing.

(d) *Progression.* The course needed to be seen to lead somewhere, that is, to progress—not simply to be a way of filling up an extra year. It did help develop more mature and independent young adults, and this was worthwhile in itself. In addition, the experience and the qualification combined lead to work, to a more specialist vocational training, or to further education. Students, parents and employers, as well as teachers, had to be helped to understand realistically the aims and possible outcomes of such a course. There is still prejudice in favour of single-subject exams at O level.

Evaluation

On this course, evaluation was to be formative (involving the students in self-assessment) as well as summative, with a record of achievements and external moderating to ensure validity. Again, such methods were seen as part of the students' learning process.

The course in detail

On the Cranford pilot course were 18 students of mixed race, sex and ability. There were no entry requirements in terms of exam results.

Structure of the course

There was an induction course of two weeks, and then the students were split into two groups. Half embarked on six weeks' work experience; half had a week's 'outward bound' course followed by five weeks in school. Then the groups changed over, the process repeating itself the following term.

The content of the in-school curriculum

Responsibility for the in-school curriculum was shared between six members of staff. As the curriculum is integrated it is therefore difficult to place in the conventional subject boundaries. However, the areas covered in school were: communication skills; social and life skills; numeracy, social, economic and environmental studies; vocational studies; individual and group guidance and counselling.

There were also group projects which gave the students the opportunity to see a process through from the idea to the end-product, for example, the production of a booklet describing 'work experience' and a slide presentation of outward-bound experience. In most areas of learning the students were given a choice of topics. They discussed their preferences. Therefore the specific content studied was always evolving—what the students were doing this year is not the same as will be done next year. The methods used depended on the needs of the particular students. The concept of a static curriculum was inappropriate.

The school experience component

There was a two-week induction course.

The first two days concentrated on social and life skills to help the individual students to reflect upon their present situation, to see where they stood, where their needs lay and where their goals might be. This was then expanded into interactive skills to help the students to get to know each other as a group. Their responses were assessed, negotiated and met as far as possible. From this, more specific verbal and written communication relevant to the workplace was explored, such as telephoning and writing a business letter. Alongside this there was an introduction to the structure and functioning of firms, and basic budgeting. In relation to this, two out-of-school investigations were started:

(a) where to invest £50, and
(b) how to find a flat, involving the decision of whether to rent or buy and the basic budgeting behind it.

Both these investigations involved information-seeking in various agencies found in the local community. Some students completed these early on whilst others found more difficulty in gaining the confidence to approach people or to sieve out the relevant information necessary.

After the induction period the group was split into two smaller groups. One group started a six-week work-experience placement at British Airways (BA) and the other group started the schoolwork element which commenced with a demanding week on an 'outward bound' course.

'Outward bound' course

This not only emphasized physical skills (for example, raft building, rock climbing, and building a shelter) but also process skills. It stressed the students' capabilities for interacting effectively in their environment, the skills of asking questions, finding out, relating specific information to particular tasks, group discussion, group decision-making, etc. Many of these skills would be applicable to certain jobs and are common across family and industry sector boundaries, such as manipulative skills (for example, rope tying, and rope bridge construction).

The whole week provided a base from which to apply their own experiences to future learning, either in the immediate or further future. Group interaction and trust, and the building of interdependent relationships, the concept of teamwork as a reality not just an ideal; these were all learning outcomes of the week's experience.

On returning to school

The first group spent a considerable amount of time exploring the process skills/social and life skills developed during the outward-bound week. They gave a presentation to fifth years, with visual aids about their experiences of outward bound.

They then began to challenge the school learning situation, wanting to take more responsibility for what they learnt. At this point, the students were given choices of area which they could explore, within the confines of the syllabus framework. They discussed and decided their preferences. Both groups drew up their own questionnaires (covering areas of social and economic elements of the course as well as job qualities of vocational preparation). In general these incorporated job-skill observation, job-quality assessment, and information-seeking on trade unions and modern technology.

Later, the students discussed the findings with particular reference to their own social skills and the various skills observed. One group wanted to know more about court procedures and their rights as employees. Visits were made to various local courts and a law centre representative discussed the areas of interest with them in school. Also as work experience was approaching for the first group, simulated workplace games were played and trade union structures and roles were explored. A BA convenor visited and explained the role. The training board showed a video of the various jobs and their skills found at BA.

Another group venture, incorporating all the interrelated skills, was the production of an information display unit based on a microcomputer (such as Prestel). This involved the students in selecting and exploring particular areas of information relevant to young people in the community as well as searching, designing programme and text layout and developing keyboard skills.

Vocational preparation

In order to provide experience of a broader range of occupations and to test the students' vocational preparedness, the school was able to 'simulate work environments' in various occupational training families. With guidance, students chose from within the areas. Some projects were undertaken as a group and involved seeing a whole process through. Others were undertaken individually under the supervision of the staff concerned.

Areas used were: the audio-visual department, school office, baby clinic, playgroup, helping the caretakers, and tuck shop.

It was helpful to this situation that Cranford is a community school and can therefore offer a wide range of opportunities.

Guidance and counselling

All members of staff were involved in these activites but there was also specific time devoted to these areas.

For instance, the students who were on work experience spent every Monday morning in school reflecting on their experiences, successes, achievements and failures in work. They gradually developed a more realistic understanding of work and a more positive awareness of their own personalities and capabilities.

The here-and-now experiences of working in a group, whether in work or at school, were analysed and discussed and any personality clashes explored. There was also individual counselling which gave students an opportunity to share their personal private concerns and helped them to build their confidence and self-respect. Some vocational counselling was obviously included here.

Timetabled social and life skills

This concentrated on group interaction and involvement of different kinds, for instance:

(a) the ability to formulate questions and listen effectively, culminating in videoed role-played interviews;
(b) individual leisure activity checklist with an exchange of information and ideas;

(c) group decision-making, role play in various work situations, for example shop steward and foreman;

(d) personality and work role clashes explored and decision-making involving persuasion, logically argued and group consensus, working out how to resolve a particular problem, for example whether or not primary-school children should take a particular bus.

The numeracy and communication elements of the course have more or less followed the City and Guilds 365 (vocational preparation) syllabus.

Communications have concentrated more on the written skills because generally the students' oral responses were satisfactory whilst the written skills required more practice. Both groups expressed a preference for what appeared to them directly relevant exercises.

The work covered the following areas:

1. Reading and understanding data in various forms and then interpreting the material, for example in the form of notices, graphs, tables, pie charts, invoices, etc.

2. Expressing written data in a graphic/tabular form, for example for use in an advertisement.

3. Organizing and expressing information in written form, for example in a letter of complaint.

4. Communicating effectively to others, for example instructions as to how to use a machine.

5. Identifying incorrect, ambiguous or badly organized material and producing an alternative, for example an account of an accident.

6. Distinguishing fact from opinion and identifying emotive phrases and bias.

There was a wide range of ability within the two groups resulting in vast differences in the standard of work completed.

Communication in a written form was an element in both the social, economic aspects of the course and the vocational—simulated work environments.

Numeracy

This was related to the needs of the work environment, that is, applying a mathematical concept to a practical realistic situation (eg What percentage has turnover fallen if it was £4000 last month and £3240 this month?). Also, areas of business were covered, such as profit and loss accounts, balance sheets, costing and pricing, as well as the use of computers and simple programs for business-type applications.

Careers guidance

Here parts of the BBC series 'Going to work' were shown—especially those relating to specific work and job skill areas. Leading on from this the students worked in detail on what they would like to do when they leave. This meant making a job choice, finding out how to obtain it, whether they were suitable and also assessing each other's potential as well as their own.

Sports and recreational activities

In these activities the students joined in with other sixth-formers. In this year's course students also have access to the science studies course which includes science and technology and politics and the media, and to the expressive arts course which includes drama, music, art and English.

Work experience at British Airways

This was negotiated initially by the Air Transport Industrial Training Board (ATITB) together with BA. The work placements were to be in a multiplicity of skill areas but unfortunately it was mainly manual and clerical jobs that were secured. Even so, these work experiences enabled the students to experience the strains of work and have helped to ease the transitional period. Some students expressed a wish to experience a broader range of occupations and some alternative placements were found, for example in catering and welfare.

At BA there were two graduate trainees who acted as contact links with the school. They were involved in establishing the aims and objectives of the course. There was a great deal of discussion with them about the students, covering not only the actual placement allocation but the way they were reacting to the particular job situation.

Frequent visits to the work areas were made by the course leader, who talked to the respective supervisors and gained an idea of the strengths and weaknesses of the particular individuals. The students themselves (in classroom discussion afterwards) were very aware of the group interaction in the workplace and which social skills make it easier to get on with the existing staff.

Also, within the 'simulated work experience' in the audio-visual department the group wrote up their work experience in the form of a booklet. Some referred to the hierarchial structure, others to the specific job tasks. They enjoyed talking about it, especially the different experience in structuring time (that is, planning the workload). In school this was often determined by teachers, whereas in work there was more flexibility.

The skills acquired in the course will be useful outside employment—hence the relevance to leisure. They should enhance the individual student's prospect for economic survival and personal development in the face of uncertain employment prospects.

The work experience component in 1982-3 has been arranged through Project Trident or personal contacts. This has the advantage of extending the range of job options available for student choice. On the other hand, more schools in the area are following our example and doing work experience and more employers are deciding not to take on work-experience students. This is partly due to the fact that employers have not enough work to give students or because they have had to cut staff and so they now do not have anybody with any time to devote to helping train work-experience young people. Therefore the number of openings available in the locality has lessened, particularly with the advent of YTS.

The school then worked with BA to set up a pilot new training initiative for which the school provides the 'off-the-job' components.

Assessments

There were regular work-experience reports and assessments plus numeracy and communication multiple-choice tests. There was also regular profiling at approximately six-weekly intervals. The profiling system used was the City and Guilds 365. We used it in both a formative and a summative way.

The advantages of profiling were that the profiling was done with the students as a learning process; it encouraged them to be involved in their own development of their personal qualities and skills; also by articulating their learning objectives they were more likely to have an idea of their career potential. The profile reports have certain levels of performance clearly defined. The students were usually unable to assess their own progess realistically. There were some drawbacks to profiling—it was time-consuming. Some students saw the levels as a pass or fail and not as a progression of their own personal development.

There were regular meetings with the course team to discuss the progress of respective students: despite reservations about the profiling system, the team found their assessments largely coincided.

The 12 students finishing the course took the City and Guilds vocational preparation 365, and all passed. Eight of these students found work, four are on job-specific further education courses. All appear to be very pleased with their progress.

Overall view of the course; what we learned

We learned that:

1. That it was better to begin the course than to plan it in a vacuum, as the course had to be flexible. There were always areas that would need to be re-negotiated with the students, employers or school. Lesson planning therefore had to be flexible, ie based on the here-and-now.
2. Initially, both teachers and students still thought in terms of school-type conventional subjects and found it difficult to adjust to the interrelatedness.
3. Traditional teaching methods were inappropriate—both teachers and students had to re-learn their roles and methods.
4. It was noticeable that the young people could be motivated and excited and made enormous progress in their development through such a course.

183

5. It showed that teachers and school can be adaptive and flexible if they so choose. There were frequent meetings between the staff to talk about subject content and how the students were getting on. Also, after the first group finished their first in-school part of the course we had a joint meeting between the staff and students to discuss their feelings about the whole six weeks. The teaching staff were very motivated and excited by the course.

The course had some minor problems:

1. Some students were more motivated for work than for school. They felt they were acquiring adult status at work but not so much at school. The school was forced to look at the implications of this.
2. Also, because these students were 16 they could leave midstream. This could cause a loss to the feeling of group identity that had been engendered, though in fact this group quickly re-formed.

The effects on the rest of the sixth-form curriculum

The school-to-work course had a profound effect on the curriculum as a whole and on teaching and learning styles:

Life skills: staff development

Although we had simultaneously introduced into the sixth-form a general studies course which included expressive arts for all, we were so impressed by the way the school-to-work course built up students' confidence and coping strategies, that we decided that all the sixth formers, including the most academic, needed these opportunities. Thus in 1982-83, a 'social and life skills' course (an unfortunate, abused term, but the only shorthand we know) was given to all sixth formers. The teaching team included experienced 'school-to-work' tutors and new members: staff were keen to join in because they saw it as exciting and releasing. After school, for ten evenings a term, we provided, through our youth leader, experiential training in group work skills for interested staff. Over 20 took this initial course voluntarily and found it both stimulating and supportive. They also found it helpful to their general classroom teaching.

An extended prevocational sixth-form

In 1981 we had 18 students on the school-to-work course (City and Guilds 365). In 1982-3 we not only repeated this course but added a BEC course (in conjunction with our local FE college) and a City and Guilds (engineering) course. Next year we added further courses, viz: a TEC (science), a City and Guilds retail distribution course, and a catering course. We are also the providers of off-the-job training for a new training initiative managed by BA. We feel that these prevocational students get a far better education this way than by repeating and failing again their O levels. We also feel that the A level students benefit from the presence of these other students. What we now have is, in fact, a comprehensive sixth-form.

Effects on the whole school curriculum

These are difficult to measure as yet. The internalization of some new important concepts by staff, the building up of their confidence to experiment with new styles, the realization of the importance and the usefulness of such curriculum frameworks as in pre-16 work, the development of the role of the form tutor, the arrangement of form rooms in a more flexible way: these developments take time, are uneven in progress and vary according to the teacher. But there is no doubt in my mind that they are happening. The work of the school is very slowly, organically and at its own pace, making an important operational shift which should benefit enormously the pupils' learning in real terms.

The latest development is that since January 1983 we have offered off-the-job training to BA trainees on a pilot youth training scheme. We were only asked to do this because of our previous record of experience of working closely with BA over a number of years and particularly on the school-to-work course. In the next section I want to return again to the young people to look at the ways they reacted to the various initiatives we took. The reader will, I am sure, be able to connect up their work with the kind of work I was doing at Mayfield. The principles behind the work are to do with showing the students/trainees respect, trust, and non-possessive warmth; with accepting and having high positive regard for them, whatever they are like initially; with high expectations of people's potential for growth; with an appreciation of *all* their qualities not simply their intellect; with offering people a feeling of choice and mastery over what they can actually do; and with building up of young people's sense of worth and value.

My role in working with the students/trainees was to do with the 'reflecting on experience'—that is how I have such a clear idea of what they thought and felt and how they progressed. I must however stress that I was only one of a team who worked very closely together; any one of us could have made similar observations. When we got together to work on joint assessments we found our views to be very similar. We are all sure that what is valuable about our various 16-19 initiatives is not the qualifications themselves but the actual experiences offered to the students or trainees. This is what makes them, at the end of the year, better people, more ready to face the world.

References

1. *A Basis for Choice* (1979) Further Education Unit
2. *Planning one year 16-17 courses* (1983) School's Council pamphlet 21

Chapter 9

Young people's responses

The school-to-work students

The 18 students who joined the first school-to-work course in September 1981 varied in background enormously, from those who had left school at Easter without any qualifications to those who had a respectable but not particularly useful clutch of CSE Grade 3s and 4s. They had their own reasons for staying on, which were not simply because they could not find work or simply that they wanted further qualificaations, though both these were true. They seemed to realize, even though they could not articulate it at first, that they needed an extra year of 'growing-up' time. They were not particularly alienated from school—though some of them had been when younger—otherwise they would not have come back at all. What appealed to them about the course was its practicality; not a repeat of the old O level/CSE failure or near miss, but *real* work experience and time to reflect on it with adult support. Young people starting work rarely get the kind of 'neutral' adult support which we provided: so often young people drift into their first jobs, lose them because they cannot handle a conflict situation with someone in authority, give up and mentally write themselves off, thus setting up a vicious spiral. Our students had the security of their home base (the school) from which they could test the temperature of the water outside for real. When they had a misunderstanding at work, they could talk it over with more than one neutral adult. They could test out various behaviours until they found the ones which brought them esteem and respect from their employers; they could discuss how to raise the delicate problem of grievance with their boss so that when they did ask they were not rebuffed and left feeling angry and unheard. At school they could make more sense of the work they were about to do. It was no longer an 'academic exercise' but had its root in reality which they had tested out for themselves.

I remain convinced that the original and real motivation for these students was their need for support in making the transition from school to work: their need for a 'space' to think about and sort out who they really were, before making a step into the world beyond school. Their original motivation was not to do with 'qualifications', for when the course was first proposed in May 1981, the City and Guilds prevocational certificate 365 had not been announced, only mooted. It was formerly established near the end of that term (Summer 1981) and we were not sure whether we would be too late to enter for it in 1981-2. More important we were not sure whether the students would want to take an exam: in the true spirit of 'negotiation', we felt it very important not to burden students with the strain and risk of failure of an examination, especially those whose experience of exams up till now had not been totally positive. So we waited until the autumn term to consult members of the course. Somewhat to our surprise (and even to our regret because we ourselves had hoped to be free from the pressure of exams!) the students all said they might as well take the exam since they would not lose anything by it if they failed; at least it gave them a chance of a 'certificate', something tangible to show an employer. It also gave a 'focus' to the work, in their eyes; though in fact it altered our syllabus hardly at all, since both our existing course and the City and Guilds course used the Mansell 'common core of skills for vocational preparation' (see Appendix) as a framework for the curriculum. The students did realize that the school would give them a 'leaving certificate' and profile stating what they had done and achieved during the year. They remained certain that they would still like the City and Guilds diploma if possible. At this point we invited a member of the City and Guilds staff to visit us, discuss what we were doing, and negotiate between us agreement that our course genuinely fitted into the City and Guilds requirements. The main adjustment we had to make was to add some 'work-related' experiences on the school site; that meant some extra work experience in our welfare clinic, playgroup, library, reprographic, catering and school keeping services etc. This we dutifully did, but neither we nor the students ever felt that 'school based' work experience was anything like as useful to the students' learning as 'real' work experience. It did extend the *range* of work experience in some cases, but was too much like 'helping at home'—inhibiting the desire to reveal a new more grown up self.

Money was never part of the basic motivation for attending this course. It was interesting that the students found themselves working alongside what were then 'YOP' trainees, who were receiving the trainee wage. We did manage to pay the students work experience expenses—this is no mean sum because 'going to work' can cost between £5-£10 a week; excess travel and sometimes rather expensive eating facilities. It is unfair and also impracticable to ask students whose parents are not well off (or even unemployed) to be out of pocket on their work experience. This is something LEAs need to come to terms with. They cheerfully hand out expenses for travel to other colleges and schools, but do not seem always to put work experience, which is a valid part of a course, in the same category. Our students barely had their out of pocket expenses paid, yet, from all accounts from the BA staff were considerably more motivated than the YOP trainees. This motivation showed in the willingness with which they undertook their responsibilities and the way they worked with their bosses and their colleagues. It is something we often discussed in groups. One member of the group put it succinctly: 'well they're in it for the money, we're in it for the experience'. This seems to me to be a most important point, and one that is borne out so far by our experience with BA trainees under a

187

pilot YTS scheme. These trainees have been initially most recalcitrant and unwilling to learn; more of them later! Suffice it to say that in my view the reason our first group of school-to-work students were so motivated—and ultimately so successful—was that the whole course was negotiated with them, based upon a negotiated agreement and match and between their needs and wishes and the requirements of work, training and exam. Their motivation came from the fact that they were patently *partners* in the learning experiences they undertook, and they felt some mastery over what was happening and some ownership of what they learnt. If only this were the case with pupil learning generally!

If we look now at the students in more detail, we can begin to see in what ways they changed over the year. The first point that has to be made is that of the 18 students, six left midstream. Any course of this nature, whether school/college based work or work based, is going to 'lose' people into work: it is something we have to come to terms with, and which will happen whatever our courses are like. It is less likely to happen in YTS, which guarantee work or which count the YTS year as part of an apprenticeship scheme. But certainly many YTS trainees and prevocational 16-19 students are going to give up during the year. What we have to ask is whether this counts as success or failure. In some cases it will be failure because what we have offered will not have met the needs of the individual concerned. However, for the young person, even to have worked this out and done something about it for him or herself, is no mean achievement! Some students/trainees discover during their year's course that they are more skilled, confident, mature, and ready for the world than they previously realized. (That does not say much for the effects of their last year of formal schooling, which may have left them feeling totally unskilled, confident and resourceless.) And when they feel ready, and look for work *successfully*, who is to stop them and say they have to finish the course?

In our first course, six students left during the year; five got jobs as, variously, a market porter, a dental receptionist, a clerk/typist, a factory worker and a car mechanic. A sixth moved to a YOP course specializing in computing because this was the field in which she wanted to specialize. The remaining 12 completed the course, eight of them going into work and four of them on to more specialist vocational courses at FE colleges. I propose now to look at the students in more detail to see in what way they progressed over the year and thereafter.

Amita

Amita had eight CSEs Grades 3 to 5, but no O level equivalents. Had she decided to repeat her CSEs or attempt O level, she would have been doomed to failure. She had learnt to type in the fifth year. Her Grade 3 maths showed some interest in numbers. But, on the face of it, she was not qualified to get a job, particularly not one in computing in which she expressed considerable interest from the start. Amita's main asset was her personality. She was well dressed, potentially very beautiful, and keen to please. Her main problem at the beginning of the year was that she did not realize how attractive or skilful she was. She was shy and somewhat anxious, becoming very worked up at the slightest set-back. She was unable to see any other point of view but her own, and she would hang on firmly to that which she knew rather than try out new things or adapt. For her, the work experience was the turning point. She worked extremely hard and, to her surprise, found not only that she was capable but also that she was popular with her boss and the other employees. So keen was she on her work experience that she went in during the holidays to offer her services. She began to dress really well, held her head high and looked at you instead of averting her gaze, sparkled with enthusiasm instead of complaining and looking downcast, and said with characteristic determination that she wanted to work on computers at BA. There were two snags about her ambition: first, BA were not taking people on before the age of 18; second, to work in computers you were supposed to have rather better initial qualifications than Amita had. She was not even sufficiently well qualified to take further basic qualifications in computers. However at BA she had been allowed to do relatively advanced work on computers; on the strength of this at the end of the year Amita managed to get herself a job in a firm where she could get more computer experience, and rumour has it that she has now actually got the job at BA. She passed her City and Guild examination with credits. She had done conscientious school work all the year. Above all, she had gained in poise, personality and determination.

Sharon

Sharon left the fifth year with three CSEs: in community studies, child care and home economics. She also had a Red Cross qualification and had recently given the kiss of life to an old man who had collapsed in the street near her. She would have loved to do nursing, child or community care, but she did not have the necessary qualifications to go further. Added to this, she had, and had always had, personal problems. She had been referred to child guidance as a child (as had several of her brothers and sisters), and she had a speech defect which was gradually going. She came from a large family in which there were several re-marriages (including her parents) and in which the extended family network was very important. Sharon had, on the surface, a loud and cheerful personality, somewhat larger than life, with a sharp sense of humour and considerable native wit. In fact, she was rather lacking in confidence, and depressed to the extent that she had several times tried to cut her wrists, including once during the course. In the group she could be either totally domineering and attention-seeking, getting on some members' nerves, or occasionally withdrawn. What was interesting was the way the group gradually took her on, confronting her, teasing her, arguing with her so that she gradually toned herself down, without losing her basic bluntness. She developed more tact. She became prepared to listen to other members points of view and to take account of them, to work more co-operatively instead of individually. She too began to look better groomed and generally smarter.

On her various work placements she was an enormous success, endearing herself to those she worked with and proving to be extremely useful and capable even though she would not have stood a chance of being appointed to work at BA normally. On one occasion her immediate boss was ill and she took over the office with great aplomb and efficiency, only ruffling feathers when she fielded a phone call from a junior Minister, and told him to 'hang on a minute duck I can't find anybody.' She did not initially have a very well developed sense of hierarchy and this was only marginally more developed at the end. What is remarkable about Sharon was how capable and likeable she was in spite of all her various handicaps. She absolutely flowered given genuine responsibility; she showed herself to be capable well beyond her qualifications, yet she must typify so many of our young people who, because of the weight given to traditional school exams, are denied access to work they could do really well. She did not sustain this achievement. She got a job as a shop assistant, a position whch certainly would use many of her skills, but not in a form which would systematically train her further. Her next best bet might be to do a YTS in retail skills—if she were eligible. We have lost touch with her, which is very frustrating. We must improve our mechanisms for post-course follow-up, but ultimately we have to accept that it is up to Sharon now to do what she wants with her life. I think she would come back if she really wanted our advice. She passed her City and Guilds exam with a credit in communication skills.

James

James came to us with five CSEs, the best being motor vehicle studies Grade 2. He had definitely 'gone off' school work, but not enough actually to leave, so he was resistant at first to anything that looked like traditional school work.

Even though the school work on this particular course was different, it was not until students had been on work experience that they realised how different it was. They tended to 'overlay' the in-school work with negative overtones from the year before, at the same time as complaining that we were treating them like children! When we tried to treat them as adults they complained that we were not helping them enough. The implications for curriculum and teaching methods for 11-16 are enormous here. It seems to me that we have swung from a perceived authoritarian approach to a perceived *laissez-faire* approach, whereas the students really want a negotiated curriculum at this stage, where they have a lot of say, but so do we. Although intellectually we understood the negotiated curriculum, it took us some time in practice to get the idea of how it worked.

James was a somewhat diffident and disengaged learner at first. He had very vague ideas about what he wanted to do—possibly something to do with cars; he was shy, clumsy and as yet unaware of his considerable charm and presence which developed over the year. He did very well on the outward bound course where he began to demonstrate qualities of leadership and physical skill. At BA, he coped with both manual work and also with a computer placement where he was allowed to do relatively advanced work. On the ramp he had been allowed to work out when the aircraft was properly loaded and whether it was safe for it to taxi forward: not tht he did this without supervision! But it did boost his confidence. He learnt to drive, partly helped by the school's driving simulator. He began to speak more coherently. In the group he could develop an argument as well as take on the views of others. He passed his City and Guilds exam with distinctions in communications and numeracy. He began work as a warehouse assistant, which does not sound like a job which gives him sufficient scope for his talent. However he came back recently with a work mate, both of them smartly turned out in their overalls; he certainly seemed to be cheerful and pleased with his progress.

Jagdeep

Jagdeep had come to England when he was about five; he had left his mother behind in India. His father had then died and he was being brought up by a collection of uncles and other brothers. His English was still limited, despite our efforts with him throughout school; his English CSE was unclassified but he had managed a Grade 2 in maths. His other CSEs were at Grade 5. He wanted desperately to be a motor mechanic and would often talk about his uncle getting him in, but nothing happened. He was a very shy boy, even depressed. In the group he was isolated at first, but gradually joined in, even though he did not say a lot. He went out with a girl for the first time during the course. Whether it was the course which gave him the confidence to do this, or the girl the confidence to improve on the course, who knows! What was *most* commendable about Jagdeep is that he also went to evening classes during the year, coming in proudly one day to show his certificate in English as a second language. His whole family of male adults came to see me on report evening saying how important it was for him to continue his education: with great determination he got himself on to a course at an FE college in engineering/technology. In Jagdeep's case the year gave him the ladder to the next stage of education.

Denise

Denise was from the beginning shy and unassuming. She had five CSEs, the best one being a Grade 2 in English. It turned out that she was deaf in one ear, but hated admitting it. The result was that she appeared not to be taking in what was happening, nor to contribute much to discussion. After she admitted it, we knew where to seat her in the group; she became more adult, suddenly very pretty and poised. On one of her work placements she was in personnel and found herself handling enquiries about early retirement—this was in the era when BA were cutting down on staff on a scale which makes falling rolls and staff deployment in schools seem like peanuts! Amazingly as a new unexperienced recruit, she did this very competently and tactfully, as well as improving her typing skills. She got a job as a receptionist where she had to do telephone work and a little typing. What altered most during the year was her self confidence and appearance. She started off as a mouse; she ended up as an elegant and attractive person.

Jaswinder

Jaswinder actually came to us from another school, which certainly was not going to have him back in the sixth since not only was he 'remedial' (that is, he had difficulties with written and spoken English), but was also rather a nuisance, being alternatively aggressive and childish. He was a large, solid, some would say fat boy, who had a knack of putting his foot in it. At times he would be belligerent and rude, and at other times he would be so anxious to please that he would agree with absolutely everything, sometimes getting his cue wrong and overstating his affirmation in the wrong place. He was a very interesting member of the group. The others were often very annoyed with him, but finally managed to talk to him straight so that he realized the effect he had on others and adapted his behaviour. He was one of those for whom the outward bound course was a turning point: he was absolutely terrified at the thought of abs-sailing, rock climbing, canoeing etc. Despite his bulk, he shook like a baby. However with the encouragement and support of the others he did do whatever was required. The effects on his self-esteem were enormous. Unfortunately on one of his work placements he was in the postal section where there were mostly women: he found this intolerable and no doubt so did they! However, he managed finally to negotiate himself out of this into a job as an 'internal' postman where *not* having to sustain relationships was an advantage! He was, however, extremely enthusiastic about the course, in fact it was he who was the mainspring behind the booklet about the course that the group wrote, typed, printed and produced. Jaswinder passed his exam with credit, worked for a short while as a salesman, then managed to get onto an FE course in technology. I would not say he had found himself yet, but he had at least moved from being an educational reject and a group reject into someone acceptable to both. That is no mean achievement! He also made progress at home: his parents, for religious reasons, were very strict about his going out. He actually attended a sixth-form disco for the first time in his life, but only managed to get permission to go because he said I was taking him home by car. He managed successfully to con me into doing this, which was a rare feat! In fact, his concern was not only to please his parents but also that he was afraid of being beaten up by skinheads on his way home.

Raj

Raj became Jaswinder's friend, but was a very different character. He had also had problems all his life. He had come to us half way through secondary school, speaking virtually no English and coming from a different part of India from most of the Asian pupils, therefore speaking a different language. Further, he had been rather badly behaved in the fourth and fifth years: he had left school at Easter in his fifth year without any examination passes—probably a realistic judgement on his part—as I doubt if he would have passed any. He needed to work because both his parents were unemployed—his father was ill—and there several other children. However, he was unable to hold down a job, largely I suspect because of his personality: he could not accept people in authority over him and he challenged everything. So he decided to come back to school. One of the first problems was to help his family reclaim family allowance for him: this piece of bureaucracy was an almost insuperable task at first; even when this was sorted out his family suffered considerable hardship, and we usually paid his expenses in advance since there was no spare money in his family to cover travel and lunch.

In the group Raj was obstreperous and demanding at first, sulky if he did not get attention, somewhat inconsiderate of others, generally questioning and challenging in an unco-ordinated and directionless way. He was in fact a handsome lad, with thick dark hair: one of his first attention-seeking acts of defiance was to get his head shaved. This resulted in the somewhat incongruous combination of a skinhead cut on an Asian—a 17-year-old Yul Brynner with dark skin. Even he must have been somewhat overwhelmed by his own audacity, for he then took to wearing a red wool hat, from which he was inseparable. We explained that woolly hats were not acceptable either at work or at school, but somehow he got away with it in both places. It was on the outward bound course that Raj really began to shine: he demonstrated exceptional qualities of leadership, courage, and physical strength—apart from the time his hat nearly went over the edge of a cliff and he with it! He took over the group in a *positive* way at last. When he returned the effect lasted. From that moment he began to mature rapidly; his sense of humour and his charm endeared him to employers and teachers alike. He got a job as a sales representative—which, in retrospect, I suppose gave him the independence and flexibility of hours which he really preferred. A year later a besuited young man with well groomed medium length hair presented himself at my door. He had an even better sales job now, with a car and enough money to keep the whole family; they and we were overjoyed and Raj was very proud. I doubt if he would have made it without a lot of work on his and our parts to help him overcome his authority problems and grow up.

Sam

Sam was a Sikh, very dignified and polite, shy and unassuming, not at all demanding and very unsure about what he should do with his life. He had done well at woodwork (CSE 1) and motor vehicle studies (CSE 2) but otherwise had the usual clutch of Grade 4s and 5s. Although he never said a great deal, he did participate more actively in the group work over the year. It was extremely pleasing that then he managed to get on to a YOP course specializing in engineering, for his real skills were on the practical side and his command of English, which no doubt had been handicapping his grades in abstract subjects, had improved enormously over the year. Like Jagdeep he

193

used the course as a confidence-builder and bridge to further more specific learning.

David

David was yet another shy and underachieving young man, with a Grade 1 in maths and six other indifferent CSEs. Initially he was rather thin and hunched, did not say much, but observed closely and took in a great deal. However in the group he took a most facilitating role, helping to integrate and to lead forward the work of the group. He did this unconsciously at first, almost writing his contribution off in his overmodest way. He gradually realized that he had considerable leadership powers. He certainly had a knack of articulating in a very dry succinct manner what was happening in the group. He blossomed visibly on outward bound and in his work experience placements on the ramp, in computers and in caretaking. He also began to reveal more of himself to others: he was a practising Christian, and also kept and bred caged birds in a most professional way. He got a job as a sales assistant in a furniture store. I am sure his sensitivity to other people's needs, his quick grasp of figures and his growing self confidence have all stood him in good stead.

Charmaine

Charmaine was one of the most intelligent of the group, with four Grade 1 CSEs plus three others at lower grades. We asked her why she wanted to do the course as she could already type and should have been able to get a job. But she was adamant that she needed the extra year's experience—she was even able to articulate that it was a set of learning experiences that she was after rather than a qualification. She was a great asset in the group, popular and efficient at work, very smart and thoughtful. We were not surprised when at the end of the year she got herself a job in a travel agency which would send her on day release for further professional qualifications. Charmaine illustrates that intelligent pupils have a need for these kinds of experiences as much as anyone else.

Claire

Claire was an interesting person. She had four average CSEs, a record of poor attendance because of intermittent ill health, and not a particularly good school record. In fact she was a strong and determined person who did not suffer fools gladly, who did nothing unless she thought it was really worthwhile and useful, who was extremely efficient and capable when she wanted to be. She was the leader of the group when the students complained about the work being too teacher directed and childish, and she spoke up for the others. As a result of this we had a lunch hour meeting between the whole group and the team of six staff who taught them. We aired our views on all sides; as a result both staff and students changed their attitudes and ways of working. Furthermore this type of open dialogue continued. For example, the student group quite rightly said that if they were going to visit an employer then *they* would decide who, why and when, they would think out the questions and design the questionnarie (if any—they thought a less structured interview might work better); and they certainly did not want some teacher's questionnaire thrust upon them. Claire's role in negotiating all this had been very helpful. Characteristically she left the course just before the examination because she had secured a post as a nanny, but she arranged to come back to sit the exam at Christmas, which she did with success. In Claire's case, we perhaps have to learnt more from her than she from us; she still took life very much on her own terms. But she had compromised a little—her attendance improved enormously and she made sure she took the exam. She is another example of a person almost written off in the conventional school system, with a personality and skills of a most original and useful nature. This extra year seemed to help redeem the five previous years. Whether it is through a prevocational education course or a youth training scheme, the hope is that all young people will mature considerably, given the opportunity of this extra year. The pity is that we do not seem able to achieve this between the years of 11-16. But that may be more to do with adolescents and their feelings that it is to do with schooling.

Parmjit

Parmjit was another remarkable girl to whom the exam system had done no justice whatsoever. Seven mediocre CSEs were no bridge to anything; they certainly did not do justice to Cherry's charm, poise, thoughtfulness and determination. Over the year she too developed her confidence, articulateness and ability to work constructively in a group. She also developed at last a very definite idea of what she wanted to do. She went on to an FE college to do a catering diploma. Much to our joy she was head waitress to a group of staff who went there to dine one evening: her professional skill and pride in her job were a pleasure to experience. I wonder why she had not been ready for that at the end of the fifth year? People do ask whether the City and Guilds diploma has any validity in terms of 'progression' to others. My answer to that is that every certificate helps. City and Guilds is a name which employers and FE know all about. But the real point is not the piece of paper but the accumulative experience over the year which results in a different person presenting him or herself.

The trainees

The next year we could no longer continue our scheme with BA in the same way. BA wanted to convert their scheme to a pilot YTS. So we continued with the school course as a City and Guilds 365 (prevocational) course, using a variety of employers for work experience. For the new BA scheme scheme we provided the 13 weeks off-the-job training. We took the 45 trainees in batches of 15 for three weeks at a time.

The contrast between the school-to-work students and the first group of BA trainees could not have been greater. We were well used to well motivated and polite students, most of whom we had known for five years. We had originally thought that the trainees would be mostly ex-pupils. In the event, we were faced with a motley group of 15 assorted 17-year-olds, all from different schools (none from ours), nearly all of whom had been on the dole for at least six months. This first group (as opposed to the next two) was particularly unmotivated—anti-education and anti-training—what the members wanted was *work*. Several had left school at Easter—or rather had been encouraged to leave; these trainees had particular problems with authority. One or two had started a sixth-form course but had not found it particularly useful or relevant, and so had left. All of them said they were bored on the dole, that they did not particularly want to do the trainees' course, particularly as the money was hardly any better, but, 'it would be better than doing nothing'. We do not have to take what they say too literally—what they admit to in front of each other is one thing, what they really feel is much more complex. Here are a few examples of their written statements made at the beginning of the off-the-job training:

'I didn't like my secondary school. I didn't get many exams—I went back for the sixth-form induction course but didn't like it. So I left. In September I started drawing supplementary benefit until I came on this course. I wanted more experience with working and because I got bored at home. When I finish the course I want to be a nurse.'

'I left school at 16 and went to technical college. I spent a year there and passed one of my five O levels. I spent the summer waiting for my results because I wanted to go back to college, but I did not have enough passes so I signed on the dole. I wanted to go on the course because I would learn something that would be of help to me in the future as I hope to join the RAF.'

'I used to work in a butcher's shop between leaving school and coming here, but I was made redundant. The careers office told me about this course and I decided to come for work experience.'

'I passed two CSEs; the rest of my results weren't mentionable. I applied for several jobs—around six; central heating, London Transport, Thames Gas, a cabinet company, a plastic mouldings company and a builders. I worked for three weeks as an apprentice laboratory technician but was laid off because I was three hours late. Then I heard about this course.'

'When I left school I went for a couple of interviews—then one day I went to the careers centre and they had a aperchan (sic) form for a trainee for BA, so I fill it in, sent it of, got a phones call to say come to interview, went to interview, had test past test, then caple of weeks later, started.'

This was clearly a mixed ability group, but the uniting factors were:

(a) a general sense of failure, but particularly in relation to their schooling
(b) problems with authority relationships
(c) unclear (or unrealistic) ideas about what they wanted to do
(d) a sense of boredom and purposelessness.

We had not wanted to segregate them from the sixth formers as if they were lepers: our mixed ability sixth-form were a friendly and outgoing group, not unwilling to share their facilities. But this was a mistake—the trainee group wanted absolutely nothing to do with anything that was like school and we finally gave them, at their request, their own space in a corner of the community lounge (which is a pub in the evening). I gather that similar groups have caused trouble at FE colleges—perhaps the problem is that they want the work experience but not the off-the-job training.

This particular group tested our skills and those of the BA staff who had done the initial induction, to the utmost! I think they needed to wreak revenge on all the bad experiences they had had at school. They dressed outlandishly, spoke coarsely and messed about in lessons and group work at first in a way our pupils or ex-pupils would not have done. The dilemma, particularly in something as relatively unstructured as the intensive group work that I was attempting to run, was whether to let this head of steam out or whether to try to control it. My instinct was to let it all come out, but then I found myself in the embarrassing position of having, as head, what might sound to others (and be) a group that was out of control. Gradually the members came to terms with each other. That was another aspect of the problem; not only did they not really want to be on the scheme, and particularly not in an educational establishment of any kind, but they did not know each other. It took them a long time to begin to trust each other, let alone the members of staff and the first week or so was spent trying to avoid work or avoid giving anything away about themselves by deviant behaviour. It was amazing (and a great relief) how much they finally settled down. When they came back for the second and third times they had changed completely. Their clothes and hair styles had become more conventionally acceptable, and they were more willing to discuss serious topics, to listen to other points of view and to risk making a contribution themselves. Inevitably, a couple left for work. But the more actual work experience they had had, the more willing they were to make sense of the off-the-job training. The satisfaction of 'holding down' a work placement undoubtedly did a great deal for their self esteem.

In discussing what the trainees were like I can only in fairness draw on my own experience. No doubt they behaved differently for different people. I was not even trying to put them through a 'social and life skills' course, which offers many concrete role-play exercises and tasks. Other colleagues were doing this, with great effect. My brief was to help the trainees to 'reflect upon their experience'. The syllabus or material was what the trainees raised for themselves. The subject matter also included the way they actually behaved in the group, which I would comment on from time to time. The kinds of topics they raised were:

(a) What had happened in their work placements: what they did, how they got on with their boss and colleagues, what they thought of BA (not always complimentary—any more than their comments about Cranford).

(b) What they actually learned from what they did, not only the specific skills but the processes and interpersonal skills; whether what they had learned would be useful in a different context.

(c) What they thought about the off-the-job training (the phrase always caused a smirk). What they had actually done and learned from that, whether it was what they wanted or needed, and if not, what they thought they did need. What they felt about being in an educational institution; what they thought about the staff, and their status in the place, their relationship with the pupils. Their views on the facilities (particularly food) and their adult status as trainees—did this give them the right to use the staff toilets?

(d) What was happening to themselves. What their experience of school had been like, how they were treated at home, in particular how they fitted in to the family. What their aspirations had been and what they were now, what their strengths and weaknesses were, whether or not it was going to be any easier to get a job at the end of the year. How they got on with each other in the group, what they thought of each other, why some members found it difficult to say much, and why others felt a need to dominate the conversation or 'muck about'.

(e) What they felt was happening in society/the world—the economic situation, unemployment and the changing nature of work, retirement, the changing patterns of family life, politics (and what difference, if any, did they make to young peoples lives); the bomb and nuclear disarmament, racial prejudice and the difficulties of living in a multicultural society, particularly in relation to mixed marriages and sexual equality of opportunity, age prejudice (why they felt that people over 40 were past it); and finally the YTS itself and whether or not it was a con.

There are several important points to make about these group discussions. It took a long time for some of the topics I have listed to be raised—and for me to raise them inappropriately, that is, before trust was established, would not have worked. The few times that I did, in an anxious, teacher-like way 'set' the topic of conversation, particularly if it was something sensitive (as most topics are, in fact) the group would either resist the topic (fight) or indulge in some other diversionary behaviour (flight). Sometimes I would start a dialogue with another member of the group (or occasionally even a monologue) but I soon found this way of behaving to be unproductive, and to let the group off doing any work themselves. The group was not for me: it was for them. Thus the principles of negotiation were again of paramount importance. In this session, above all, it was important for the group to set the agenda, and the furthest I could go was to list some possible topics and ways forward. Until the group members took up a topic for themselves, no real work was done.

The second point to make is about understanding what the group members were actually saying, as opposed to what they said. This is a rather subtle skill, about which it is easy to be deluded! It was, for example, very disconcerting to find everything we did at Cranford subject to criticism and scorn. However when we discussed BA, they got the same treatment, not only for their contribution to off-the-job-training, but even for the work! When it finally became clear that these alienated and negative attitudes applied also to their families, society in general, the place of young people in society and the future, it became clear that they told you more about these young people themselves felt than about the actual situations they were in. There were some things about our course which needed improving or changing, and no doubt the same applied to the BA contribution. However, in fact what we had initially was a group of very frightened, alienated young people who had already labelled themselves as failures and who felt the whole world was against them. As they gained confidence through the work experience and the off-the-job training, they began to feel that they did have some skills and something to contribute to society. In spite of their anti-school feelings, and their view that they wanted nothing at all to do with the pupils, they felt very sore when they were not allowed to join in the many end of term activities: sports, staff show, final assembly and merit awards etc. Obviously, they had to keep to their programme of work—but you could see that they were beginning to wonder whether even a school was not such a bad place after all. For various reasons they had not seen their own schools in this light. They were always given access to the sixth-form social facilities and activities in their lunch hour: they could use the school cafeteria, the sixth-form cafeteria or go out to lunch, as they preferred. They did use the staff toilets, but more as a gesture to assert their adult status. The group we tried to integrate with the sixth-form hated mixing; we stopped trying with the next two groups who then spontaneously made positive relationships with the other 16-19s if and when they wanted, but on their own terms.

So, in the group, it was important for staff to be able to take what was happening at several levels. The trainees needed to hit back at adults for various reasons: the important point was to accept it, but not to lie down and take it to the point of feeling inadequate and deskilled oneself (though there were times when we did). We had to accept this anger and hostility without actually condoning it, but without also either repressing it or ruling it out of order. However it was important eventually to challenge back: ask them what would *you* do if you were planning this training? What is it that you want to learn that you are not learning? If and when we took this line, it was important not to do it in a superior 'so there' kind of way, which immediately made them feel deskilled again. It had to be done in a genuine spirit of concern and inquiry. You will recognize throughout what I have been saying, the original counselling qualities of trust, respect, empathy and congruence. There is absolutely no difference in essence between my work done recently with trainees and the work done as a counsellor years ago.

One exercise which the trainees did enjoy once a sufficient degree of trust was built up (and this normally took some time) was to discuss each others' strengths and weaknesses. Sometimes they did this in pairs or in threes, but they preferred to do it all together (this was not so pleasing and showed that they were still very dependent on the whole group structure and not yet able to stand alone without it). Recognizing that they were curious to hear about each other, I occasionally managed to get them to work in smaller groups and then feed in to the whole group. Working with a group of 15 meant that the trainees had to be very patient in waiting their turn. That they did manage this is one step forward!

In these sessions all sorts of fascinating facts emerged. Usually, and not really surprisingly, there was a direct connection between the role the trainee took in the group and the way they behaved or were treated at home. The trainees were very blunt with each other, in many ways being able to take comments from their peers, which they would have felt insulted by and would have resisted from adults. Perhaps yet again this simply illustrates the wish of young people for having some control over their own lives, and of being able to make a contribution to each other for themselves, instead of always 'being told' by adults. If we look at just a few examples it will be clearer what I mean:

The general view was that *Susan* was very confident—so confident that she was insensitive to other people's feelings. She spoke her mind too easily; this often upset other people who then resented her because they felt hurt. She could be an extremely pleasant and considerate person, but only when she really liked you. Then she would be understanding and even be a very good listener. She was not very good when she met people for the first time—she would usually say the wrong thing. However, she had a strong and warm personality; all she needed to learn was more personal confidence. Susan was mildly surprised to find out how much she antagonized people. She defended her right to be truthful and not to bottle up her feelings, but she recognized that, in making herself feel more comfortable by letting everything out, she was sometimes hurting other people even when she did not mean to. She agreed to think about this.

The group thought that *Michael* was a real laugh, a great character, full of fun, always getting the group to enjoy itself. This was fine at first, but why was he so attention-seeking? He seemed to need to prove himself by always being the centre of attention. He tried to make out he was sexually very potent and attractive—a stud. If this was really the case, why did he go on about it so much? He seemed cheerful, but actually he was rather stubborn; he liked to be right, and though he would sometimes accept being in the wrong, was he not, in fact, with all this attention/affection seeking rather insecure underneath?

I hasten to add that nothing came quite as bluntly as this, but what was amazing was to find *Michael* accepting that there was something in what the group said, and being able to articulate for the first time some of his own vulnerability. Accepting his 'whole' self—his good bits and his bad bits—

helped him to make a more realistic contribution to the course. There are dangers in this method being undertaken too soon and too insensitively—the skill is in getting the young people to look at their strengths so that they feel good enough to examine their weaker points in the spirit of 'What is it about myself that I would like to improve'.

In fact *David* was very keen to be part of the crowd and join in, but was not actually sufficiently confident to do things without group approval: he needed to join in more for himself, not simply to follow. *Paul* did anything for a laugh but actually took things very much to heart and was ultra-sensitive: he needed to develop a thicker skin and more confidence in himself. *Graham* talked a great deal (a lot of it rubbish) but it was a smokescreen to cover up his basic shyness. *Christopher* was a good leader and a good mixer, but he was quite nervous and twitchy, really. *Sharon* was too quiet, she had views that were worth hearing, so why didn't she say anything much? *Lynne* allowed herself to be the subject of a lot of sexual teasing, but there was much more to her than that; she needed to speak up for her ideas. And so on.

It is clear that it might have been very negative to have left these young people wallowing in a sense of their own shortcomings. However, the point is that at the stage when these views came out, the members of the group stopped blaming everyone else for their problems and began to take responsibility for themselves. This was at a stage when there was a possibility that they could actually do something abut their shortcomings, particularly as they would not be doing it alone but would have group support in changing their behaviour. At the base of almost all the problems was a lack of personal confidence. This had manifested itself either in various attention-seeking behaviours, or silence. Once they were able to admit to each other some shared feeling, they were able to do something about it.

Clearly for the person running such a group there are a lot of risks and difficulties. I would have been very lost without my counselling experience. For adults seeking to do this kind of work, it is important if possible for them to try to get some experience of being in a group themselves. At Cranford, we offered support to staff in several ways. First the team which taught the students/trainees met as often as possible to compare notes. Second, we ran three kinds of group training sessions over a period of two years. To do this we used skills already available in our staff group. Our counsellor ran two six weeks courses on counselling skills. Our youth leader ran an eight week course on social and life skills. Our director of development (the senior teacher in charge of professional staff development) ran a six week 'curriculum in action' course which resulted in staff observing each others' lessons. All these courses were held after school on a Thursday evening from 4 to 6pm. They were attended by some 30 staff who, through sharing experiences and undertaking practical experiential tasks together, began to build a sense of mutuality and common support, at the same time as building their confidence to deal with interactions with individuals, with groups and with classes. We are not limiting our efforts to work in this way to the 16-19 age group but are hoping eventually to use this way of working throughout the whole school.

In describing the various ways I have worked with young people on prevocational courses and YTS, I would not wish to make it sound as if counselling skills are the only skills needed. There are a great many practical skills and competencies to be taught and learnt, which I have not described at all. What I *have* described is that part of the work which I call 'reflecting upon experience' in which counselling skills are of paramount importance. However, what I have also tried to describe is a 'counselling approach to learning and training' which I recognize as being at the core of all these prevocational schemes. Fundamental to this approach is respect for the learner, a 'negociated' curriculum, self-appraisal and goal-setting, which leads to greater personal confidence and effectiveness. By taking responsibility for themselves our young people cease to be a charge on our schools, our work places and our society and begin to contribute in their turn. Thus, feeling useful instead of parasitical, our young people regain a sense of their own worth.

Prevocational courses and YTS which are mechanistic, trivialized and impersonal will not help our young people to become mature adult workers. Such courses will increase, not decrease, the problems of our society. Schemes which are based on young people's needs and managed on the basis of the counselling skills and approaches I have outlined in this book, will do much to release that energy and potential in young people which our society needs so much.

Postscript

I am certainly not going to write a conclusion to this book. Even since finishing the new section, there have been considerable developments both at the micro level of the school and the borough where I work, and at the macro level, in the launching of the first YTS, and the slow unveiling of the prevocational Certificate of Education. It is in the nature of the work I have been describing that it is constantly evolving, developing, and adapting. If we add to this the environmental and economic holocaust surrounding education and training, then only a fool would predict anything but unpredictability! We move from vague predictions about preparing for a life of change, to that change of life itself, which can be as we all know, an uncomfortable stage of development for both sexes! In such turbulent times it is important to have a framework of beliefs and values, of principles and practices which give sense and meaning to what would otherwise be a series of 'ad hoc' reactions. My port in this storm is the framework of counselling principles, which place at their centre, the needs of the young person (or old person for that matter) and the necessity for the counsellor/facilitater to be genuine, empathic, and 'non-possessive'. If we can all of us put aside sectional interests and work together to build the confidence, the creativity, the capability and the coping qualities of our young people, then this is the best we can do for them, for the economy and ultimately for ourselves. If we manipulate young people merely to meet our temporary 'ad hoc' needs, if we fail to harness their energy, their expertise, their idealism and their practicality, then we shall fail as a nation. I am confident that young people will respond to genuine demands made upon them in a spirit of unselfish care and concern. Therein rests our future. Therein rests my case.

Appendix

Further education curriculum review and development unit

A common core of skills for vocational preparation

An appendix to *Basis for Choice* gives a series of aims and objectives which it is suggested might be the core of studies on a vocational preparation course. It was not suggested that this checklist was in any way prescriptive; indeed its dynamic nature has always been stressed, as has its responsiveness to local conditions.

There have already been suggestions that the checklist should be modified to include, for instance, computer familiarization, and what follows is an amended version of the checklist.

The prescribed objectives are described in terms of a combination of observable performances to be expected of students and learning experiences which they should be offered. The commentary in italics following each objective is not prescriptive, but offers illustrations, examples and suggested methods.

For convenience, the objectives are grouped under the headings of the core aims. Some referencing has been used to indicate where an objective/experience may contribute to another aim. The grouping of the objectives/experiences is not intended to represent, necessarily, the order or organization of the learning. Neither does the number of objectives in any group necessarily represent weighting. Some difficult time-consuming and important activities may be stated quite briefly.

Aim 1

To bring about an informed perspective as to the role and status of a young person in an adult society and the world of work.

The students should:

1.1 Describe a typical organizational structure of at least two different types of workplace or organization, and relate this structure to their respective funtions.

This should include: identification of component functions (eg: sales, store-keeping, production, maintenance, professional services, administration, book-keeping) and who performs them (eg: a department v one man as part of his job) distinguishing between large and small-scale organizations, and productive and service industries (eg: garage and clothing factory).

1.2 Visit a place of work, relevant to their interests, and describe:

    a.   the working conditions and tasks of new entrants

    b.   the range of decisions which can legitimately be made by these young workers

    c.   to whom they are responsible

    d.   with whom they have regular working relationships

    e.   training and career prospects: entry requirements.

The information should, preferably, be gained by interviewing young workers, perhaps using a tape recorder or questionnaires (ref. Aims 2, 3 and 6.2).

1.3 Interview at least two adult workers about their entry to working life and the factors which influenced their subsequent job progress.

eg: relatives, friends or workers in jobs of interest (This may be done in pairs if strangers are to be interviewed).

1.4 Make comparison of different working situations, using the information gained by themselves and others.

Students might compare notes in discussion, with regard to both similar and different jobs. Note should be taken of any variations in perception or experience due to differences in the cultural background of those interviewed. There may be a need for tutors to compensate here for lack of information due to inadequate interviewing skills.

1.5 Describe the relevant trade union organizations within a particular firm or organization, and their method of operation: identify and discuss any differences between the systems observed, and the significance and functions of trades unions in general.

Students should be able to use correctly such terms as: differentials, collective bargaining, closed shop, shop steward.

1.6 Describe the basic management structure within a particular firm or organization; identify the channels of communication to and from the young workers, and the area of responsibility of their immediate supervisors.

eg: whom to see about a day off, faulty equipment, pay queries. Who has the authority to give instructions and about what?

1.7 Use the knowledge and insights gained as a basis for analysing factors influencing job choice, job satisfaction and relative rewards.

eg: (factors influencing rates of pay) skill, unionization, social status, difficult conditions, age, qualifications eg: (factors influencing job satisfaction) responsibility, prospects, social environment, usefulness, wage levels. A suitable method might be for students to rank a list of jobs according to a selection of factors, and then to discuss the differences between their own judgements and the actual position as reflected in wage rates, etc.

Many of these objectives may be achieved simultaneously with some of those in 9.2 (politics), 9.12 (economics), 10.4, 10.5 (technology), 2 (career choice) and 6.3 (communication skills).

Aim 2

To provide a basis from which a young person can make an informed and realistic decision with respect to his or her immediate future.

The students should:

2.1 Participate in the construction of self-profiles, which analyse and evaluate their own characteristics, preferences and capabilities.
eg: ability to relate to colleagues or strangers, physical fitness, willingness to travel, reaction to routine, aptitude for calculation, any sensory or physical disabilities (ref. 3.1).

2.2 Present their self-profiles to colleagues and compare them with those of the rest of the group. *Including: checking self-image against the perception of others; comparing the reactions of others to similar factors. This may enable the teacher to establish a group identity, and the students to gain practice at relating to others in a group (ref. 6.3.r).*

2.3 Obtain, by a variety of means, information on the characteristics of the range of job opportunities available to them and how to gain access to these opportunities.
eg: (characteristics) entry qualifications, working conditions, training, prospects, job location
eg: (methods) consulting reference books, interviewing people, visiting job centres, listening to local radio, consulting careers officers (ref. 6.3.d, 6.3.e).

2.4 Relate this information to their own profiles, and discuss the alternatives open to them. *Use could be made of the careers service here, and attention paid to changes in the students profiles during and since their time in school. Care may be needed to avoid sex-stereotyping.*

2.5 Recognize the risk of future unemployment, understand its causes, and know the steps they can take to mitigate its effects on them personally (including knowledge of government schemes, voluntary opportunities, entitlement to benefit, the possible advantages of mobility and the possibilities of self employment. *eg: (causes and risks) decline of industries, and regional variations in job opportunities; technological developments (ref. 10.5, 10.4)*
eg: (schemes and opportunities) YOP and FE courses; useful unpaid work (CSV, local hospitals and community projects); social security regulations; the possibilities and difficulties of moving to another area; the possibilities of co-operatives and the

knowledge and skills necessary to advertise and sell one's own labour, or to set up one's own business (ref. 9.10, 8.2).

2.6 Experience at least three different types of task, and evaluate their responses to them. *(eg: a heavy physical task (mixing concrete), manipultive task (assembly work), clerical task (filing). They should preferably come from more than one sector of employment. This job sampling may well be conducted in conjunction with the activities required under Aim 3.*

Aim 3

To bring about continuing development of physical and manipulative skills in both vocational and leisure contexts, and an appreciation of those skills in others. Work in connection with objectives 3.1—3.4 in particular, will form part of the Induction Phase but all the objectives in this section should be worked towards throughout the year and also in the course of vocational and job specific studies.

The students should:

3.1 Develop an awareness of their physical and manipulative abilities through experience of both vocational and leisure activities, and understand the implications of these for future job choice.
This is a general objective to which much of the practical activity in the course should contribute. It should also influence the self profiles (ref. 2.1, 2.2). The leisure activities should include a choice of group and individual activities designed to satisfy a variety of student preferences (team games, gymnasium activities, dancing, pottery, etc).

3.2 Experience the physical demands of some occupations, assessing (a) their reactions to physical conditions and (b) their ability to learn to cope with them, *eg: guided experience of being out of doors, standing, lifting and carrying (in the course of workshop activity, as an approach to physical education, etc).*

3.3 Experience the manipulative demands of some occupations, assessing their reactions to these demands, and their ability to learn to cope with them. *eg: handling/constructing laboratory apparatus; making small-scale constructions, working accurately, and at speed; using a keyboard.*

3.4 Experience the effect of working for an extended period of time between breaks, and the demands made on their concentration and physical stamina. *eg: work-place sessions as opposed to school periods.*

3.5 Perform tasks to a set standard and in a given time, working co-operatively when appropriate. *eg: including appreciation of: the difference between the application of set standards of work, and the 'grading' of tasks by teachers in schools.*
—the need to 'pace' one's effort.
—the need to protect the safety of colleagues.

3.6 Understand the properties and uses of a range of materials, and practice using a variety of tools and processes appropriate to these materials. *eg: wood, paper, metal; cutting, joining, assembling, copying; appropriate safety procedures–all in the context of vocational and creative leisure activities (ref. 10.4).*

3.7 Work on tasks where measuring and estimating of materials and time are required, to ensure accuracy and precision. *eg: typing, picture-framing, wallpapering.*

3.8 Work on tasks where aesthetic judgements of shape and colour are required. *eg: choosing materials or designing for appearance as well as strength; painting for appearance as well as protection.*

3.9 Observe a skilled practitioner at work, in an area of their choice, and appraise the judgement and skills involved. *eg: (areas) typing a letter; panel beating, connecting a tap; bathing a child; plastering 'throwing' a pot. Social and aesthetic judgements may also be involved, as may the abiity to plan (ref. 8.2). The appraisal is probably best developed through group discussion.*

3.10 Be introduced to examples of complex equipment, in order to develop confidence in its use in the future. *eg. machine tools, electronic equipment, microcomputers.*

Aim 4

To bring about an ability to develop satisfactory personal relationships with others.

The students should:

4.1 Experience, directly and vicariously, a variety of personal encounters and a range of responses in them. *eg: (encounters) receiving instructions; being asked for help, receiving a complaint–in direct experience (such as those involved in 1.2 and 1.3), role-play, film or literature eg: (responses) aggression; sympathy; evasion.*

4.2 Describe several patterns of behaviour, and analyse the inter-action in terms of the roles of those involved. *eg: (patterns) use of authority or status; effect of aggression or appeasement; use of reason or emotional pressure eg: (roles) parent and child; supervisor and worker; student and teacher.*

4.3 Identify and practise alternative responses. *eg: being agressive, conciliatory, submissive, understanding, distant–probably in role-play–(possibilities of video).*

4.4 Consider the merits of these responses in various situations, and with regard to various types of encounter.*eg: dealing with authority, the family, the peer group, individuals of the opposite sex (probably through group discussion) (ref. 5.5).*

4.5 Predict the changes in role likely to occur for them in the near future. *eg: student to wage earner, child to parent.*

4.6 Be aware of contemporary social conventions in various contexts likely to be met, and be able to adopt behaviour appropriate to their own goals. *eg: at work, eating out, in a library; self-presentation at interview; attitudes to those in authority; language and behaviour whilst in contact with the public (ref. 5.4).*

4.7 Describe some of the categories by which they classify other people, and become aware of the indicators they and others use to allocate individuals to a category. *eg: (categories) old/young, friendly/unfriendly; kind/unkind; social classes, cultural groups, sexes.*
eg: (indicators) dress: accent; non-verbal behaviour.

Aim 5

To provide a basis on which the young person acquires a set of moral values applicable to issues in contemporary society.

With reference to:
    a.   their present situation
    b.   a predictable future working situation
    c.   some wider current issues

The students should:

5.1 Be prepared for common moral dilemmas. *eg: individual v group loyalty, what constitutes 'stealing' at work, quality of workmanship, tax evasion, 'a fair day's work for a fair day's pay', sexual or racial discrimination.*

5.2 Give reasons for certain moral 'rules' and decisions. *eg: keeping promises, returning lost property, being faithful.*

5.3 Apply relevant moral terms to specific situations. *eg: integrity, corruption, cheating, fairness; in contexts such as sport, examinations, strikes, 'perks' at work.*

5.4 Describe the prevailing moral code of given groups. *eg: cultures, ages, social groups, occupations (eg: soldiers, doctors, sexes).*

5.5 Formulate their own codes of behaviour in relation to certain issues and dilemmas, coping with clashes of principles. *eg: honesty versus loyalty, in relation to issues, such as those described above.*

5.6 Describe and analyse the moral consequences of actions. *eg: driving without insurance, the conception of a child; concealing information at interview (ref. 9.1.d).*

It is anticipated that many of these objectives (especially perhaps 5.1, 5.3 and 5.6) might be dealt with in the course of such things as practical sessions, or discussions about economic issues or work experience.

Aim 6

To bring about a level of achievement in literacy, numeracy and graphicacy appropriate to ability, and adequate to meet the basic demands of contemporary society.

6.1 *Numeracy*

The students should be able to:

a. Add, subtract, multiply and divide whole numbers, basic functions and basic decimals

b. Given an awareness of their own abilities and future needs, decide when to use calculators, tables, pencil and paper or mental arithmetic, and be prepared to learn any required techniques
What does their intended job require (a) of necessity, (b) for convenience? What are their personal needs?

c. Interpret place value

d. Convert fractions to decimals and vice versa

e. Use standard units of measurement, read graduated scales, and make approximate conversions between imperial and metric units
eg: through the interpretation of plans and preparation of materials in the course of a project

f. Read the 24-hour clock, and train/bus timetables, make estimations of time
eg: planning journeys (ref. 8.2)

g. Interpret and use tables of figures
eg: bank statement, temperature conversion, football results

h. Make approximations and estimations, and assess the accuracy of results obtained by a calculator

i. Apply and interpret ratio and proportion *eg: preparing mixtures, scale on maps, wage increases*

j. Calculate averages *eg: average wage rates*

k. Calculate percentages *eg: VAT, discounts, tax rates*

l. Make elementary algebraic substitutions *eg: using a formula to determine one unknown*

m. Describe the properties of common shapes, and measure angles

6.2 *Graphicacy*

a. Make calculations and estimations of perimeter, area and volume of right-angled figures, circles and cylinders *eg: estimating quantities of materials*

b. Interpret and present graphs, charts and maps, choosing an appropriate form for their purpose *eg: understanding of gradient of axes; pi-charts, bar-charts, etc. in the context of newspapers, textbooks, student projects (ref. 10.1)*

c. Appreciate perspective in space, photography, etc

6.3 *Communication*

The student should:

a. Read and understand data in a wide variety of forms and identify the points of a given text relevant to a particular purpose *eg: instruction manuals, notices, letters, labels (see also 6.1 and the rest of 6.2) eg: read a manual in order to know action to take in case of a breakdown*

b. Be able to read and understand written questions and requests *eg: questionnaires, memos, worksheets*

c. Be able to distinguish fact from opinion, identify emotive and ambiguous statements, and identify instances where expert advice is relevant to a matter of opinion *eg: sales literature (including comparison of products); political speeches (ref. 9.1) eg: medical opinion on when to return to work (as opposed to an opinion on what is funny)*

d. Find and use information from a variety of given sources, including electronic information sources *eg: dictionaries, catalogues, indexes, encyclopedias, Prestel etc (ref. 9.17)*

e. Listen to, and understand information and requests given orally *(ref. 3.5, 4.1)*

f. Be able to communicate competently in written form: organize content, write effectively and with observation of the conventions of legibility, spelling, punctuation and grammar. *eg: formal letters and reports, informal notes and messages*

g. Explain and describe events, processes and opinions sensibly and clearly in writing *eg: accident reports, operating instructions, arguing a case*

h. Make notes for own use *eg: on visits, from books, during talks*

i. Be able to express tabular or graphic data in written form or vice versa *eg: diagrams, charts, sketch maps, statistics (ref. 6.2)*

j. Fill in forms correctly *eg: driving licence applications, job applications, insurance claims*

k. Speak audibly and give clear verbal explanations of processes/ opinions/events to a variety of audiences *eg: friends, acquaintances, strangers, etc.*

l. Make a disciplined contribution to group discussion *eg: following some procedure: accepting and responding to others' views*

m. Use the telephone effectively

n. Experience and practise various kinds of verbal encounter, and evaluate their own strengths and weaknesses *eg: negotiating, advising, persuading, justifying, using simulations, role-playing, mock-interviews, etc (ref. 1.3, 4.1)*

o. Experience membership of, and practice communication in, a variety of groups *eg: formal, informal; large, small; decision making, task-centred; competitive and co-operative (ref. 9.2)*

p. Experience various roles in these groups *eg: leader, recorder, participant, chairman*

q. Experience the communication requirements of certain jobs and evaluate their reactions to them, and their ability to learn *eg: with children, in an office; with customers; with VIP's (ref. also 2.1, 2.3)*

r.   Participate in planning and creating an example of a particular form of communication, matching the form to the purpose *eg: TV (video) programme; audio tape; newspaper; exhibition*

s.   Critically appraise examples in a medium of communication with which they have experience *eg: TV, records, radio, books; identifying style, imagery, the message being transmitted, the audience for whom it is intended, influence of the technology, etc.*

Aim 7

To bring about competence in a variety of study skills likely to be demanded of the young person.
It is suggested that these study skills should be introduced as a specific group learning activity early in the induction phase, but that subsequent practice should come from following the course itself. This practice should subsequently be reinforced and evaluated on a tutorial basis.

The students should:

7.1 Learn how to take notes, or use given notes for their own purposes. *eg: when preparing an essay; when hearing a talk. Different strategies are possible*

7.2 Know how to gain access to appropriate works of reference. *eg: location in library; use of index*

7.3 Appreciate when to 'skim-read' and when to read for detail, and practise both techniques.

7.4 Practise discussions and questioning. *eg: with teachers, with colleagues, with experts, co-operative learning*

7.5 Gain some appreciation of effective learning strategies and how to deploy them for their own benefit in the planning of their learning. *eg: aids to memory, such as mnemonics; simply psychology of learning, such as knowledge of learning plateaux, attention spans, and methods and effects of practice*

7.6 Experience a variety of learning situations and evaluate their reactions to them. *eg: formal talks, group work, programmed learning, individual study with text books, using a library, role-plays and simulations; identifying which methods suit them best, for a given purpose. (These situations will normally occur naturally in the rest of the course; a separate session may be required only to evaluate them.)*

Aim 8

To encourage the capacity to approach various kinds of problems methodically and effectively, and to plan and evaluate courses of action.

The students should:

8.1 Examine and appraise given faults, problems or events, working individually or in a group.
eg: faulty equipment, college over-crowding, a fall in sales, by:

a. Thinking up alternative solutions or explanations
eg: 'brainstorming' sessions in groups, listing alternatives without evaluation ('lateral' or 'divergent' thinking)

b. Identifying what evidence would support a statement or a guess and what would cast doubt on it *eg: logical deduction of consequences, probable implications*

c. Considering or eliminating alternatives, in a systematic way *eg: the need to hold some variables constant or have a 'control' taking into account previous experience; the probability of certain causes; distinguishing between cause and correlation*

d. Generalizing as appropriate from previous experiences or data
eg: including discussion of the degree of confidence which is justified, the effects of further evidence, etc
Special sessions in problem-tackling or scientific method may appeal to some students. Others will respond better if these objectives are dealt with in the natural course of activities and discussion occurring in the rest of the course. In the latter case, students should still be made aware of what constitutes a scientific approach, and in either case, experience should be given of problems which do not have one clear solution, as well as those which do.

8.2 Experience the process of planning an event or course of action, working individually and in groups.
eg: a journey by public transport, a visit to a factory, making an object, applying for a job, buying a vehicle, by:

a. Identifying the nature of a problem, and collecting relevant information *eg: factors involved; factual data available; sources of expert advice*

b. Working out alternative strategies and predicting their likely outcomes *eg: as a pencil and paper exercise; as a topic for group discussion*

c. Choosing and implementing a plan, and adapting it to circumstances as appropriate

d. Evaluating the effectiveness of the plan, and identifying lessons to be learned *student performance should be judged with regard to this, rather than success or otherwise of the plan*

e. Develop the capacity to learn with computer assisted methods, using appropriate equipment

Aim 9

To bring about sufficient political and economic literacy to understand the social environment and participate in it.

Section 9.1 describes a procedure by which the political dimension of issues which arise during the course can be analysed. It is not intended that these objectives should be learned in isolation. The issues may arise among the students, or through an account in a case-study, the press, TV, etc.

The students should:

9.1 Appraise a policy dispute by:

a. Identifying the cause of disagreement *eg: goals, values, methods (especially if allocating resources), results (ref. 9.11)*

b. Saying what further information they need; and where it can be found *(ref. 6.3.d)*

c. Identifying where and by whom any decision will be made *eg: in a local authority, by the housing committee; in the college, by the Academic Board*

d. Indicating who is likely to be affected by various policies and in what way *eg: identify likely supporters/opponents (ref. 5.6)*

e. Describing alternative ways of influencing the decision, and evaluating their relative merits *eg: by forming pressure groups, writing letters, visiting, organizing petitions, writing to newspapers; evaluating through discussion (ref. 8.2)*

f. Describing the issue using some basic political terms *eg: conflict, power, consent-dissent, order-disorder, rules, compromise, consensus*

9.2 Analyse and appraise some groups to which they belong, and describe the methods by which decisions are reached in them
eg: family, youth-club, class, student union; formal and informal groups

9.3 Develop an awareness of the workings of formal decision-making groups by:
ie: groups which have rules of procedure

a. Experiencing membership of such a group. *eg: class meetings, or in role-play simulation*

b. Experiencing/discussing different systems of voting *eg: for nationwide referenda, general elections, class representative, goal of the month*

c. Listing the conventional order of items on an agenda, and explaining their meaning and usage *eg: minutes, standing items, AOB*

d. Visiting and observing a public decision-making body in action *eg: local council, college, Academic Board*

9.4 Gain a basis for evaluating national politics by being able to:
   a. Name the major political parties, their leaders, and describe major or and/or distinctive items of policy *eg: analysis of statements, actions, manifestos (ref. 6.3.c); critical evaluation of media reports*
   b. Describe, in general terms, how local and central government relate, and the role of the EEC *eg: probably approached through case study of a given issue*
   c. Indicate which Departments of Government are responsible for decisions which may affect the students personally *eg: fundings of the college, repair of roads, law on speed limits*

9.5 Check and explain a payslip. *eg: deductions, tax-coding*

9.6 Balance income against expenditure and keep necessary records.

9.7 Make value-for-money calculations and estimations.
When shopping; various sizes of product, special offers in shops (ref.6.1)

9.8 Plan an estimated personal budget for a typical working week in their intended jobs. *eg: travel costs, meals, entertainment, accommodation, etc. (ref.11.5)*

9.9 Describe the function and use of a bank account, the Giro, building society, HP and credit cards. *eg: comparative interest rates; conditions of use, etc*

It is recommended that the achievement of the following objective be promoted through the use of a simulation or business game, which enables students to discover the various factors involved from experience or as a result of their own investigations (ref.8.2). Presentation of the material in the form of a series of lectures, or a conventional text book, would not be appropriate

9.10 Investigate how a business is run by identifying the factors involved in:
   a. Deciding what to sell *eg: market research, effect or competition, design of product*
   b. Choosing location *eg: availability of labour, raw materials, transport; location of customers and competitors*
   c. Borrowing money *eg: banks, shareholders*
   d. Employing people *eg: wages, national insurance, legislation*
   e. Buying raw materials *examples from manufacturing and service industry*
   f. Calculating overheads *eg: rent, rates, advertising, office staff, maintenance, etc*
   g. Selling product *eg: functions of sales staff, customer relations; determining prices*
   h. Calculating profit/loss *eg: simple accounting*
   i. What happens to profit/loss *eg: interest payments, taxation, reinvestment, dividends*

9.11 Discuss the factors influencing the variable price of certain items, and arguments for and against state intervention. *eg: houses, fresh fruit, fuel*

9.12 Explain a selection of firms or organizations in basic economic terms. *eg: capitalist, co-operative, nationalized, enterprises*

9.13 Investigate the sources of central and local government income, and where it is spent. *eg: case studies, use of reference texts, interpretation of tables and graphs*

9.14 Read some common legal documents and be able to answer simple comprehension questions on them. *eg: guarantees, HP contracts, rental agreements*

9.15 Visit a court of law, and discuss its procedures, personnel and atmosphere

9.16 Demonstrate knowledge of their rights with respect to arrest and bail, by role-playing typical incidents and evaluating alternative courses of action. *eg: an incident involving the police (a) when the individual has broken the law and (b) when the individual is in the right*
eg: discussion of principle v expediency, rights and duties; discussion with police representatives (ref. 4.4)

9.17 Use a simple reference text to determine their rights/duties in specific cases relating to the law as it affects the consumer, the motorist, the employee. *eg: NCCL guide, Department of Employment publication (ref.6.3.d)*

9.18 Distinguish between criminal and civil law, know the usual order of proceedings through the courts, and compare the function of tribunals. *perhaps via case-studies*

9.19 Be aware of sources of legal aid and advice

Aim 10

An appreciation of the physical and technological environments and the relationship between these and the needs of man in general and working life in particular.

The students should:

10.1 Participate in a group conducted survey of local amenities, which identifies some characteristics of the locality. *eg: surveys of leisure facilities, open or unused spaces, distribution of shops or industry*

10.2 Visit a social welfare centre as a basis for discussing personal and community responsibility for others. *eg: old folk's homes, centres for the handicapped, day centres (ref. 4.1, 4.6)*

10.3 Identify and assess the nature of environmental problems, through such issues as housing and transport. *eg: (a) use local photographs, sketches and taped interviews to argue for and against various forms of housing and (b) undertake a costing exercise of daily travel to support cases for and against private and public transport schemes (ref.8.2) referring to the notions of continuity, change, cause, effect, etc as appropriate (ref.8.1.d)*

10.4 Examine at least two different industries or places of work, identifying:
eg: a production and a service industry

    a.   the enterprises, their use and dependence on energy. *eg: what fuels are used, and for what, the ecological and environmental implication of their use*

    b.   the production methods and materials which are used. *eg: mass production, batch production, unit production; the processes which are mechanized and how this compares with the recent past and predictable future (ref.1.3); the effect on this of changes in materials*

    c.   the division of labour and the nature of individual jobs; *the effect of fully automatic, semi-automatic or manual control on the nature of jobs; the effect of the use of power, production methods and materials on working conditions, skills required, etc (ref. 1.2)*

10.5 Appraise the implications of some current developments in technology. *eg: as observed in the above industries as currently highlighted in the news. Discussion of economic, social environmental and psychological implications (eg: Capital investment required, scale/location of industry, effect on employment and ownership, pollution, power requirements, changes in status of jobs, etc)*

Aim 11

To bring about a development of the coping skills necessary to promote self sufficiency in the young people.

The students should:

11.1. Be able to plan and prepare adequate meals *eg: including budgeting, shopping and costing (ref.9.2)*

11.2 Use and maintain every-day machinery and equipment. *eg: fit an electric plug, use a launderette, iron a shirt. Willingness, and confidence, and a knowledge of how to learn these things are intended, rather than comprehensive practice*

11.3 Apply simple principles of health-care, hygiene and physical fitness to their every-day lives. *eg: knowledge of the effect of drugs (coffee, aspirin, tobacco, 'hard' drugs, etc); symptoms, prevention and treatment of common ailments and diseases; access to facilities and activities for developing and maintaining fitness (ref. 3.2)*

11.4 Practise simple first-aid techniques. *eg: dealing with cuts, sprains, burns, etc. Know when to call in expert help*

11.5 Investigate and use sources of information regarding the finding and maintenance of accommodation. *eg: use of press adverts, agencies, rental and purchase, regulations and procedures; do-it-yourself manuals*

Aim 12

To bring about a flexibility of attitude and a willingness to learn, sufficient to manag future changes in technology and career.

Introduction
There may be said to be four elements necessary to produce this flexibility;

   a. **Possession of commonly used and transferable skills and capacities**

   b. **Realization of the need for flexibility**

   c. **Ability to identify the underlying principles of a process or activity**

   d. **Experience of and confidence in one's ability to transfer learning from one context to another**
     It is hoped that many of the transferable capacities— element (a)—are already embodied in the other core objectives. Element (b) will be encouraged by the economic and technological objectives included under Aims 9 and 10. The need for (c) is part of the rationale behind the prescription of much experiential learning and project/case study/simulation activity in the core. Element (d) entails the following general objectives, which will relate to much of the activity in the course as a whole, affecting the teaching approach as much as the content.

The students should:

12.1 Whenever they develop a particular capacity in a given context. *eg: measuring up; estimating materials; following an instruction manual; giving instructions; fault finding*

   a.   Identify other contexts in which the capacity could be useful
     eg: similarity between: assembly instructions and recipes; and adjusting bikes or sewing machines

   b.   Be given practice at applying relevant aspects of previous learning to a new situation. *Having identified a transferable skill, practise transferring and adapting it*

   c.   Identify any other activities at which they are likely to be successful, on the evidence of this learning. *As a contribution to the self profile (ref.2.2, 2.4). What do they enjoy doing? What kind of learning comes easily to them?*

Bibliography

Counselling in Britain: theory and practice

Counselling in Schools (1967) Schools Council working paper no 15 HMSO 1967

Daws, P *et al* (1970) *'Who cares?' A Discussion of Counselling and Pastoral Care in Schools* Council for Educational Advance

Daws, P, Rayner, J, Atherley, R, Fuller, J, Juniper D, (1967) 'The Counselling Function: A Symposium' *Educational Research* February

Fuller, J, (1967) 'School Counselling: A First Enquiry' *Educational Research* February

Gill, J (1967) 'Counselling in Schools' *Trends in Education* April

Hamos, P (1965) *The Faith of the Counsellors* Constable

Hamblin, D H, (1974) *The Teacher and Counselling* Basil Blackwell

Hamblin, D H, (1978) *The Teacher and Pastoral Care* Basil Blackwell

Hamblin, D H, (1983) *Guidance 16-19* Basil Blackwell

Holden, A (1972) *Counselling in Secondary Schools (with special reference to authority and referral)* Constable

Holden, A, (1969) *Teachers as Counsellors* Constable

'Horizontal Notebook on Pupil Counselling in Great Britain' (1967) *The New Era* November

Hughes, P M (1971) *Guidance and Counselling in Schools: A Response to Change* Pergamon

Jackson, R and Juniper, D F (1971) *A Manual of Educational Guuidance* Holt, Rinehart and Winston

Lawrence, D (1973) *Improved Reading through Counselling* Ward Lock Educational

Lytton, H (1969) 'Counselling and Psychology in Britain' *Bulletin of British Psychological Society* October

Lytton, H and M (1974) *Craft Guidance and Counselling in British Schools* 2nd ed (revised) Edward Arnold

Milner, P (1974) *Counselling in Education* Dent

Moore, B M (1971) *Guidance in Comprehensive Schools: A Survey* NFER

Nelson-Jones, R (1982) *The Role and Practice of Counselling Psychology* Holt, Rinehart and Winston

Palmer, E (1965) *Student Guidance* Longmans

Proctor, B (1978) *Counselling Shop* Burnett Books in association with Andre Deutsch

Venables, E (1971) *Counselling* National Marriage Guidance Council

Williams, K (1973) *The School Counsellor* Methuen

Working Party Report on Counselling Services in Schools (1969) National Association for Mental Health

American theory

Arbuckle, D S (1965) *Counseling: Philosophy, Theory and Practice* Allyn and Bacon

Blocher, D (1974) *Developmental Counseling*, Ronald Press

219

Boy, A and Pine, J (1963) *Client-centered Counseling in the Secondary School* Houghton Mifflin

Hamrin, S and Paulson, B (1950) *Counseling Adolescents* Science Research Associates

Krumboltz, J *ed* (1966) *Revolution in Counseling* Houghton Mifflin

Krumboltz, J and Thorenson, C E (1976) *Counseling Methods* New York, Holt, Rinehart and Winston

Counselling adolescents in school

Lindsay, G *ed* (1983) *Problems of Adolescence in the Secondary School*

Loughary, J (1960) *Counseling in Secondary Schools: A Frame of Reference* Harper

Lytton, H (1968) *School Counseling and Counsellor Education in the US* NFER

Rogers, C (1951) *Client-centered Therapy* Houghton Mifflin

Rogers, C (1961) *On Becoming a Person* Houghton Mifflin

Rogers, C (1978) *On Personal Power* Constable

Stefflre, B *ed* (1965) *Theories of Counseling* McGraw Hill

Sue, D W *ed* (1981) *Counseling the Culturally Different–Theory and Practice* Wiley

Truax, C and Carkhuff, R (1968) *Towards Effective Counseling and Psychotherapy: Training and Practice* Aldine

Tyler, L (1961) *The Work of the Counselor* Appleton Century Crofts

Warters, J (1964) *Techniques of Counseling* McGraw Hill

Further theories and techniques of counselling, casework and groupwork

Berne, E (1966) *Games People Play* Penguin

Biestek, F and S J (1961) *The Casework Relationship* Allen and Unwin

Ferard, M and Hunnybun, N (1962) *The Caseworker's Use of Relationships* Tavistock Press

Harris, T (1973) *I'm Ok, You're Ok* (Pan)

Heywood, J (1964) *An Introduction to Teaching Casework Skills* Routledge and Kegan Paul

Jones, A and Holdsworth, R (1978) Counselling Skills Library: a set of 5 audio cassettes on counselling (Holdsworth Audio-Visual, 18 Malbrook Road, London SW15 6UF)

Jones, A, Marsh, J and Watts, A G (1974) *Male and Female–Choosing Your Role in Modern Society* Hobsons Press

Jones, A, Marsh, J and Watts, A G (1976) *Living Choices: Home and Family in Modern Society* Hobsons Press

Jones, A, Marsh, J and Watts, A G (1980) *Time to Spare–Leisure in Modern Society* Hobsons Press

Kaye, B and Rogers, I (1968) *Group Work in Secondary Schools and the Training of Teachers in its Methods* Oxford University Press

Klein, J (1956) *The Study of Groups* Routledge and Kegan Paul

Moran, M (1968) *Pastoral Counselling for the Deviant Girl* Geoffrey Chapman

Perls, F B, Hefferline, R, and Goodman, P (1973) *Gestalt Therapy* Penguin

Rich, J (1968) *Interviewing Children and Adolescents* Macmillan

Richardson, E (1967) *Group Study for Teachers* Routledge and Kegan Paul

Rogers, C (1971) *Encounter Groups* Penguin

Schutz W M (1973) *Joy: Expanding Human Awareness* Penguin

Sprott, W (1958) *Human Groups* Pelican

Thompson, S and Khan, J H (1970) *The Group Process as a Helping Technique* Pergamon

Timms, N (1964) *Social Casework: Principles and Practice* Routledge and Kegan Paul

Wallis, J (1960) *Counselling and Social Welfare* Routledge and Kegan Paul

Wallis, J (1968) *Marriage Guidance: A New Introduction* Routledge and Kegan Paul

Adolescence: theory and background

Bazalgette, J (1971) *Freedom, Authority and the Young Adult* Pitman
Bazalgette, J (1978) *School Life and Work Life: A Study of Transition in the Inner City* Hutchinson
Chandler, E M (1980) *Educating Adolescent Girls* Unwin Education
Davies, B and Gibson, A (1967) *The Social Education of the Adolescent* ULP
Dunn, N (1963) *Up the Junction* MacGibbon and Kee
Eppel, E and M (1966) *Adolescents and Morality* Routledge and Kegan Paul
Erikson, E (1968) *Identity: Youth and Crisis* Faber and Faber
Fyvel, T (1961) *The Insecure Offenders* Chatto and Windus
Goetschius, G and Tash, M (1967) *Working with Unattached Youth* Routledge and Kegan Paul
Hadfield, J (1962) *Childhood and Adolescence* Penguin
Hamblett, C and Deverson, J (1964) *Generation X* Tandem
Hemming, J (1967) *Problems of Adolescent Girls* Heinemann
Hersov, L A and Schaffer, D *eds* (1978) *Aggression and Antisocial Behaviour in Childhood and Adolescence* Pergamon Press
Hurlock, E (1951) *Adolescent Development* McGraw Hill
Jones-Davies, C and Cave, R G *eds* (1976) *The Disruptive Pupil in the Secondary School* Ward Lock Educational
Josselyn, I (1959) *The Adolescent and His World* Family Service Association of America
Miller, D (1970) *The Age Between: Adolescents in a Disturbed Society* Cornmarket Hutchinson
Morse, M (1965) *The Unattached* Penguin
Musgrove, F (1964) *Youth and the Social Order* Routledge and Kegan Paul
Odlum, D (1978) *Adolescence* Wayland
Pringle, M K (1974) *The Needs of Children* Hutchinson
Schofield, M (1965) *The Sexual Behaviour of Young People* Longmans
Spicer, F (1977) *Adolescence and Stress* Forbes Publications
Wall, W (1968) *Adolescents in School and Society* NFER
White, R K and Lippitt, R (1960) *Autocracy and Democracy: An Experimental Inquiry* Harper

Books about personal relationships and life skills

Barnes, K *15 + Facts of Life* Family Doctor Series British Medical Association
Barnes, K (1958) *He and She* Penguin
Button, L (1981) *Group Tutoring for the Form Teacher* Hodder and Stoughton Educational
Boys' Questions Answered National Marriage Guidance Council
Cave, R and Conochie, D (1965) *Living with Other People* Ward Lock Educational
Cave, R and O'Malley, R (1967) *Education for Personal Responsibility* Ward Lock Educational
Dallas, D M (1972) *Sex Education in School and Society* NFER
David, K (1982) *Personal and Social Education in Secondary Schools* Longman for Schools Council
Girl's Questions Answered National Marriage Guidance Council
Hacker, R (1961) *The Opposite Sex* Pan Piper
Hamblin, D *ed* (1981) *Study Skills* Blackwell
Harris, A (1967) *Questions about Sex* Hutchinson Educational
Harris, A (1968) *Questions about Living* Hutchinson Educational
Hopson, B and Scally, M (1981) *Lifeskills Teaching* McGraw Hill

Ingleby, A (1964) *Learning to Love* Robert Hale
Is Chastity Out? National Marriage Guidance Council
Lancashire Education Authority (1980,81) Active Tutorial Work Books 1-5 Blackwell
Morton, R *VD and Diseases Transmitted Sexually* Family Doctor Series British Medical Association
Pilkinton, R *Facts of Life for Parents* Family Doctor Series British Medical Association
Prince, G *Teenagers Today* Family Doctor Series British Medical Association
Rayner, C (1968) *A Parent's Guide to Sex Education* Mini Corgi
Richards, L (1963) *Design for Living for Boys* Basil Blackwell
Richards, M (1963) *Design for Living for Girls* Basil Blackwell
Rogers, C (1973) *Becoming Partners and Its Alternatives* Constable
Sex Education in Perspective National Marriage Guidance Council
Spock, B (1963) *Problems of Parents* Bodley Head
Vaughan, P (1969) *Family Planning* Queen Anne Press
Where on Drugs: A Parent's Handbook Advisory Centre for Education
Wood, A *Drug Dependence* Corporation of Bristol and Bristol Council of Social Service
Your Teenagers National Marriage Guidance Council
For the full booklist of the National Marriage Guidance Council write to Bookshop, the National Marriage Guidance Council, Rugby.

Services relating to young people

A New Training Initiative (1981) Manpower Services Commission. May
Behavioural Units (1979) HM Inspectorate, DES
Berg, I and Hersov, L *ed* (1979) *Truancy: Problems of School Attendance and Refusal*
Carroll, H M C (1977) *Absenteeism in South Wales* Studies of pupils, their homes and their secondary schools Faculty of Education, University College, Swansea
Carter, M (1967) *Into Work* Penguin
The Education of Maladjusted Children (1965) Department of Education and Science pamphlet no 47 HMSO
Guide to the Social Services Family Welfare Association
Kahn, J (1964) *Unwillingly to School* Pergamon Press
Maclean, I (1966) *Child Guidance and the School* Methuen
Making Experience Work (1979) Guidelines for Youth Opportunities Programmes Manpower Services Commission
Psychologists in Education Services (1963) the Summerfield Report (HMSO 1968)
Report of the Committee on Local Authority and Allied Personal Social Services (1968) the Seebohm Report HMSO
Report of the Committee on Maladjusted Children (1956) the Underwood Report HMSO
Rutter, M (1979) *15,000 Hours* the Rutter Report Open Books
Training Opportunities for Women (1975) Manpower Services Commission
Truancy and Behavioural Problems in some Urban Schools (1979) HM Inspectorate, DES
Venables, E (1971) *Teachers and Youth Workers: A Study of their Roles* Evans Methuen Educational
Vocational Preparation for Young People (1975) Manpower Services Commission
Watts, A G *ed* (1982) *Schools, YOPs, and the New Training Initiative* CRAC
Willmot, P (1967) *Consumer's Guide to the British Social Services* Penguin
Youth Training Scheme: Scheme Design and Content April 1983
Young People and Work (1977) the Holland Report Manpower Services Commission
Youth and Community Work in the 70s (1969) HMSO

General background

Argyle, M (1967) *The Psychology of Interpersonal Behaviour* Penguin
Balogh, J (1982) *Profile Reports for School Leavers* Longman for Schools Council
Berne, E (1966) *Games People Play* Deutsch
Carstairs, G (1963) *This Island Now* Hogarth Press
Children and Their Primary Schools (1967) the Plowden Report HMSO
Clegg, A and Megson, B (1968) *Children in Distress* Penguin
Craft, M *et al* (1967) *Linking Home and School* Longman
Douglas, J (1964) *The Home and the School* MacGibbon and Kee
Goacher, B (1983) *Recording Achievement at 16+* Longman for Schools Council
15 to 18 (1959) the Crowther Report HMSO
Half our Future (1963) the Newsom Report HMSO
Hamblin, D *ed* (1981) *Problems and Practice of Pastoral Care* Blackwell
Higher Education (1963) the Robbins Report HMSO
HMI: Aspects of Secondary Education (1979) HMSO
HMI: Teaching in Schools: The Content of Initial Training (1982) DES
HMI: The New Teacher in School (1982) HMSO
Institute of Manpower Studies: *Foundation Training Issues* (1982) February
Institute of Manpower Studies: *Youth Skills Project* (1983)
Institute of Manpower Studies: *Training for Skill Ownership—Learning to Take it With You* (1983)
Jackson, S (1967) *A Teacher's Guide to Tests and Testing* Longman
Pringle, M (1966) *Investment in Children* Longmans
Marland, M (1974) *Pastoral Care* Heinemann
Richardson, E (1973) *The Teacher, the School and the Task of Management* Heinemann Schools Council (1981) *The Practical Curriculum* working paper 70 Methuen Educational
Richardson, E (1975) *Authority and Organisation in the Secondary School* Macmillan Education
Warnock Report (1981)
Watts, T (1983) *Education, Unemployment and the Future of Work* Open University
Wootten, B (1959) *Social Science and Social Pathology* Allen and Unwin

Manpower services commission research and development series

Youth Unemployment and Special Measures (1981) An annotated bibliography. Linda Skeates, Andrew Rix, Graham Smith, Department of Industrial Relations and Management Studies University College Cardiff, January
Urainee Centred Reviewing (TCR) (1981) Helping trainees to help themselves. Barbara Pearce, Elizabeth Varney. CCDU Leeds University. David Flegg, Peter Waldman ITRU Cambridge. November
Young People on YOP (1981) A national survey of entrants to the Youth Opportunities Programme. Trevor Bedeman, Juliet Harvey. December
Trainees Come First (1981) The organizational structure of Community Projects YOP Schemes. Pauline Brelsford, Andre Rix, Graham Smith. University College Cardiff. December
The Benefit of Experience (1981) Individual guidance and support within the Youth Opportunities programme. Edward G Knasel, A G Watts and Jennifer M Kidd
The Benefit of Experience (1982) Individual guidance and support within the Youth Opportunities Programme. Edward G Knasel, A G Watts, Jennifer M Kidd. National Institute for Careers Education and Counselling. April
Ethnic Minorities (1982) Their involvement in MSC Special Programmes Rodney Stares, David Imberg, John McRobie. Economic and Social Research. February
CEP is Working (1982) The report of a study of the Community Enterprise

Programme, Clare Short, Andrew Sawdon, Sheila Tucker. Youthaid. March
Training Workshops (1982) The way they work in YOP. Michaela Dungate March
Learning at Work (1982) The Tavistock Guide. Linden Hilgendorf, Rosemary
Welchman. July
Experience is not enough (1982) A review of staff development practices relevant to
individual guidance and support in the Youth Opportunities Programme.
Edward G Knasel NICEC

Further education unit (FEU) publications

*Experience, Reflection, Learning: Suggestions for Organisers of Schemes of Unified
Vocational Preparation* (April 1978)
A Basis for Choice (July 1979)
Supporting YOP (July 1979)
Beyond Coping: Some Approaches to Social Education (1980)
Developing Social and Life Skills: Strategies for Tutors (January 1980)
Vocational Preparation (January 1981)
*ABC in Action: A Report from an FEU/CGLI Working Party on the Piloting of 'A Basis
for Choice'* (September 1981)
*How Do I Learn? An Experimental Programme to Introduce Young People and their
Teachers to the Many Ways of Learning* (December 1981)
Tutoring: The Guidance and Counselling Role of the Tutor in Vocational Preparation (June
1982)
*Teaching Skills: Towards a Strategy of Staff Development and Support for Vocational
Preparation* (June 1982)
NTI: Joint Statement by MSC/FEU No.1 General Principles (September 1982)
Profiles: A Review of Issues and Practice in the Use and Development of Student Profiles
(September 1982)
Basic Skills (November 1982)
Who Cares?: A Curriculum Policy for Caring Courses at the Initial Level (November
1982)
*A Basis for Choice: Report of a Study Group on Post-16 Pre-employment Courses 2nd
Edition* (December 1982)
Progressing from Vocational Preparation: Towards a Solution (December 1982)
Towards a Personal Guidance Base (March 1983)
TRADEC1: An Evaluation of Trades Education Schemes (March 1983)
FEU Guidance Notes No.3 Curriculum Implications of the 21 Hour Rule (May 1983)
Supporting YTS (May 1983)
Copies of these documents (which are free of charge) are obtainable from the
Publications Despatch Centre, Department of Education and Science, Honeypot
Lane, Canons Park, Stanmore, Middlesex. HA7 1AZ.
A complete list of FEU publications is also available from the above address.

Index